NEW X MEN

NEW ⊗ MEN

WRITER: *Grant Morrison*
PENCILER: *Marc Silvestri*
INKERS: *Batt, Joe Weems, Billy Tan, Eric Basaldua & Tim Townsend*
COLORISTS: *Steve Firchow, John Starr, Matt Milla, Frank D'Armata, Beth Sote* *& Brian Buccellato*
LETTERERS: *Virtual Calligraphy's Rus Wooton & Chris Eliopoulos*
COVER ART: *Marc Silvestri, Joe Weems & Steve Firchow*
ASSISTANT EDITORS: *Stephanie Moore & Cory Sedlmeier*
EDITOR: *Mike Marts*
Special Thanks to Jim McLauchlin & Matt Hawkins

COLLECTION EDITOR: *Jennifer Grünwald*
EDITORIAL ASSISTANTS: *James Emmett & Joe Hochstein*
ASSISTANT EDITORS: *Alex Starbuck & Nelson Ribeiro*
EDITOR, SPECIAL PROJECTS: *Mark D. Beazley*
SENIOR EDITOR, SPECIAL PROJECTS: *Jeff Youngquist*
SENIOR VICE PRESIDENT OF SALES: *David Gabriel*
SVP OF BRAND PLANNING & COMMUNICATIONS: *Michael Pasciullo*

EDITOR IN CHIEF: *Axel Alonso*
CHIEF CREATIVE OFFICER: *Joe Quesada*
PUBLISHER: *Dan Buckley*
EXECUTIVE PRODUCER: *Alan Fine*

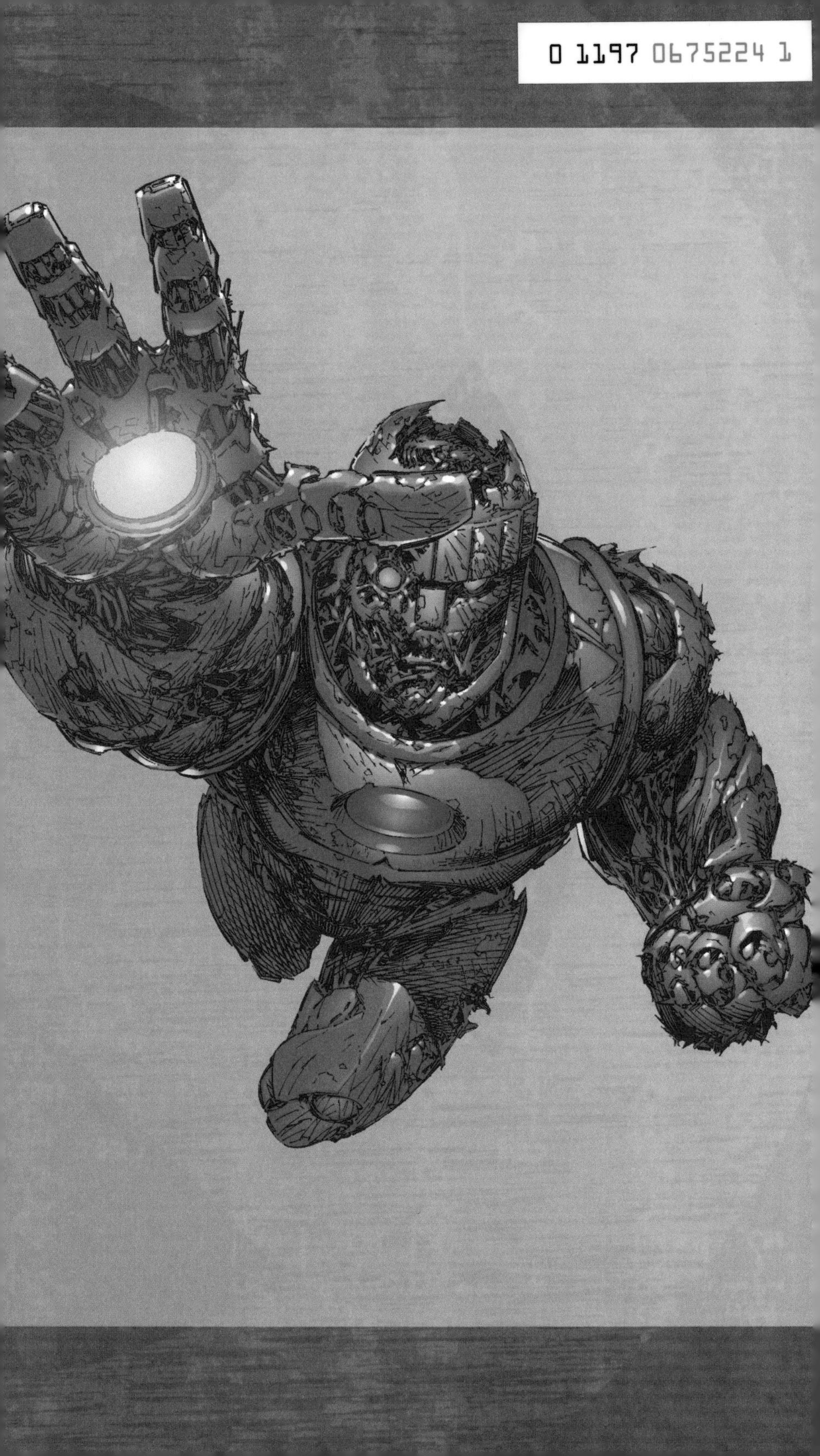

#151

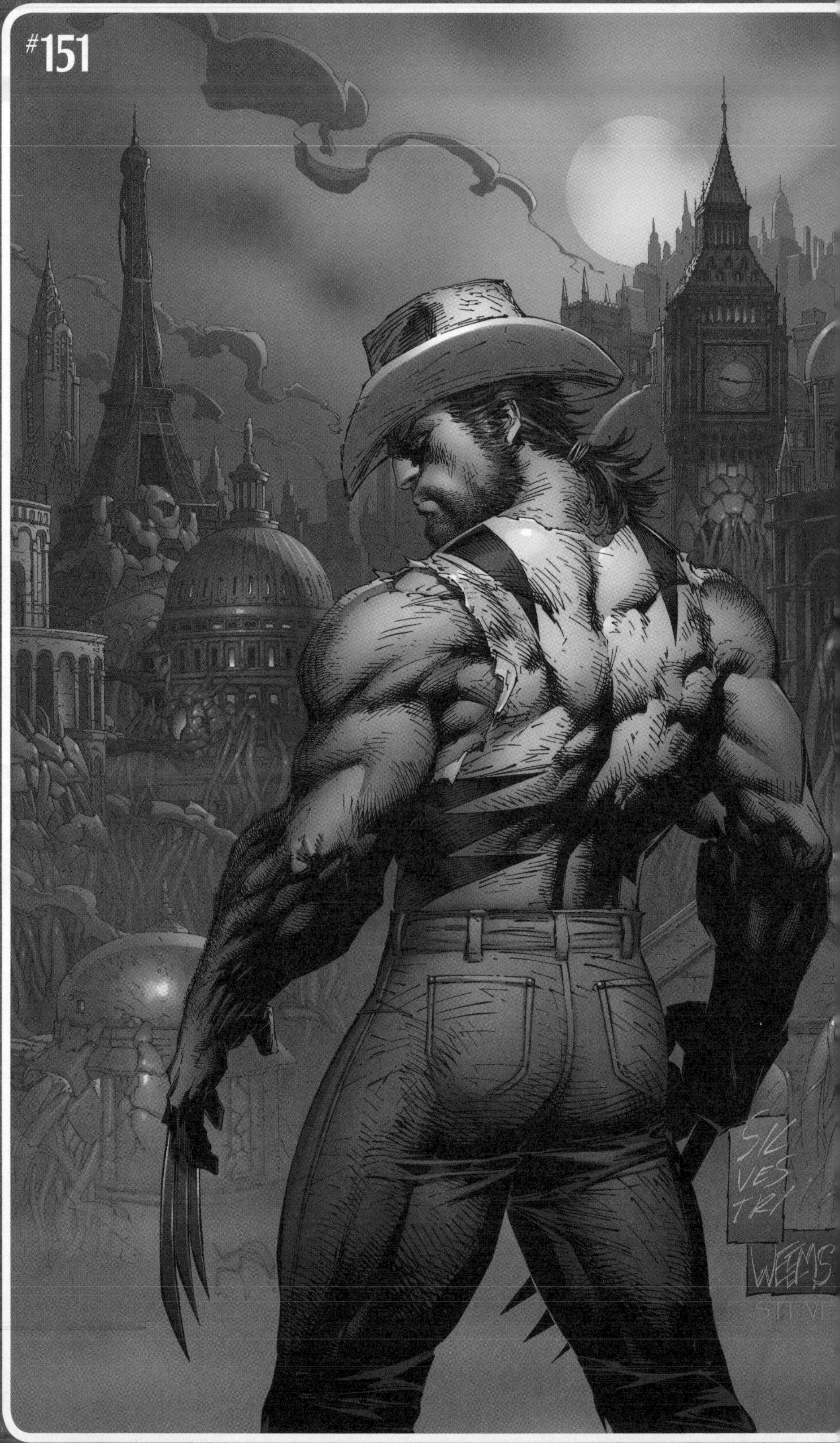
SIL
VES
TRI
WEEMS

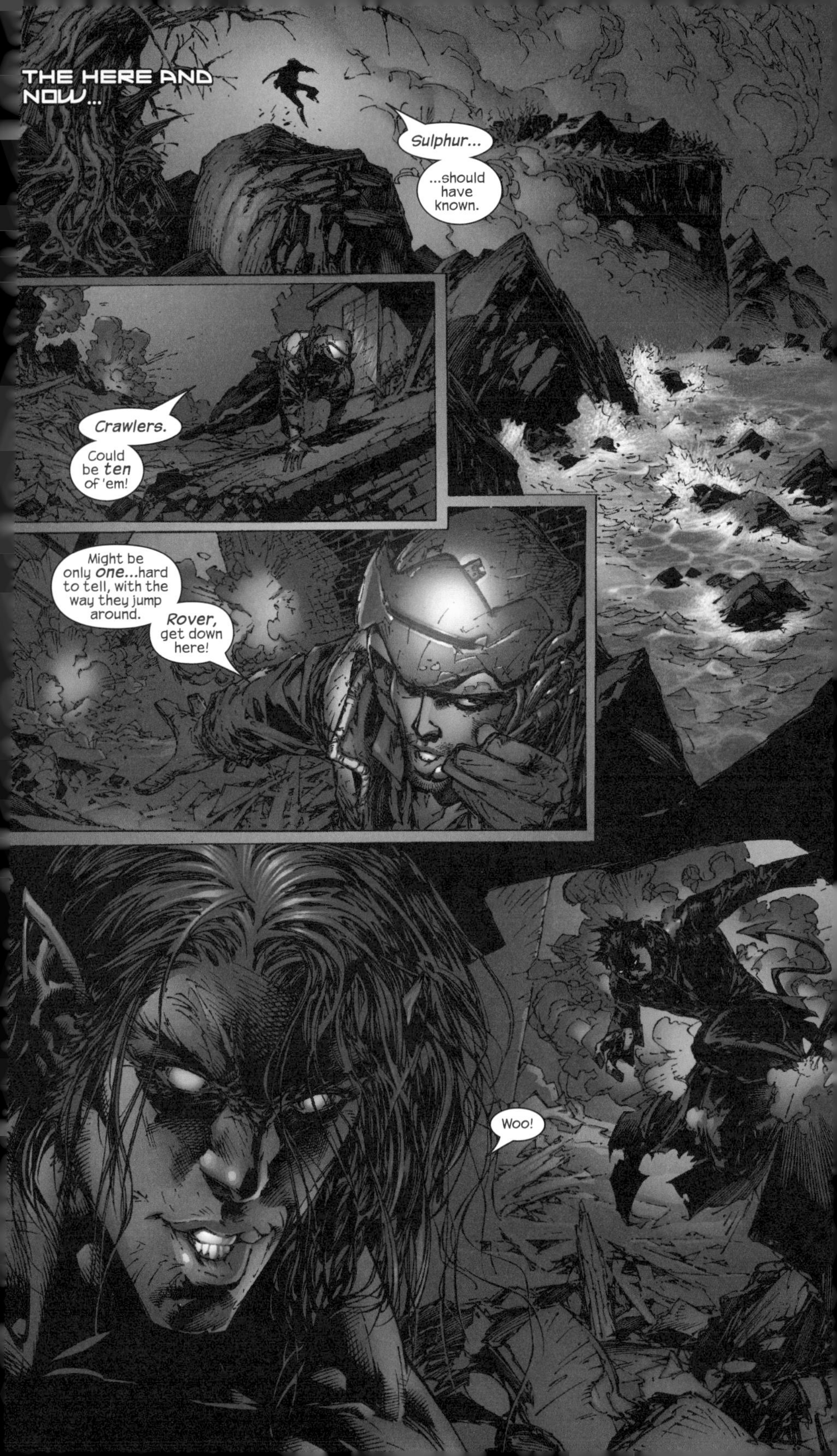
THE HERE AND NOW...
Sulphur...
...should have known.
Crawlers.
Could be ten of 'em!
Might be only one...hard to tell, with the way they jump around.
Rover, get down here!
Woo!

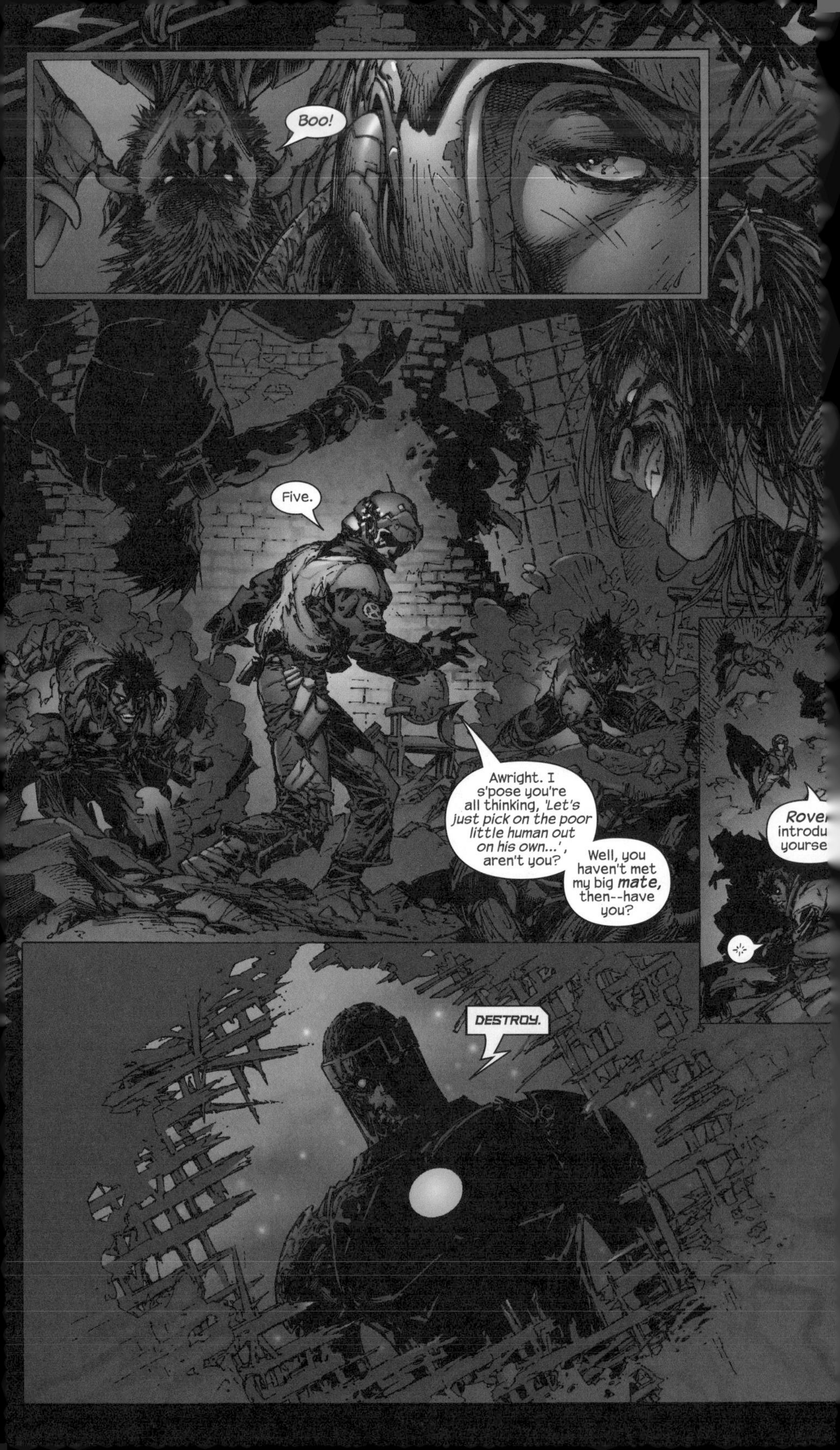
Boo!
Five.
Awright. I s'pose you're all thinking, *'Let's just pick on the poor little human out on his own...'*, aren't you?
Well, you haven't met my big ***mate,*** then--have you?
DESTROY.

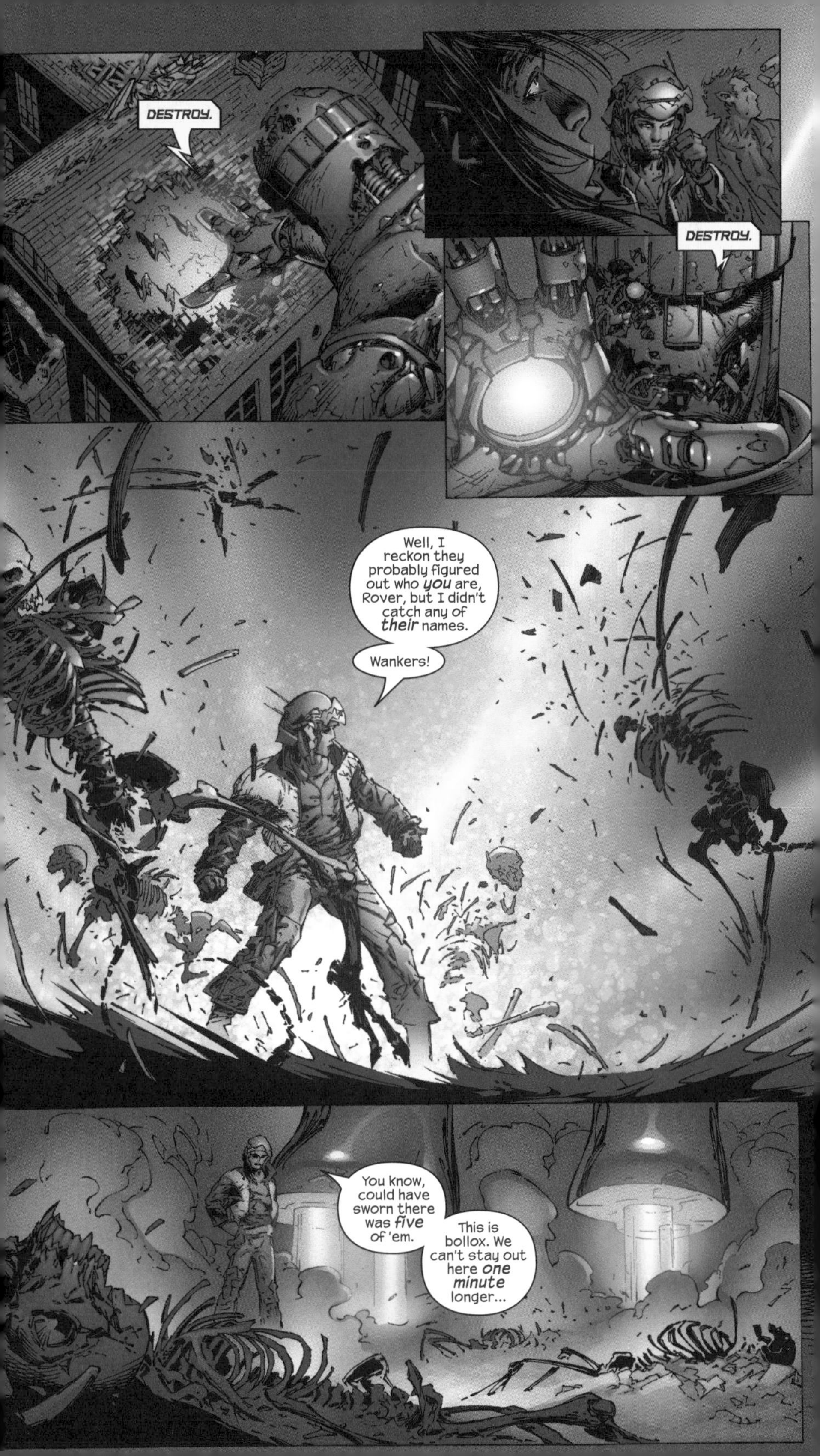
DESTROY.
DESTROY.
Well, I reckon they probably figured out who *you* are, Rover, but I didn't catch any of *their* names.
Wankers!
You know, could have sworn there was *five* of 'em.
This is bollox. We can't stay out here *one minute* longer...

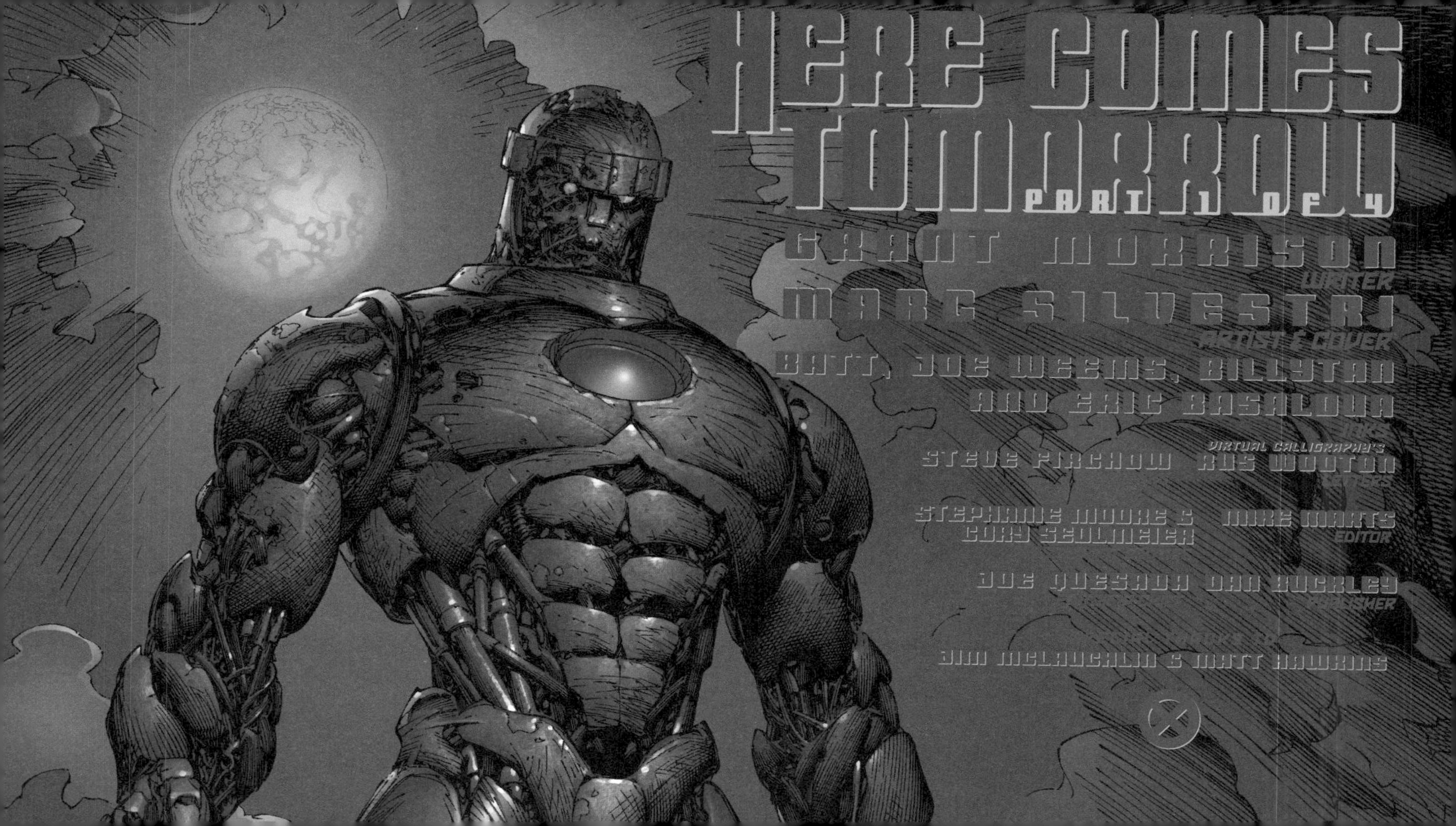

HERE COMES TOMORROW
PART 1 OF 4
GRANT MORRISON
WRITER
MARC SILVESTRI
ARTIST & COVER
BATT, JOE WEEMS, BILLYTAN AND ERIC BASALDUA
INKS
STEVE FIRCHOW
VIRTUAL CALLIGRAPHY'S RUS WOOTON
STEPHANIE MOORE & CORY SEDLMEIER
MIKE MARTS
EDITOR
JOE QUESADA
DAN BUCKLEY
DIM MCLAUCHLIN & MATT HAWKINS

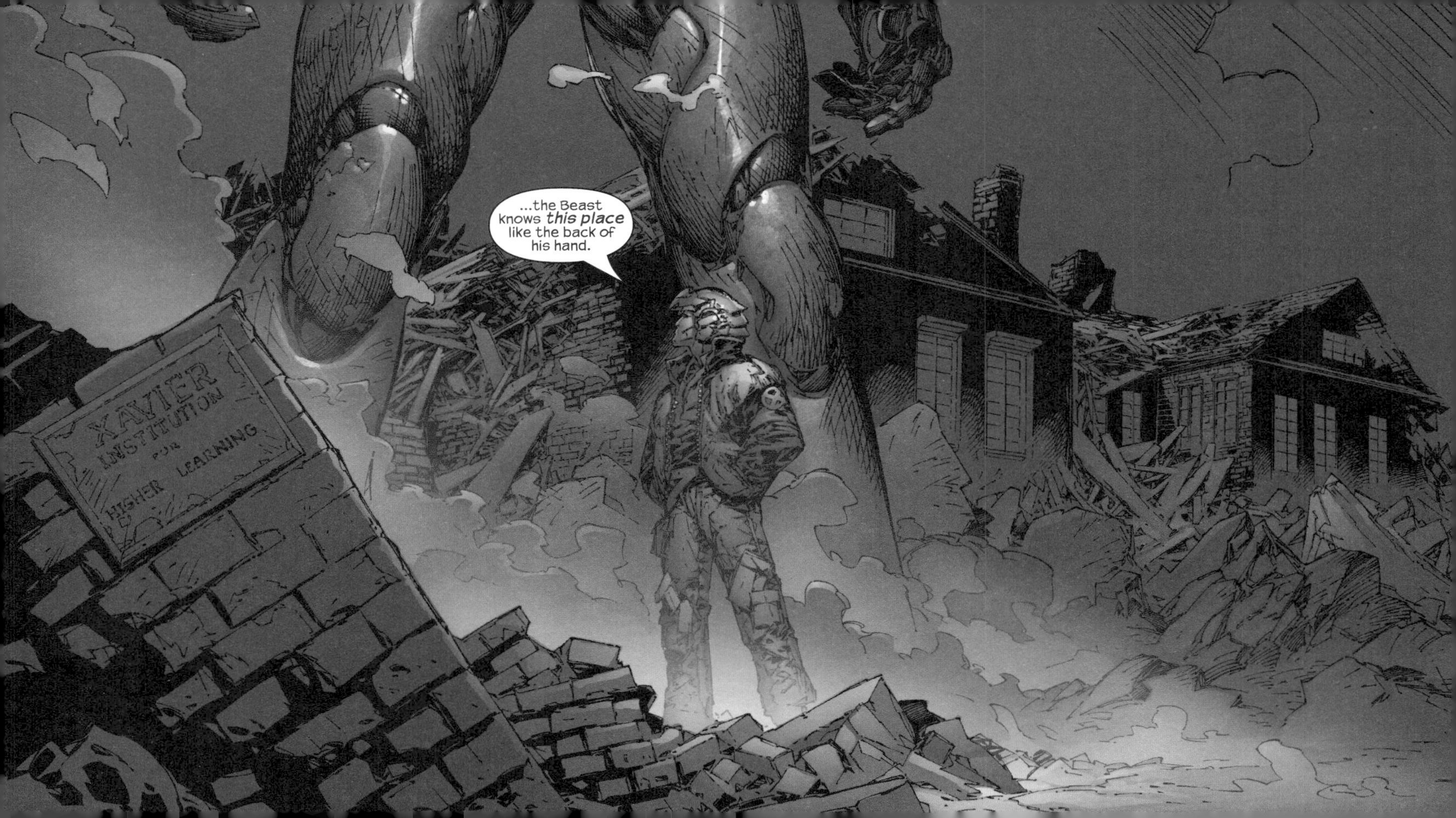
...the Beast knows this place like the back of his hand.
XAVIER INSTITUTION FOR HIGHER LEARNING

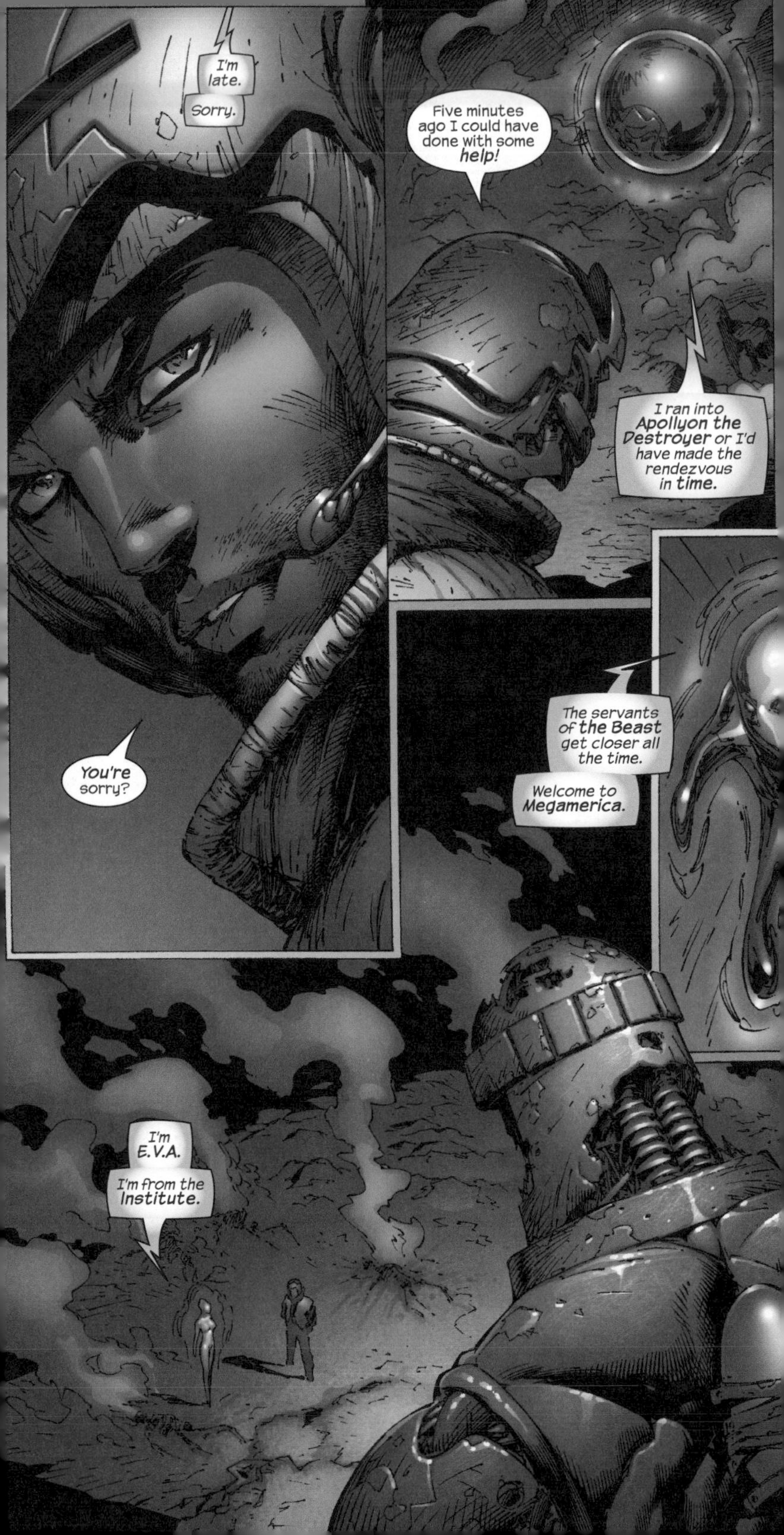

I'm late.
Sorry.
Five minutes ago I could have done with some help!
I ran into Apollyon the Destroyer or I'd have made the rendezvous in time.
You're sorry?
The servants of the Beast get closer all the time.
Welcome to Megamerica.
I'm E.V.A.
I'm from the Institute.

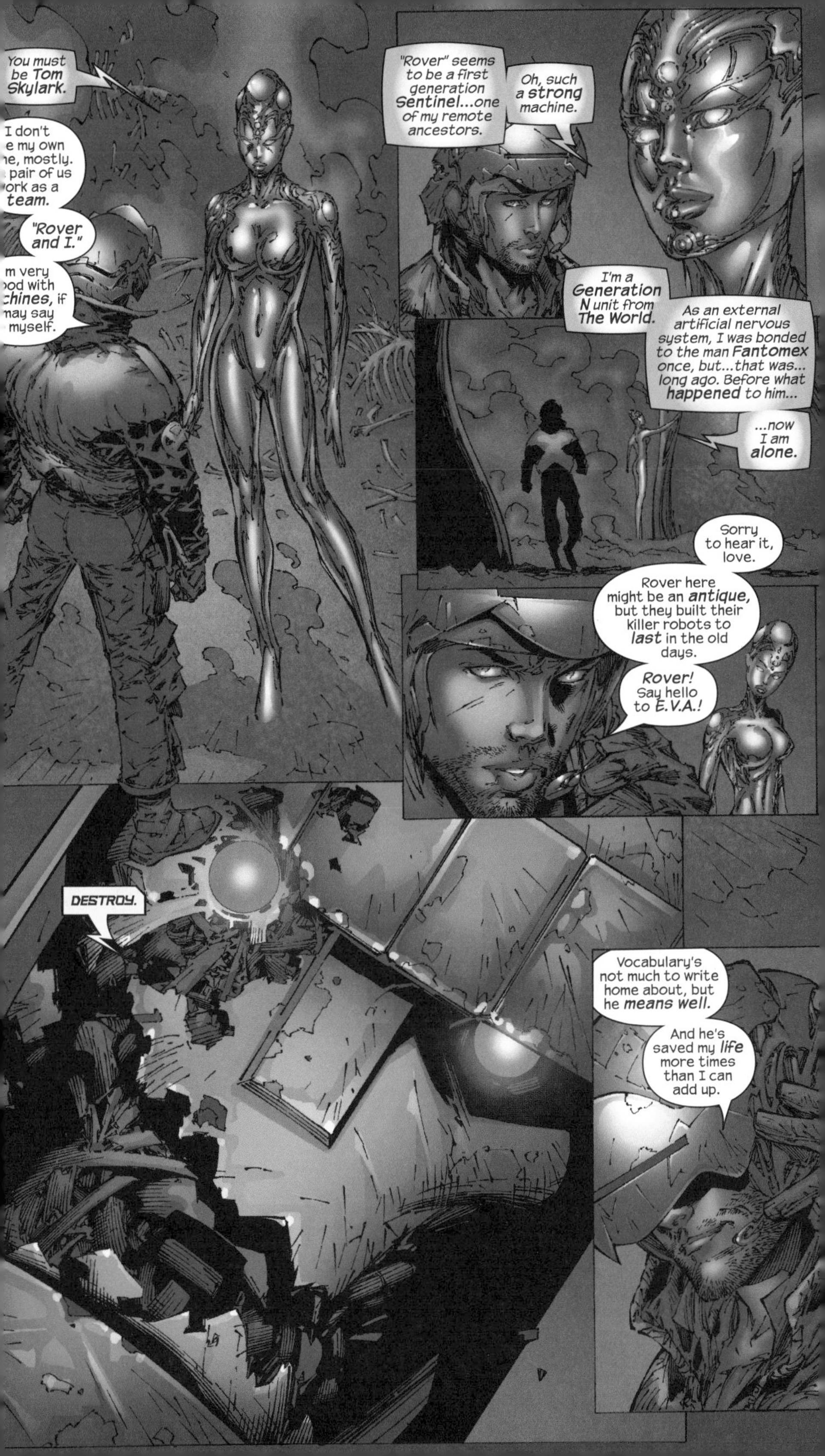

You must be Tom Skylark.
I don't e my own ne, mostly. pair of us ork as a team.
"Rover and I."
m very ood with chines, if may say myself.
"Rover" seems to be a first generation Sentinel...one of my remote ancestors.
Oh, such a strong machine.
I'm a Generation N unit from The World.
As an external artificial nervous system, I was bonded to the man Fantomex once, but...that was... long ago. Before what happened to him...
...now I am alone.
Sorry to hear it, love.
Rover here might be an antique, but they built their killer robots to last in the old days.
Rover! Say hello to E.V.A.!
DESTROY.
Vocabulary's not much to write home about, but he means well.
And he's saved my life more times than I can add up.

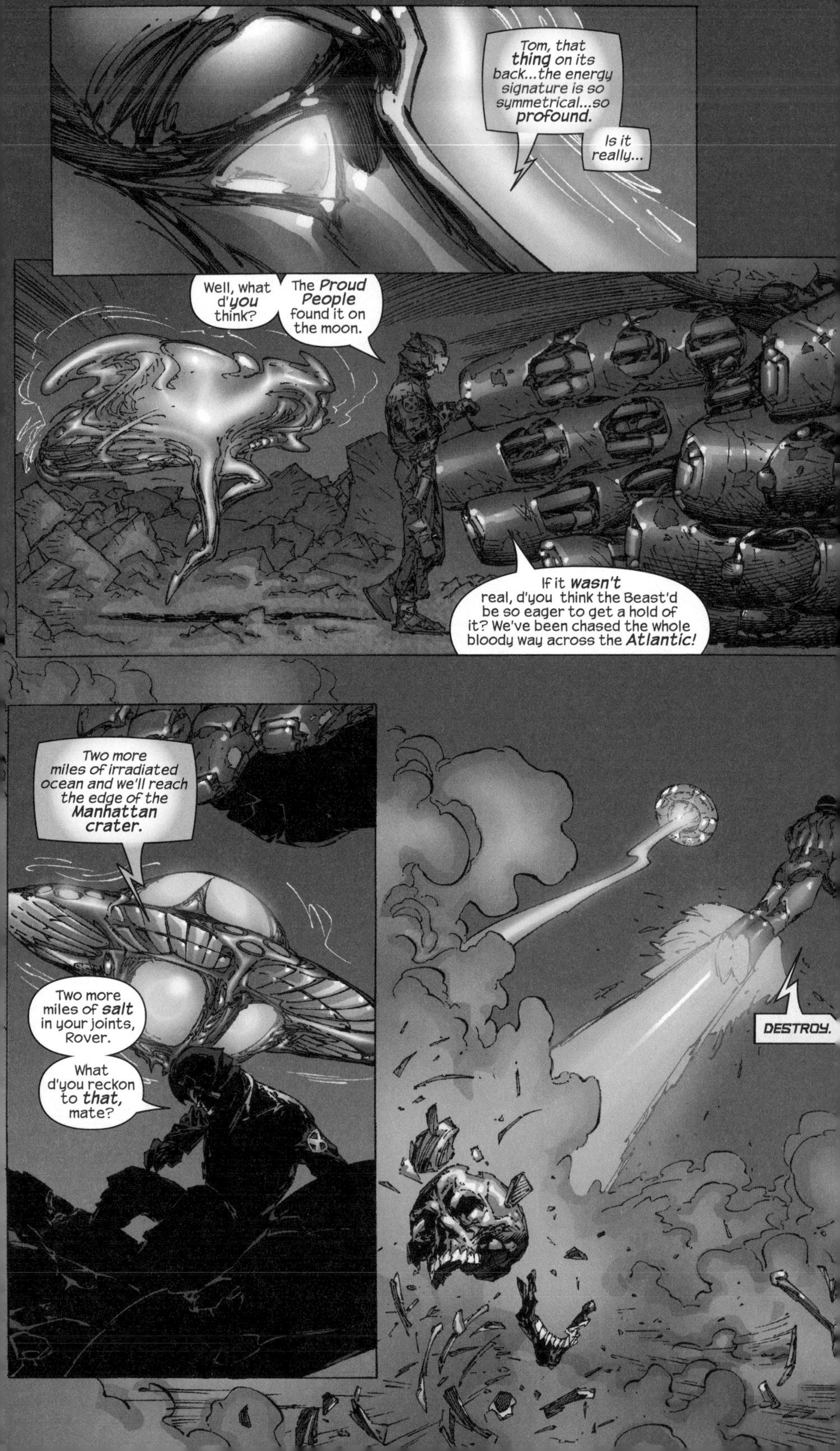
Tom, that thing on its back...the energy signature is so symmetrical...so profound.
Is it really...
Well, what d'you think?
The Proud People found it on the moon.
If it wasn't real, d'you think the Beast'd be so eager to get a hold of it? We've been chased the whole bloody way across the Atlantic!
Two more miles of irradiated ocean and we'll reach the edge of the Manhattan crater.
Two more miles of salt in your joints, Rover.
What d'you reckon to that, mate?
DESTROY.

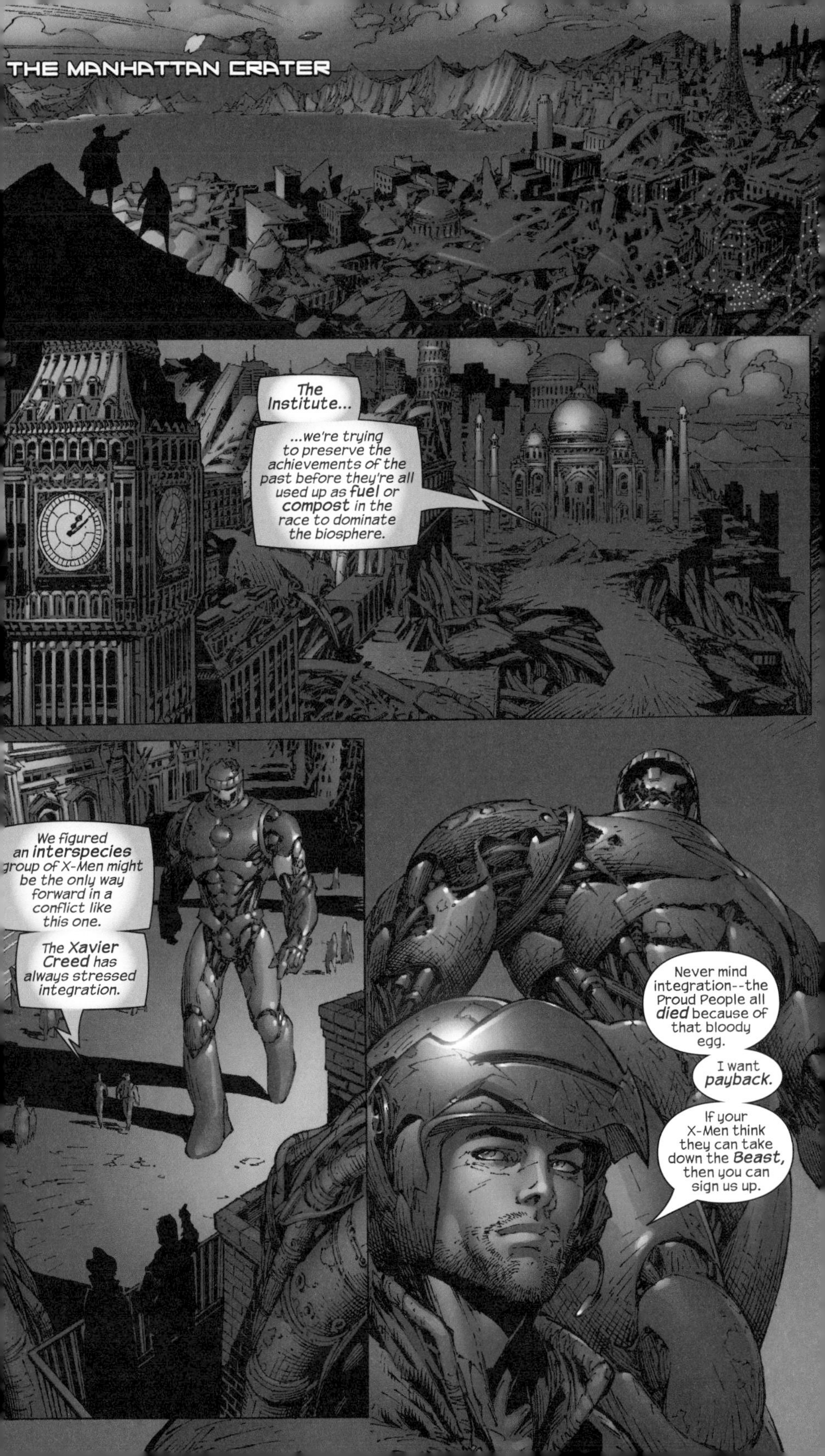
THE MANHATTAN CRATER
The Institute...
...we're trying to preserve the achievements of the past before they're all used up as **fuel** or **compost** in the race to dominate the biosphere.
We figured an **interspecies** group of X-Men might be the only way forward in a conflict like this one.
The **Xavier Creed** has always stressed integration.
Never mind integration--the Proud People all ***died*** because of that bloody egg.
I want ***payback.***
If your X-Men think they can take down the ***Beast,*** then you can sign us up.

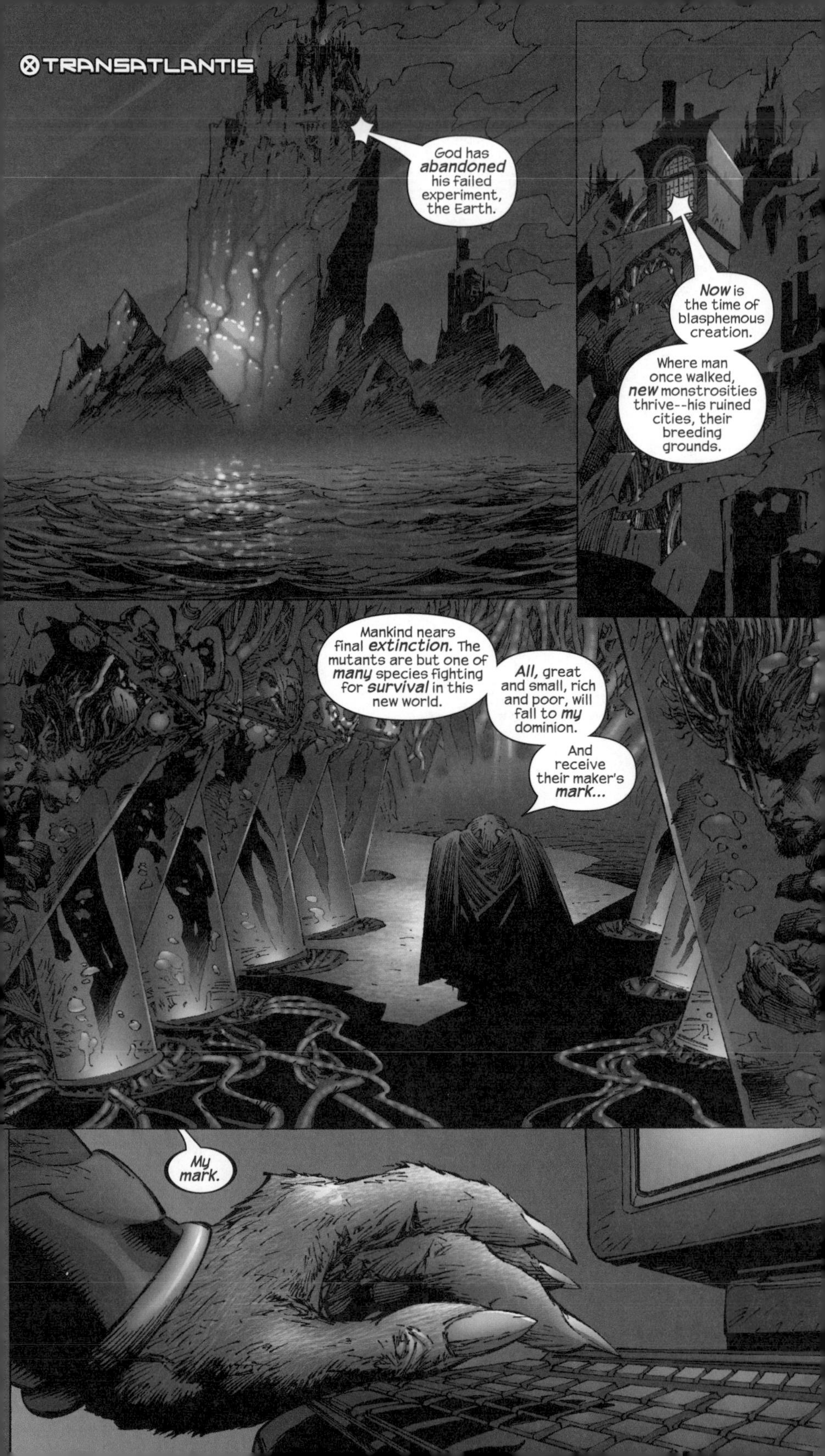
TRANSATLANTIS
God has *abandoned* his failed experiment, the Earth.
Now is the time of blasphemous creation.
Where man once walked, *new* monstrosities thrive--his ruined cities, their breeding grounds.
Mankind nears final *extinction.* The mutants are but one of *many* species fighting for *survival* in this new world.
All, great and small, rich and poor, will fall to *my* dominion.
And receive their maker's *mark...*
My mark.

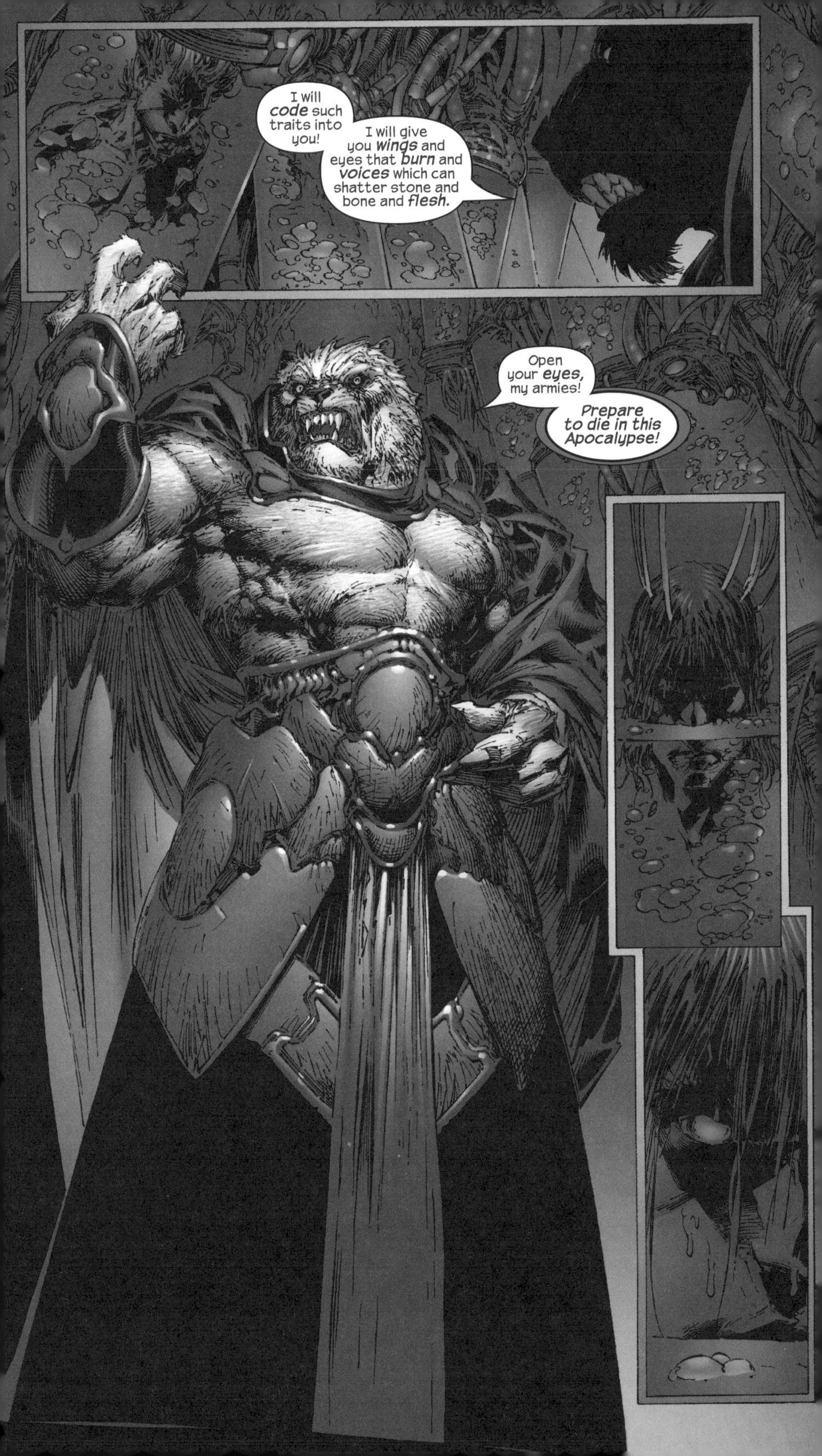

I will code such traits into you!
I will give you wings and eyes that burn and voices which can shatter stone and bone and flesh.
Open your eyes, my armies!
Prepare to die in this Apocalypse!

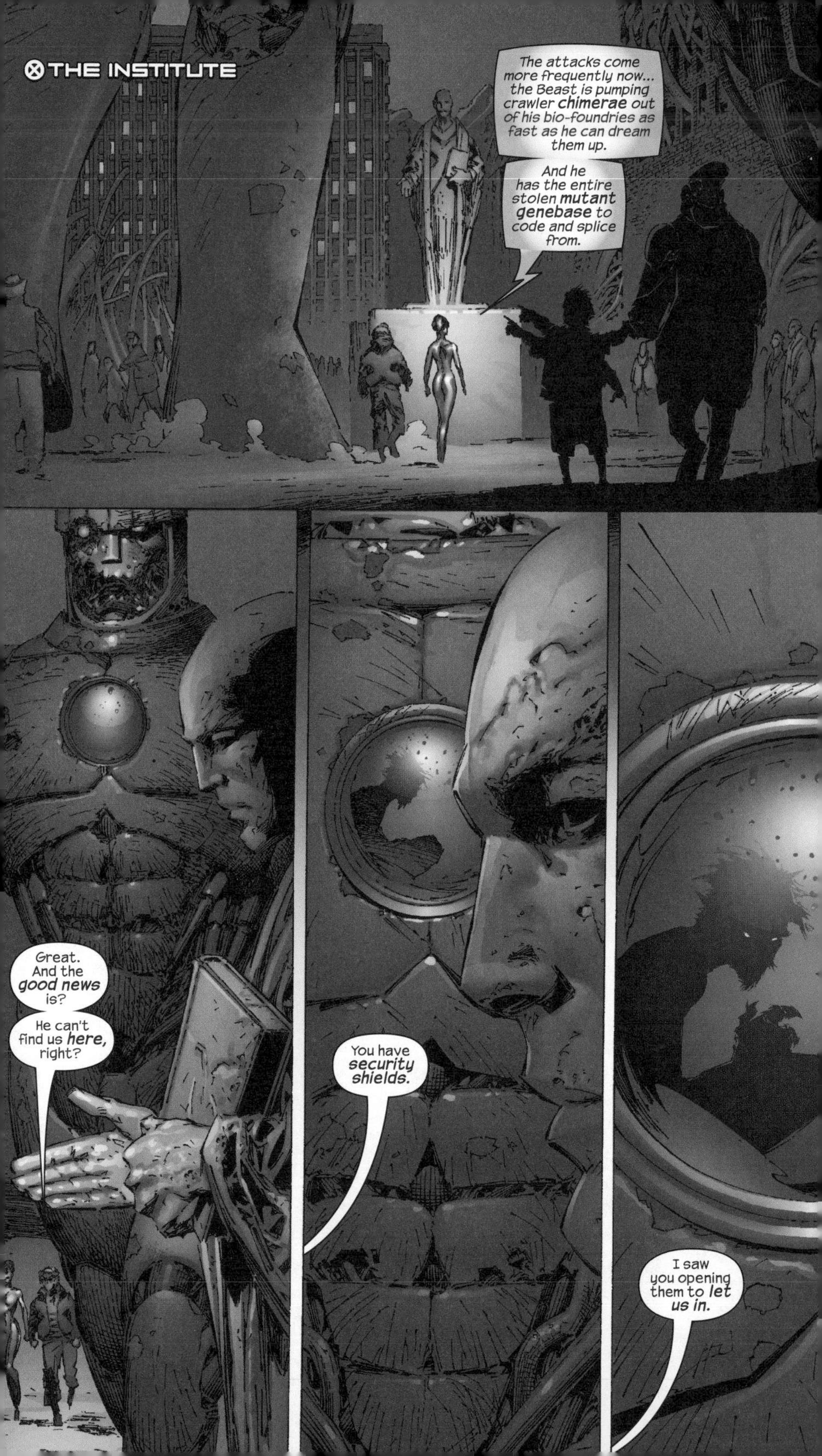
THE INSTITUTE
The attacks come more frequently now... the Beast is pumping crawler chimerae out of his bio-foundries as fast as he can dream them up.
And he has the entire stolen mutant genebase to code and splice from.
Great. And the good news is?
He can't find us here, right?
You have security shields.
I saw you opening them to let us in.

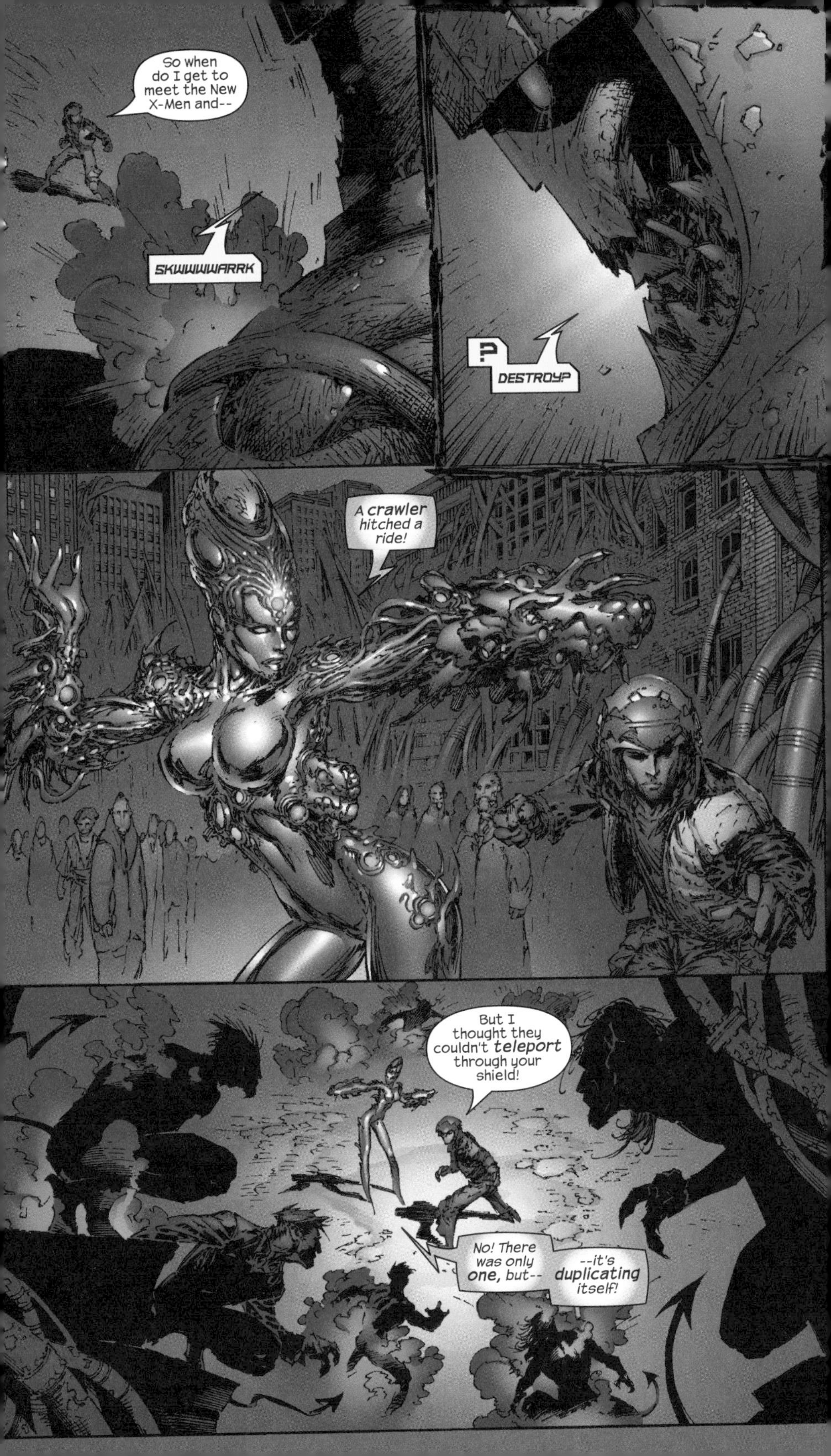
So when do I get to meet the New X-Men and--
SKWWWWARRK
?
DESTROY?
A crawler hitched a ride!
But I thought they couldn't teleport through your shield!
No! There was only one, but--
--it's duplicating itself!

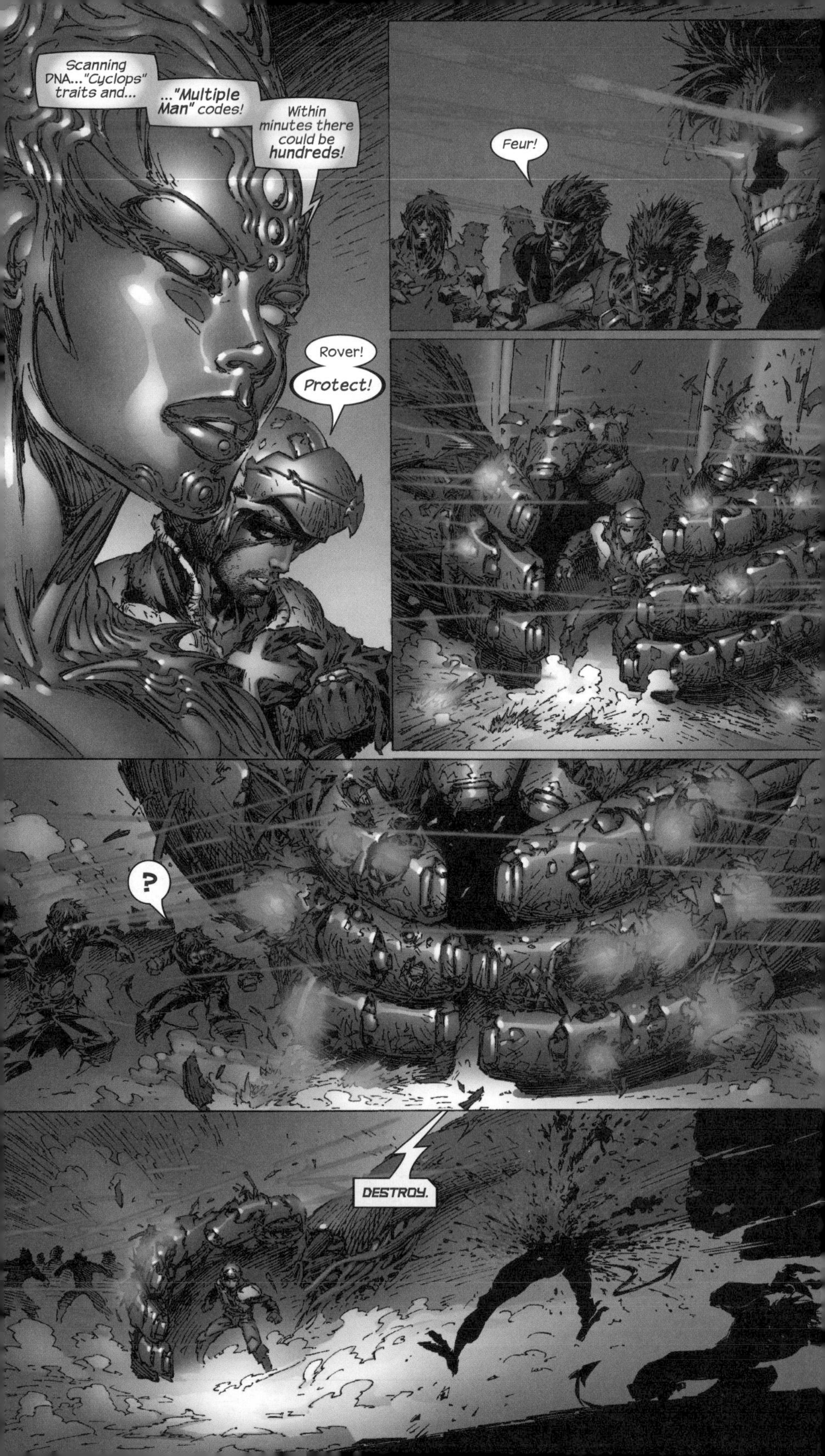
Scanning DNA..."Cyclops" traits and...
..."Multiple Man" codes!
Within minutes there could be hundreds!
Feur!
Rover!
Protect!
?
DESTROY.

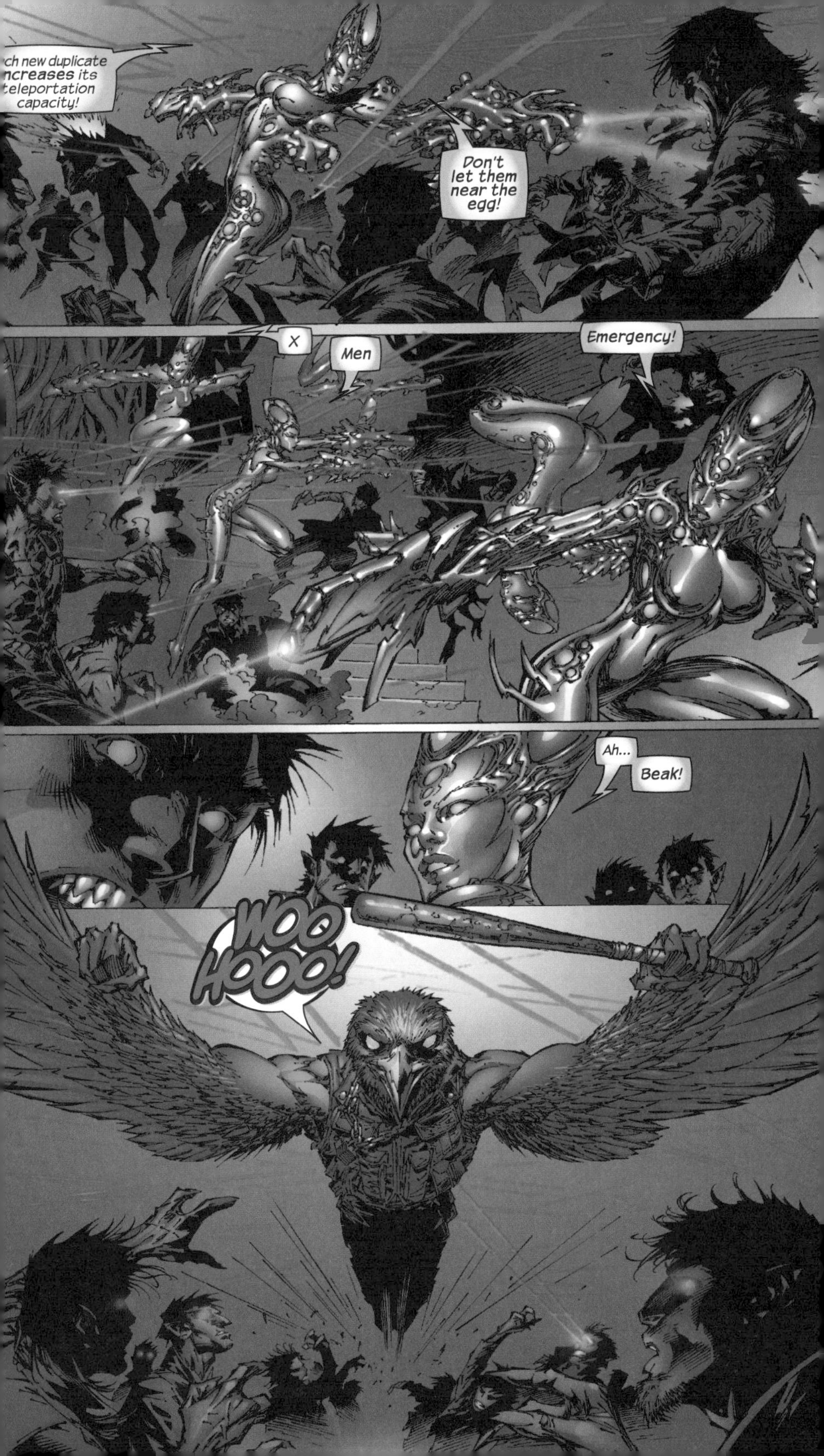

ch new duplicate ncreases its teleportation capacity!
Don't let them near the egg!
X
Men
Emergency!
Ah...
Beak!
WOO HOOO!

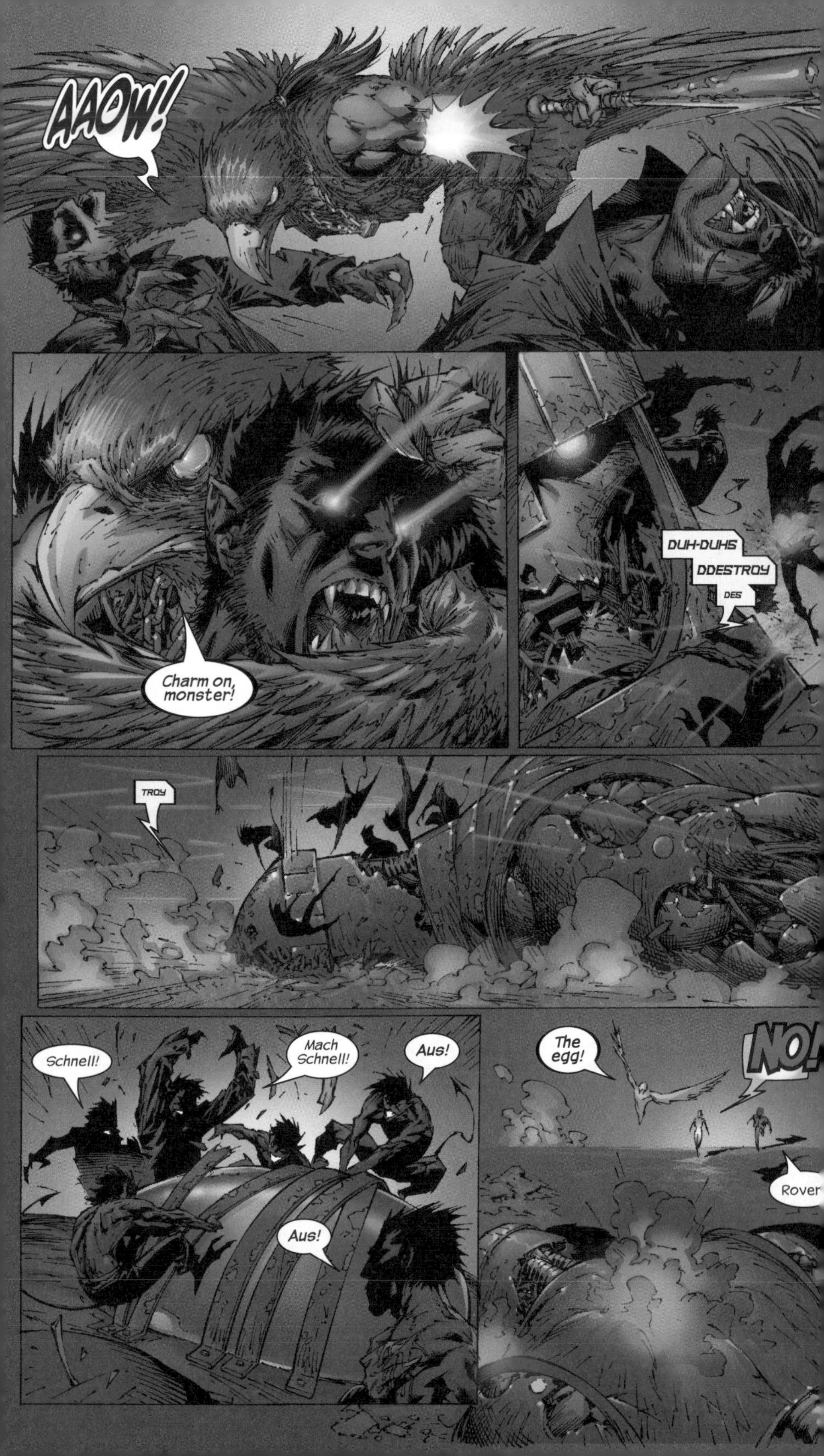
AAOW!
Charm on, monster!
DUH-DUHS
DDESTROY
DES
TROY
Schnell!
Mach Schnell!
Aus!
Aus!
The egg!
NO!
Rover

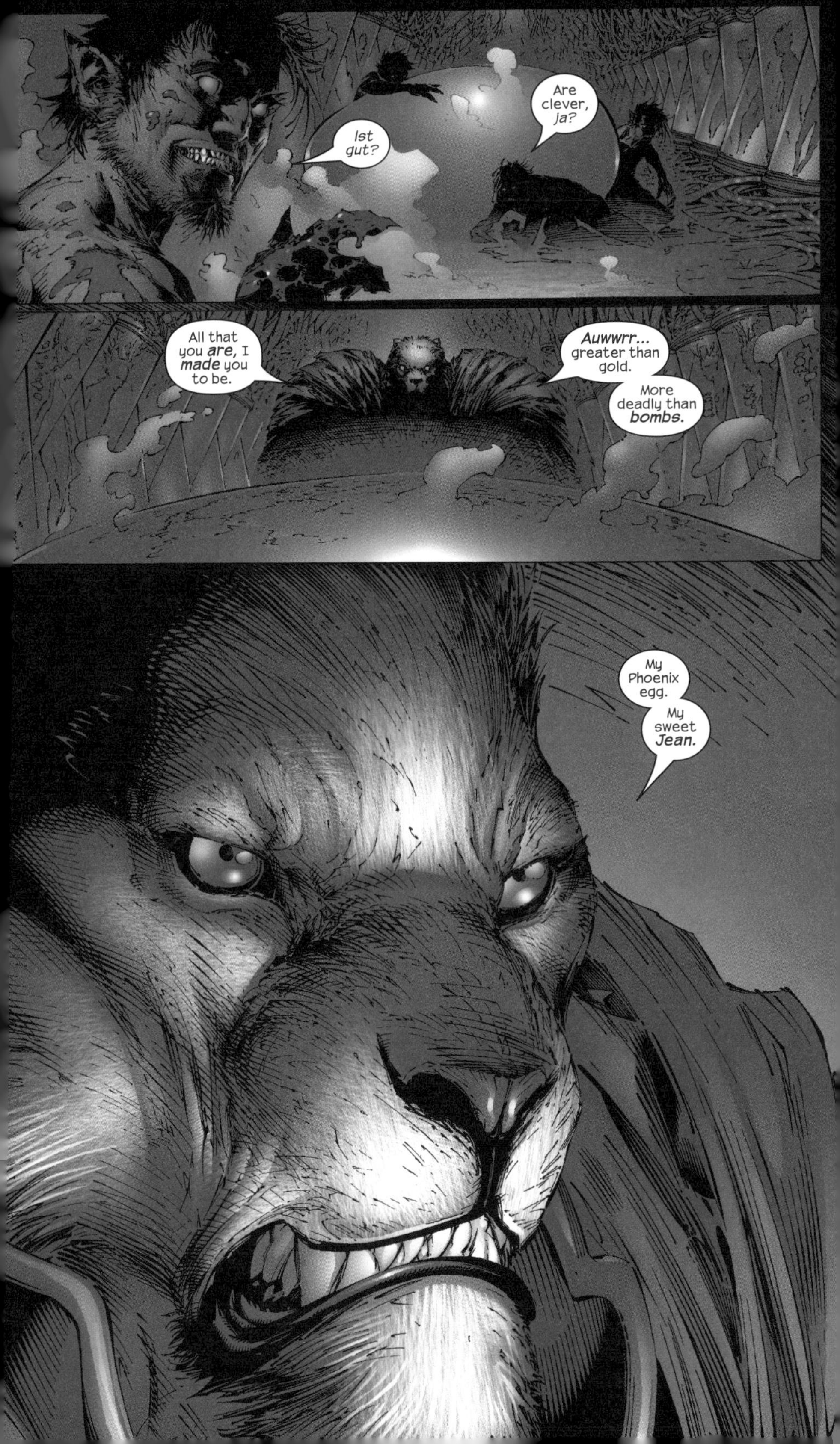

Ist gut?
Are clever, ja?
All that you are, I made you to be.
Auwwrr... greater than gold.
More deadly than bombs.
My Phoenix egg.
My sweet Jean.

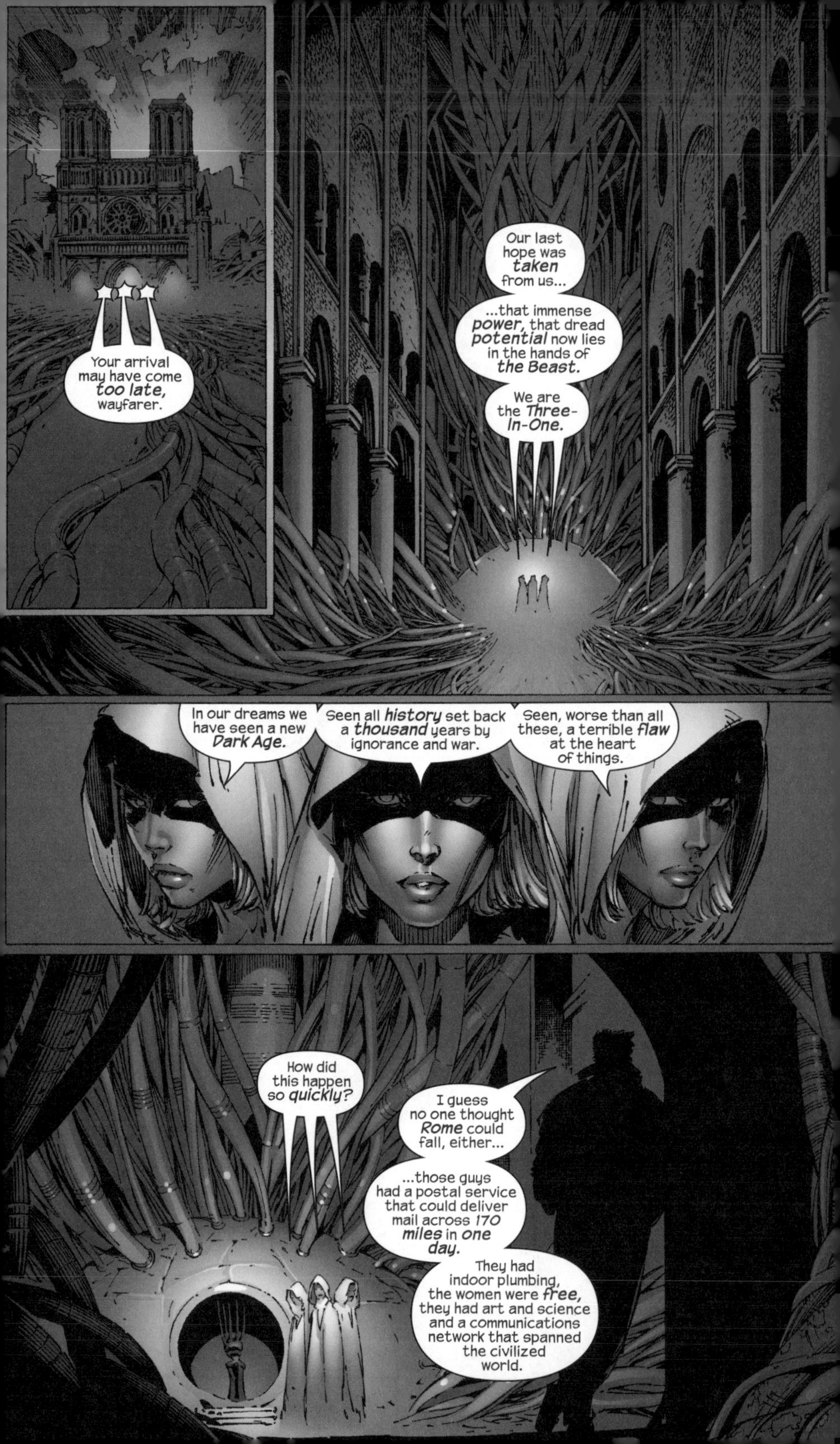
Your arrival may have come too late, wayfarer.
Our last hope was taken from us...
...that immense power, that dread potential now lies in the hands of the Beast.
We are the Three-In-One.
In our dreams we have seen a new Dark Age.
Seen all history set back a thousand years by ignorance and war.
Seen, worse than all these, a terrible flaw at the heart of things.
How did this happen so quickly?
I guess no one thought Rome could fall, either...
...those guys had a postal service that could deliver mail across 170 miles in one day.
They had indoor plumbing, the women were free, they had art and science and a communications network that spanned the civilized world.

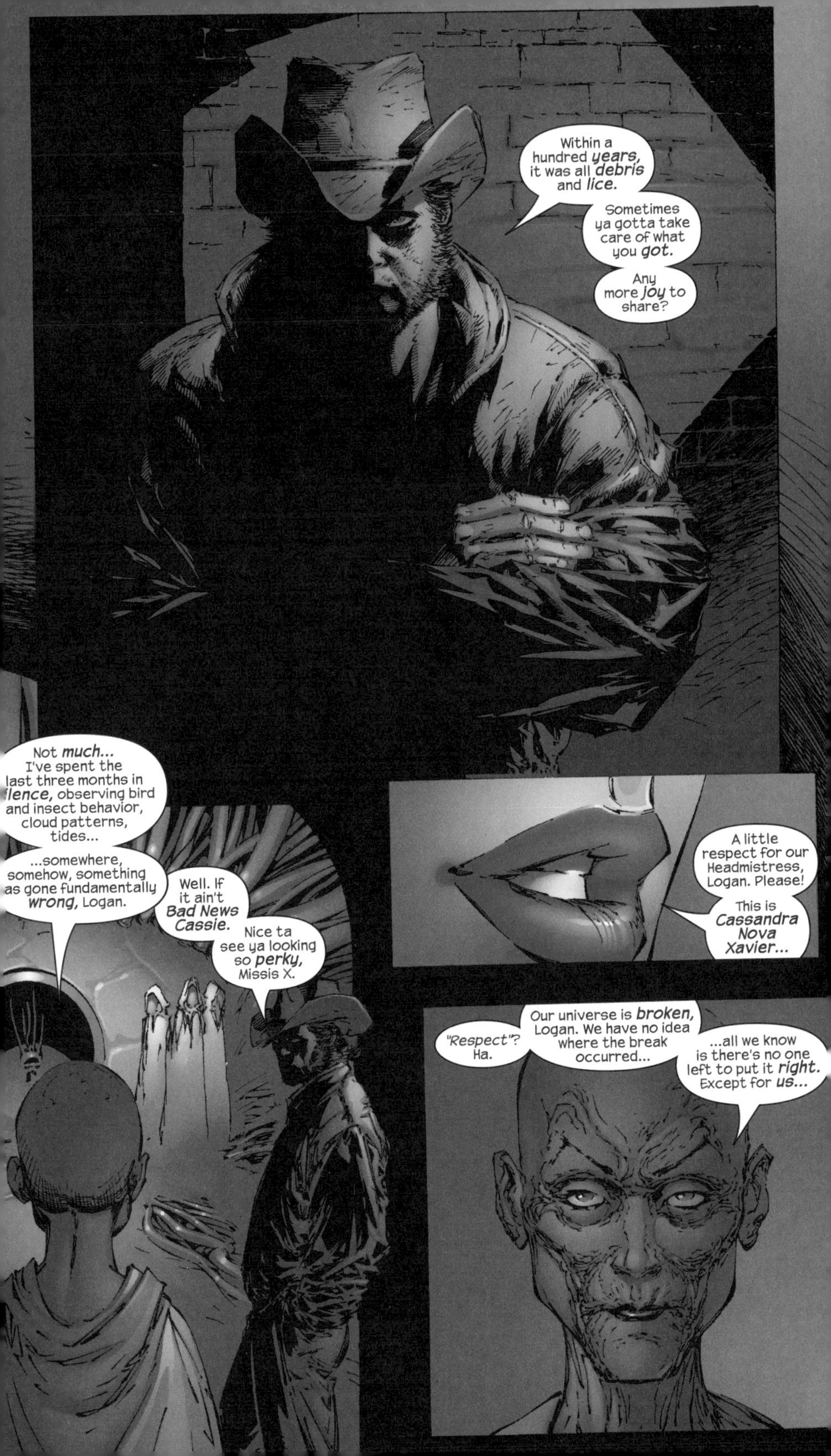
Within a hundred *years,* it was all *debris* and *lice.*
Sometimes ya gotta take care of what you *got.*
Any more *joy* to share?
Not *much*... I've spent the last three months in lence, observing bird and insect behavior, cloud patterns, tides...
...somewhere, somehow, something as gone fundamentally *wrong,* Logan.
Well. If it ain't *Bad News Cassie.*
Nice ta see ya looking so *perky,* Missis X.
A little respect for our Headmistress, Logan. Please!
This is *Cassandra Nova Xavier...*
"Respect"? Ha.
Our universe is *broken,* Logan. We have no idea where the break occurred...
...all we know is there's no one left to put it *right.* Except for *us...*

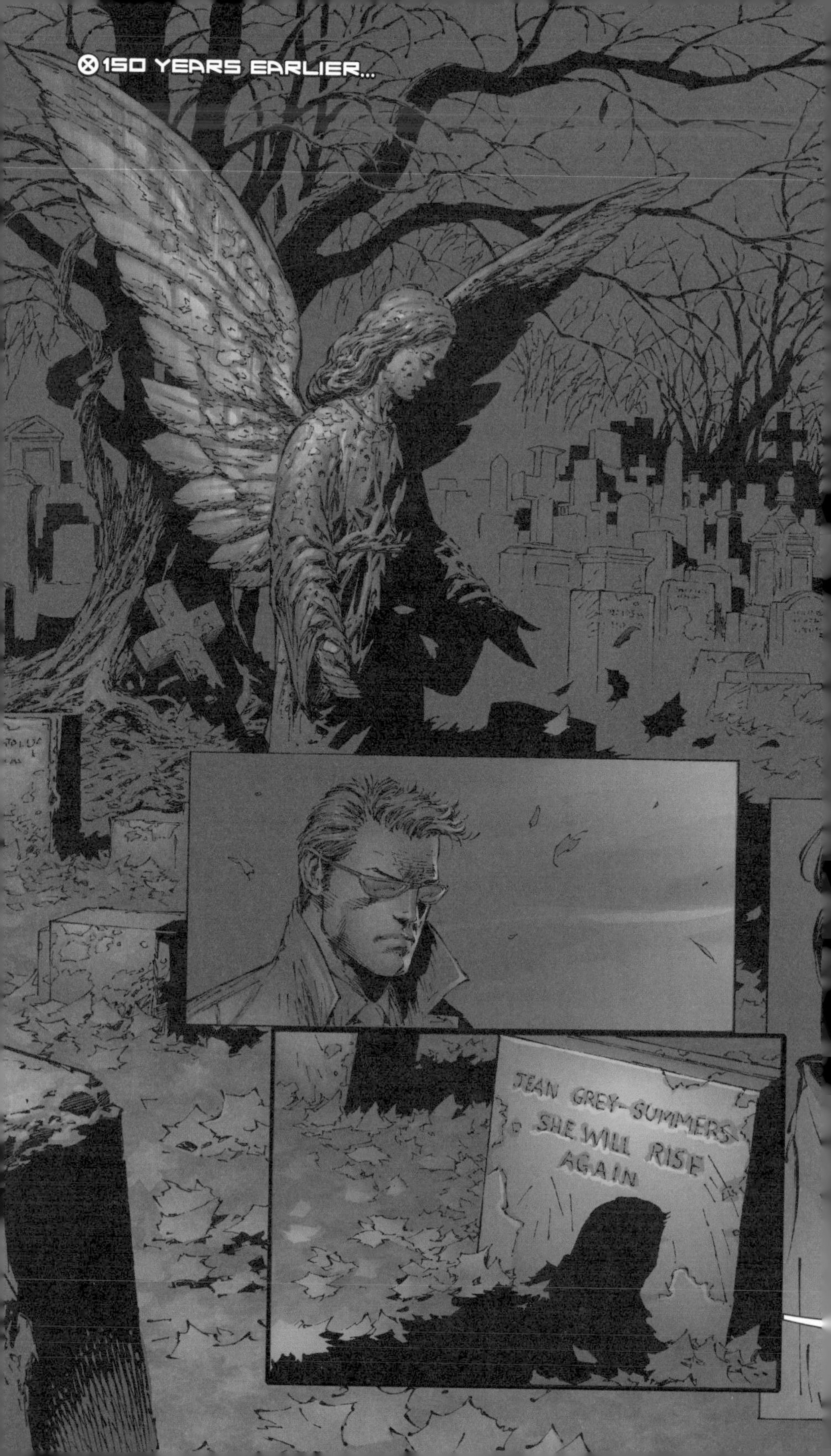
150 YEARS EARLIER...
JEAN GREY-SUMMERS
SHE WILL RISE AGAIN

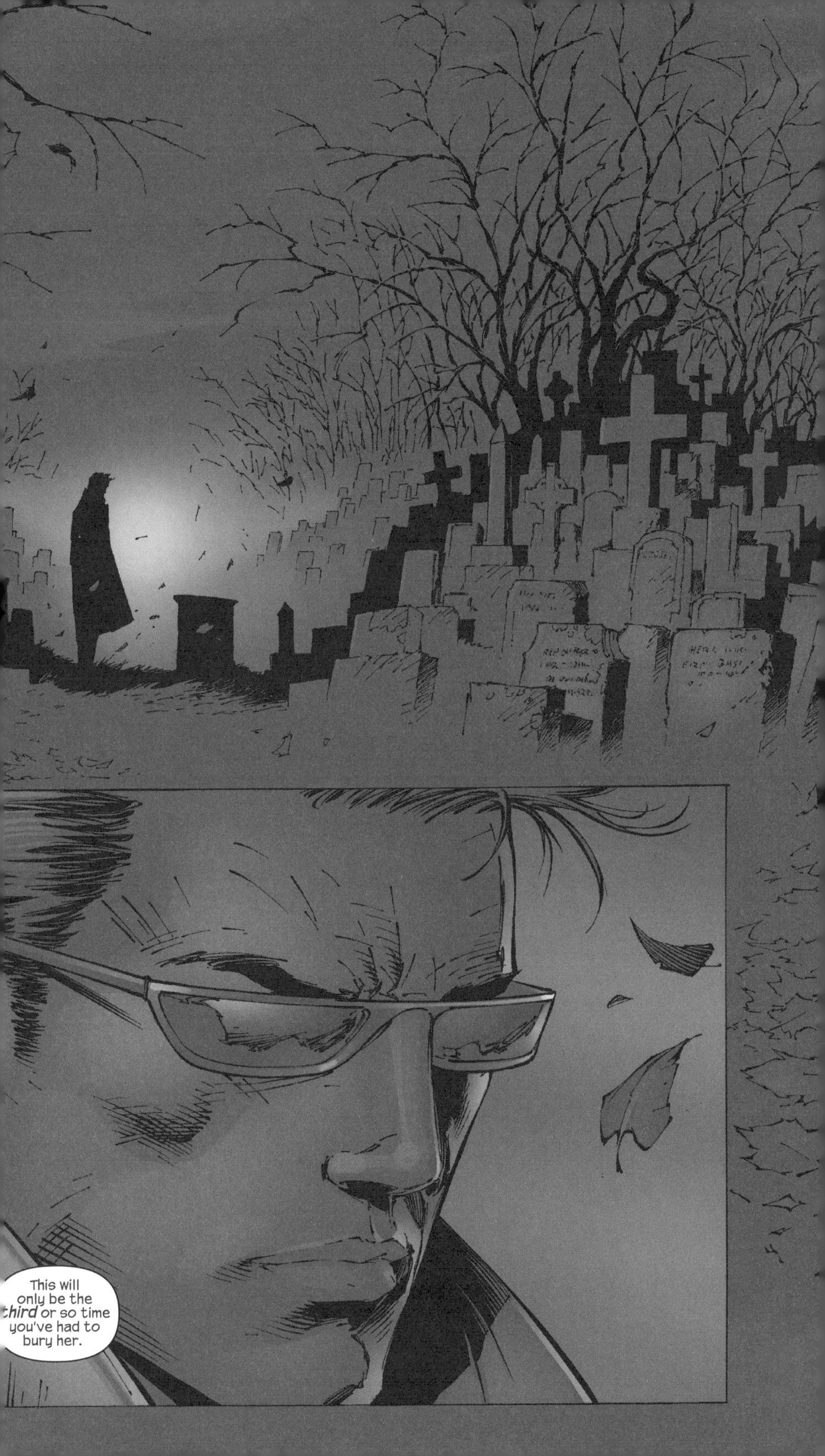
This will only be the *third* or so time you've had to bury her.

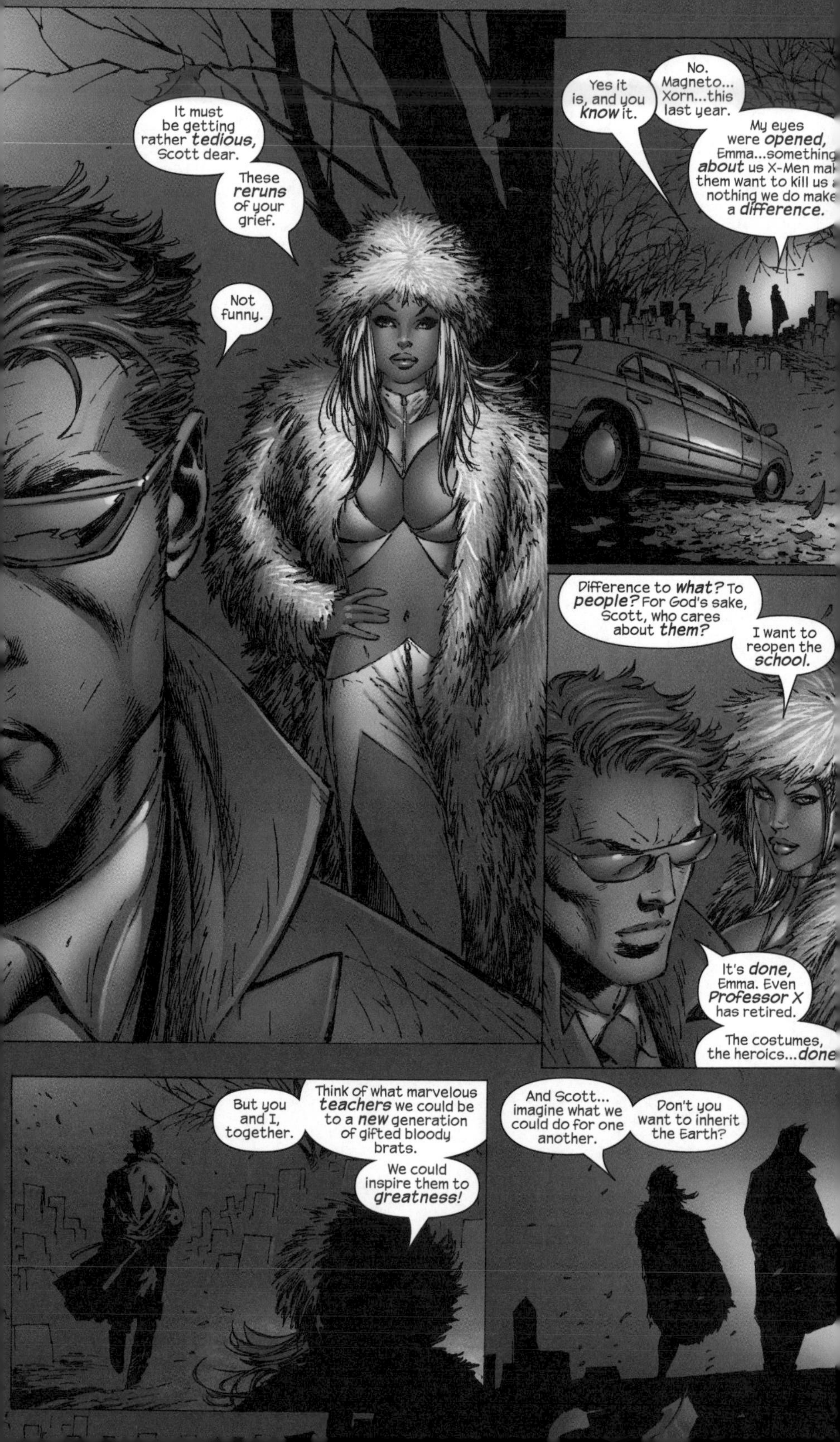
It must be getting rather tedious, Scott dear.
These reruns of your grief.
Not funny.
Yes it is, and you know it.
No. Magneto... Xorn...this last year.
My eyes were opened, Emma...something about us X-Men mak them want to kill us a nothing we do make a difference.
Difference to what? To people? For God's sake, Scott, who cares about them?
I want to reopen the school.
It's done, Emma. Even Professor X has retired.
The costumes, the heroics...done
But you and I, together.
Think of what marvelous teachers we could be to a new generation of gifted bloody brats.
We could inspire them to greatness!
And Scott... imagine what we could do for one another.
Don't you want to inherit the Earth?

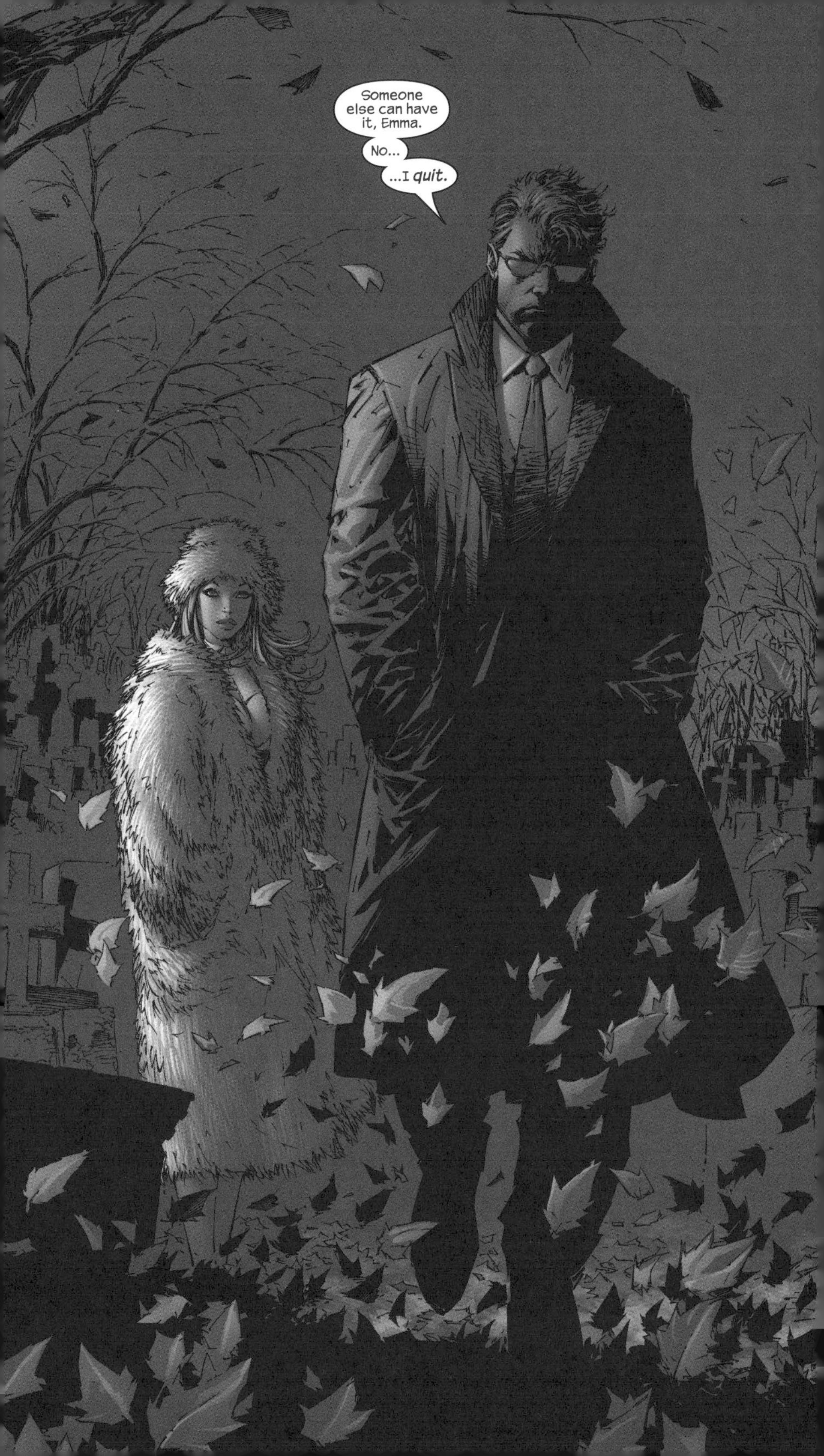

Someone else can have it, Emma.
No...
...I quit.

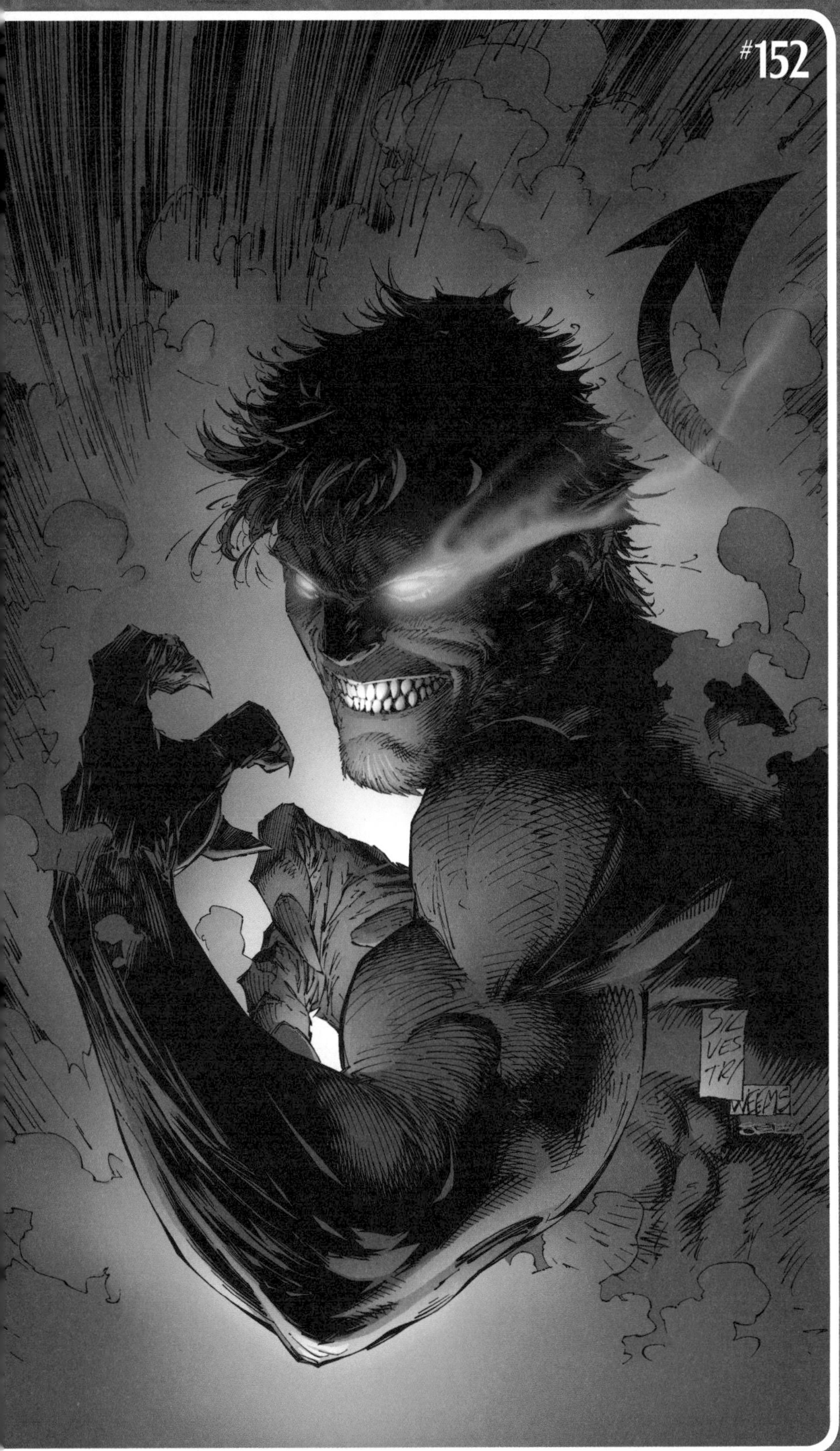
#152

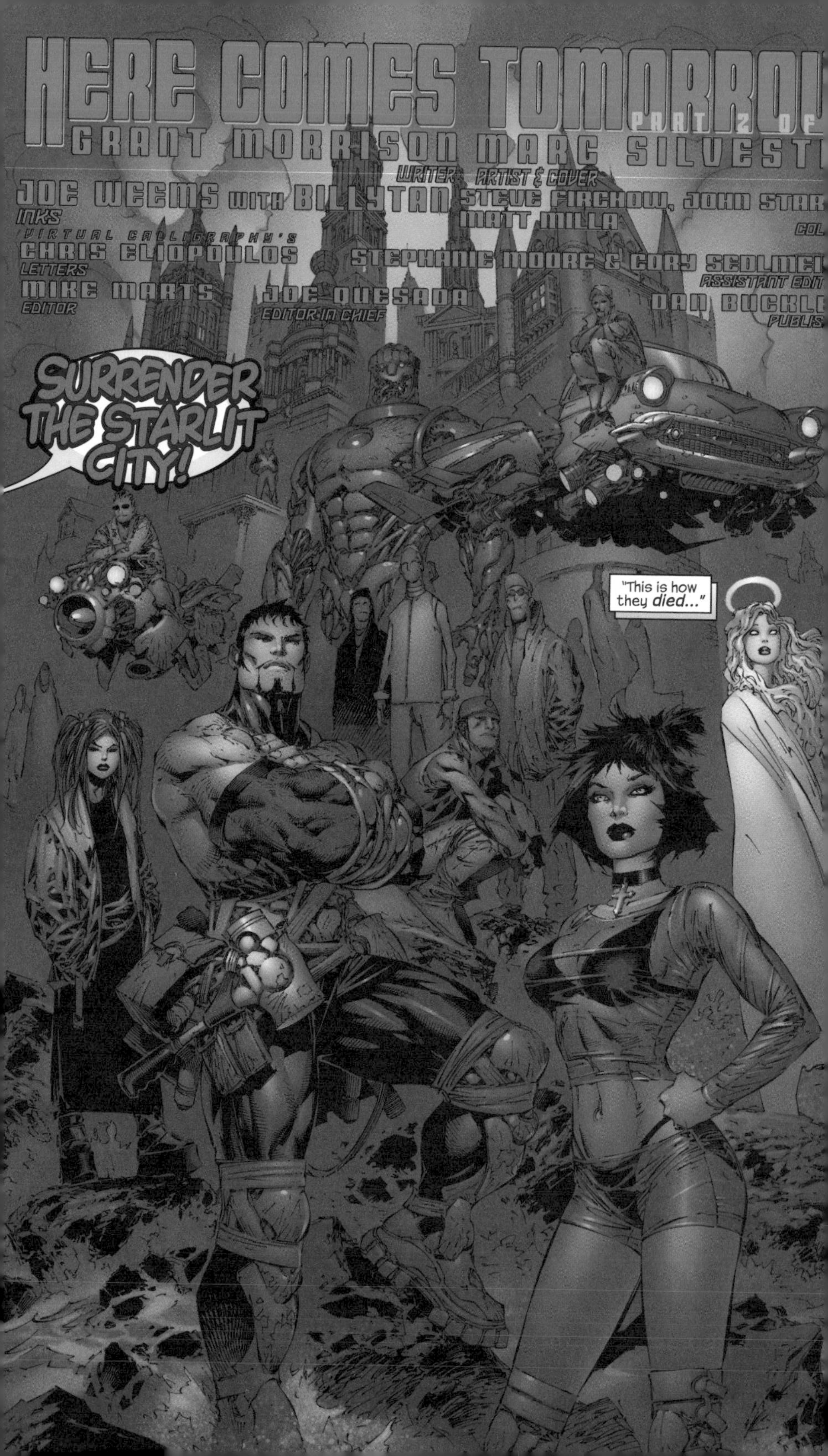
HERE COMES TOMORRO
PART 2 OF
GRANT MORRISON
WRITER
MARC SILVESTR
ARTIST & COVER
JOE WEEMS WITH BILLY TAN
INKS
STEVE FIRCHOW, JOHN STAR
MATT MILLA
COL
VIRTUAL CALLIGRAPHY'S
CHRIS ELIOPOULOS
LETTERS
STEPHANIE MOORE & CORY SEDLMEI
ASSISTANT EDIT
MIKE MARTS
EDITOR
JOE QUESADA
EDITOR IN CHIEF
DAN BUCKLE
PUBLIS
SURRENDER THE STARLIT CITY!
"This is how they *died*..."

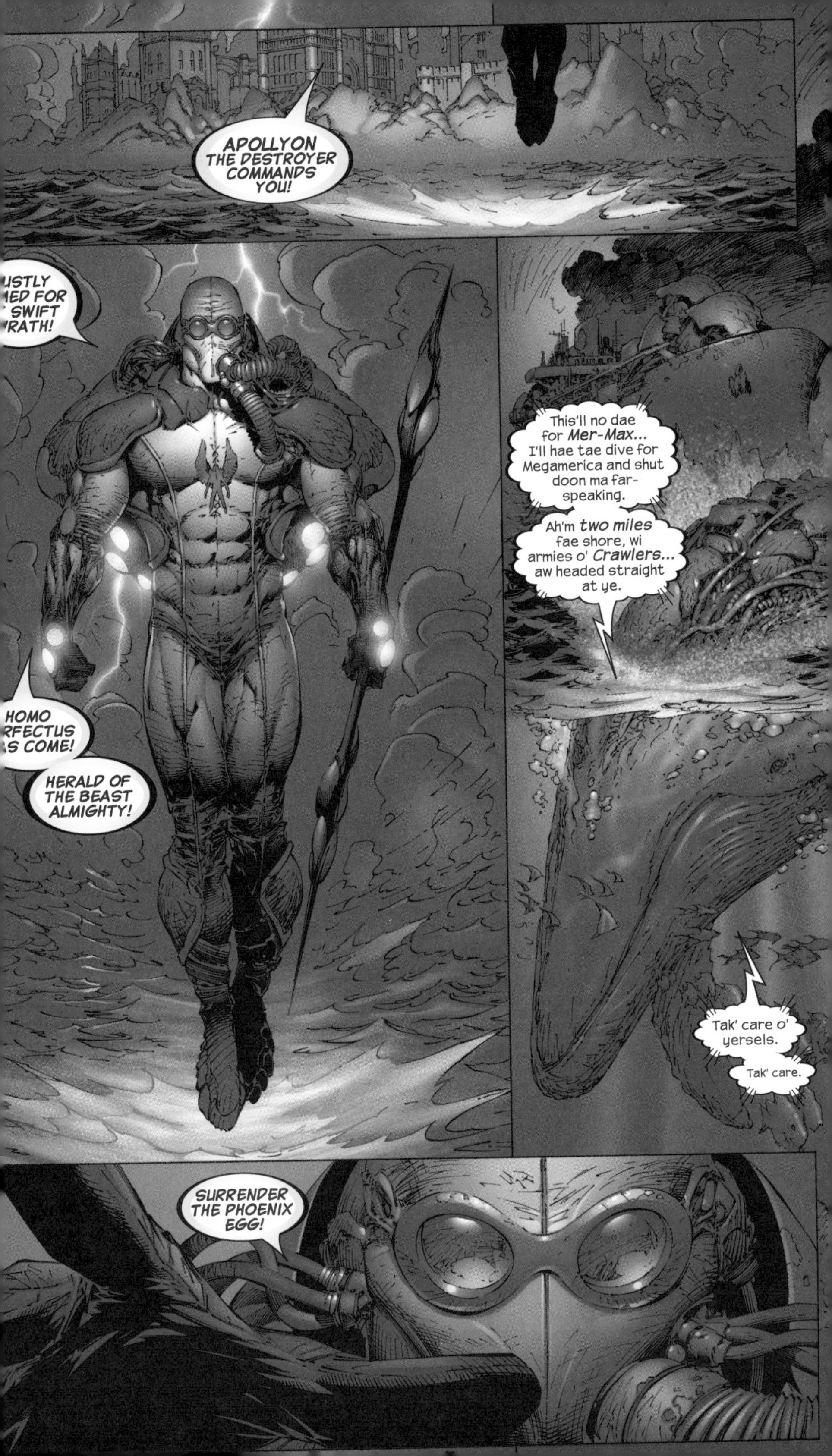

APOLLYON THE DESTROYER COMMANDS YOU!
USTLY MED FOR ' SWIFT RATH!
This'll no dae for Mer-Max... I'll hae tae dive for Megamerica and shut doon ma far-speaking.
Ah'm two miles fae shore, wi armies o' Crawlers... aw headed straight at ye.
HOMO RFECTUS 'S COME!
HERALD OF THE BEAST ALMIGHTY!
Tak' care o' yersels.
Tak' care.
SURRENDER THE PHOENIX EGG!

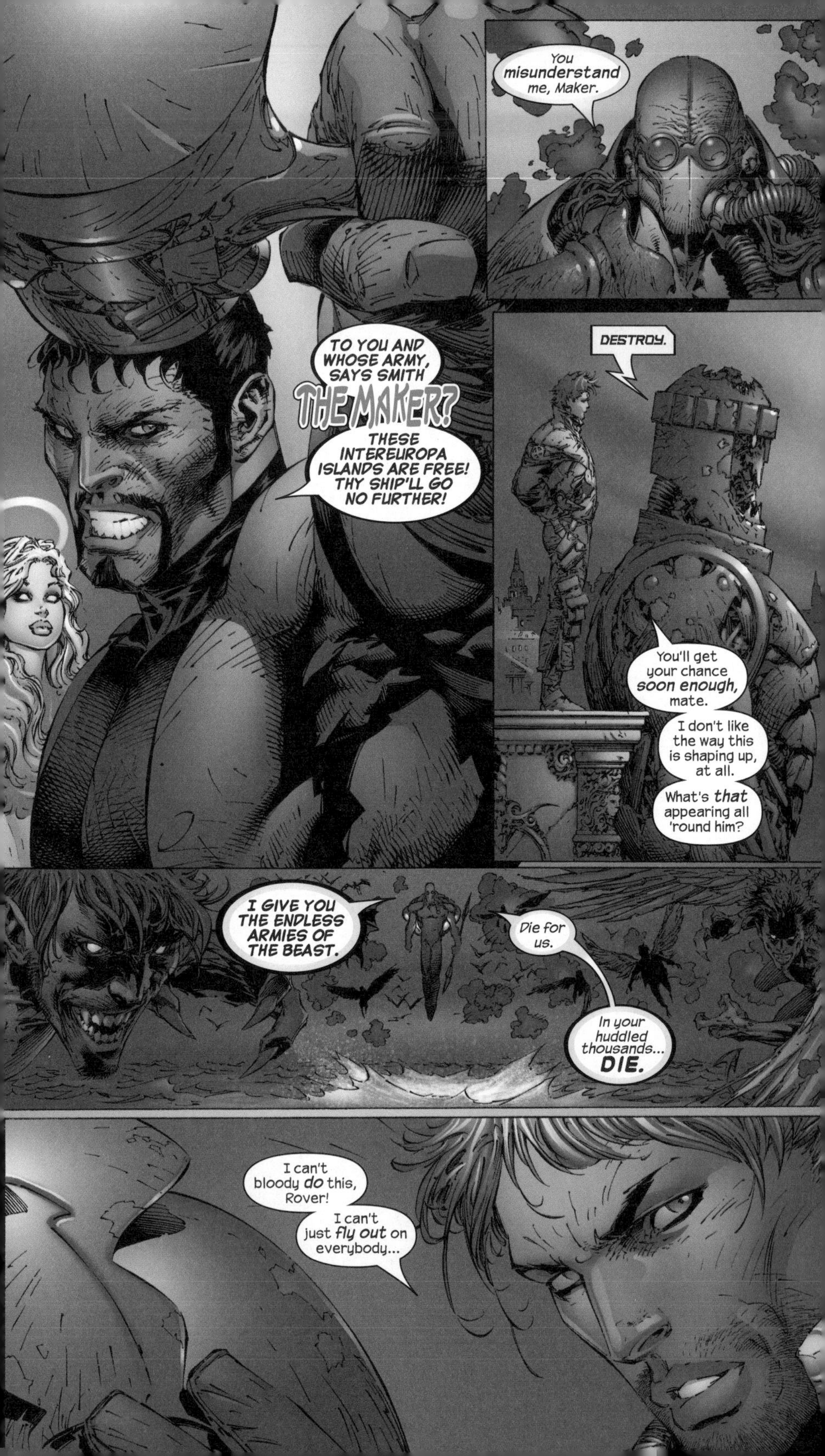
You misunderstand me, Maker.
TO YOU AND WHOSE ARMY, SAYS SMITH
THE MAKER?
THESE INTEREUROPA ISLANDS ARE FREE! THY SHIP'LL GO NO FURTHER!
DESTROY.
You'll get your chance soon enough, mate.
I don't like the way this is shaping up, at all.
What's that appearing all 'round him?
I GIVE YOU THE ENDLESS ARMIES OF THE BEAST.
Die for us.
In your huddled thousands... DIE.
I can't bloody do this, Rover!
I can't just fly out on everybody...

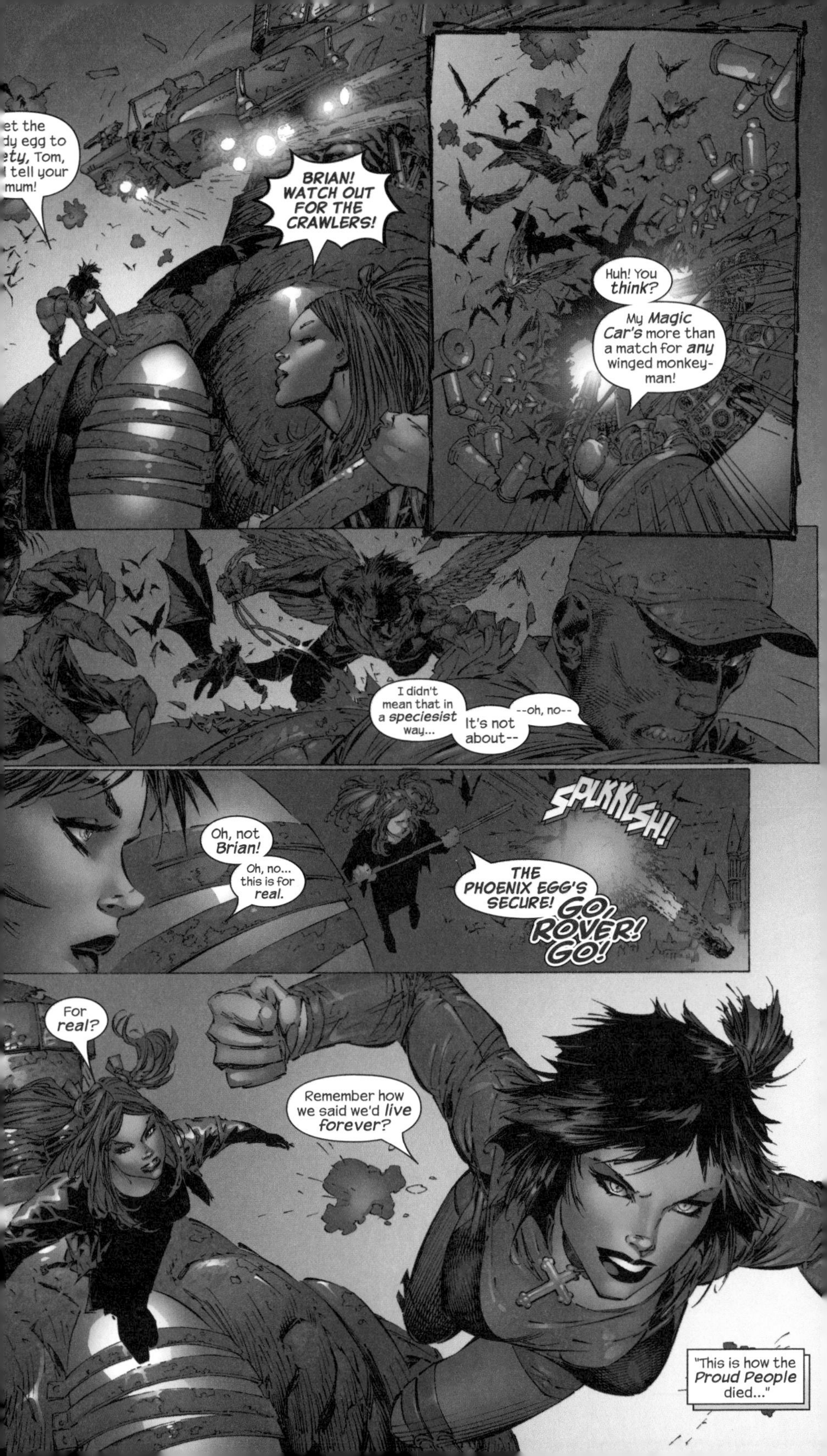
et the dy egg to ety, Tom, tell your mum!
BRIAN! WATCH OUT FOR THE CRAWLERS!
Huh! You think?
My Magic Car's more than a match for any winged monkey-man!
I didn't mean that in a speciesist way...
It's not about--
--oh, no--
Oh, not Brian!
Oh, no... this is for real.
SPLKKLSH!
THE PHOENIX EGG'S SECURE! GO, ROVER! GO!
For real?
Remember how we said we'd live forever?
"This is how the Proud People died..."

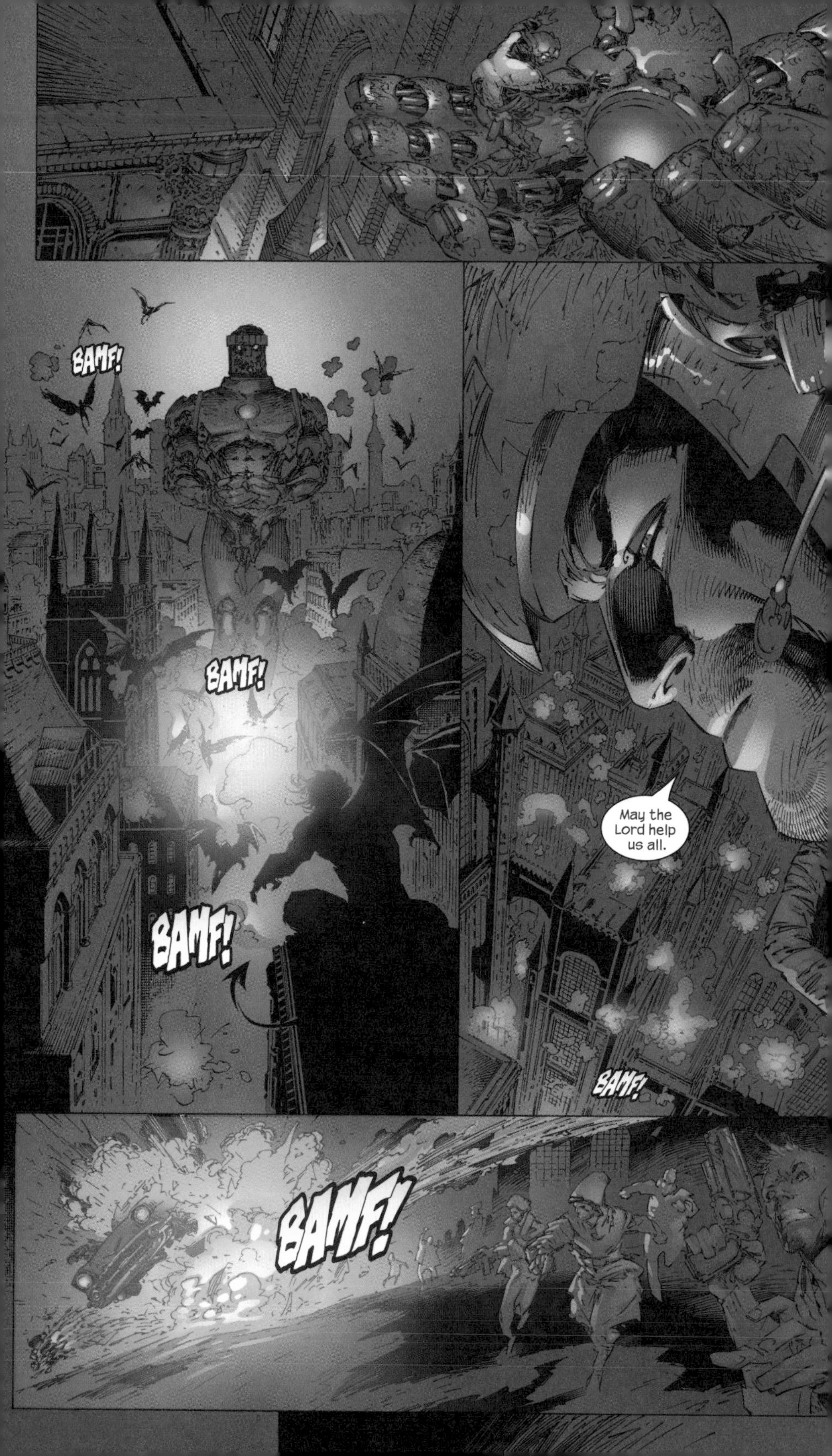

BAMF!
BAMF!
BAMF!
May the Lord help us all.
BAMF!
BAMF!

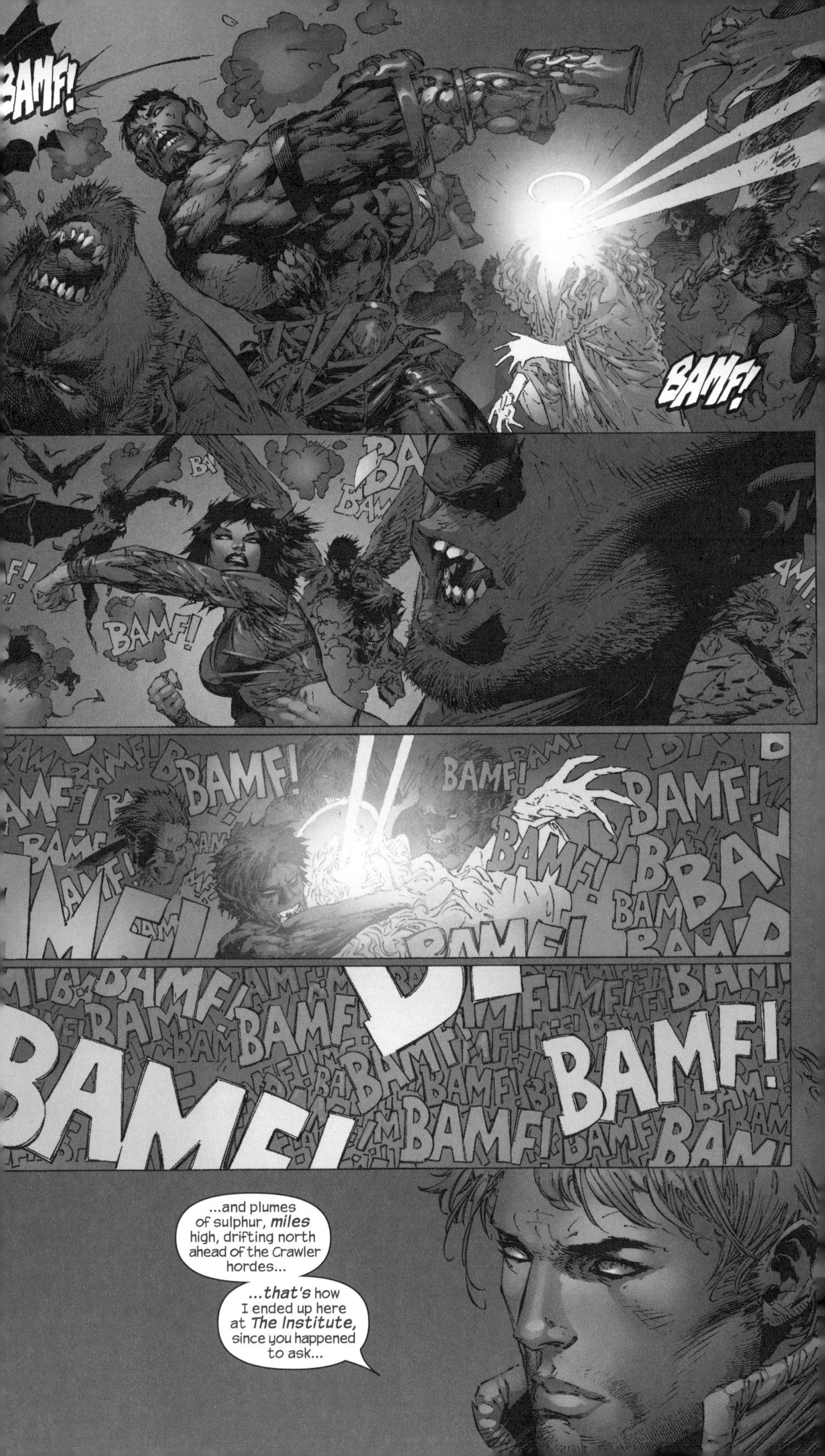

BAMF!
BAMF!
BAMF!
BAMF!
BAMF!
BAMF!
BAMF!
BAMF!
BAMF!
BAMF!
...and plumes of sulphur, *miles* high, drifting north ahead of the Crawler hordes...
...that's how I ended up here at *The Institute,* since you happened to ask...

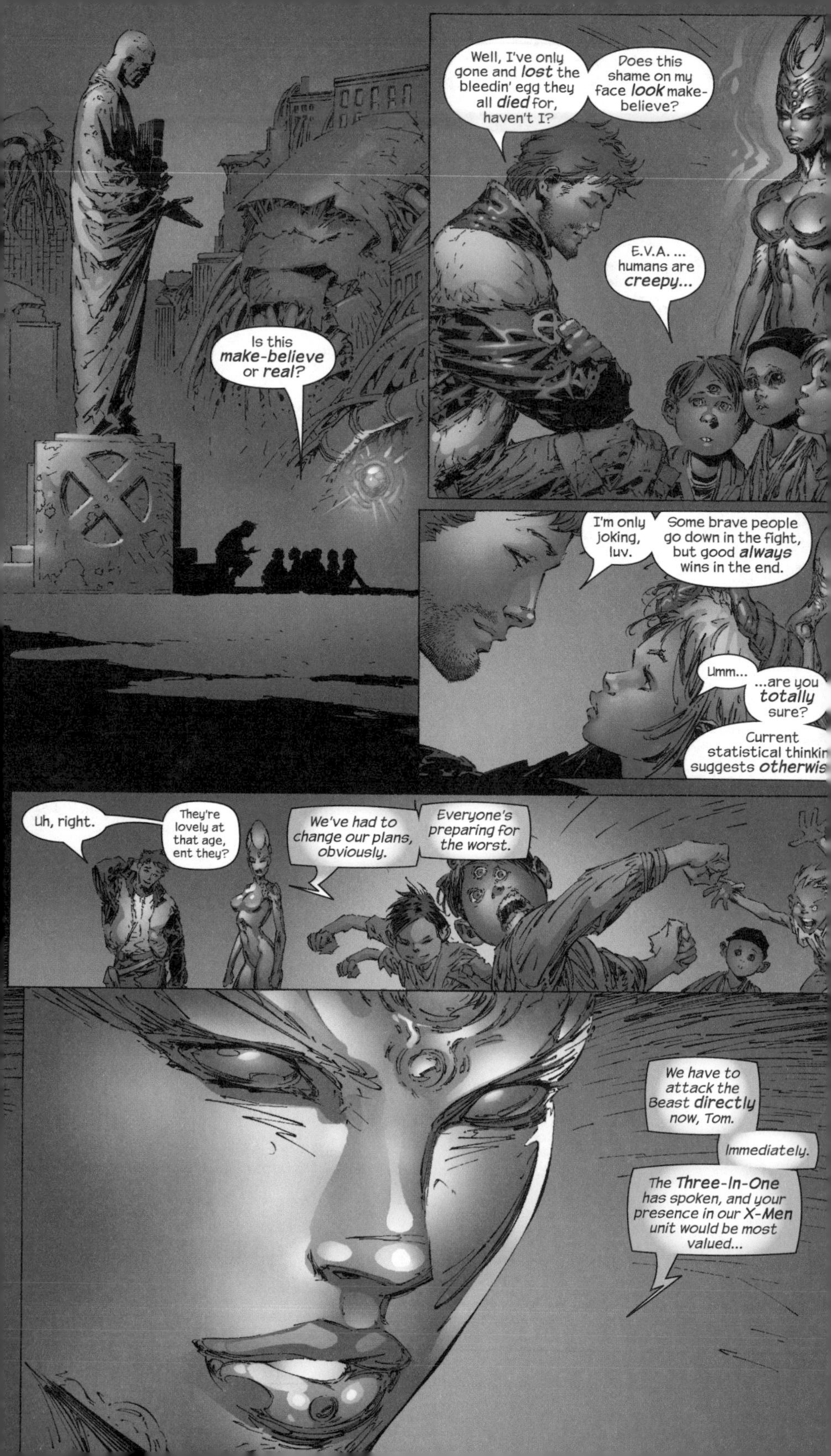
Is this make-believe or real?
Well, I've only gone and lost the bleedin' egg they all died for, haven't I?
Does this shame on my face look make-believe?
E.V.A. ... humans are creepy...
I'm only joking, luv.
Some brave people go down in the fight, but good always wins in the end.
Umm...
...are you totally sure?
Current statistical thinkin suggests otherwis
Uh, right.
They're lovely at that age, ent they?
We've had to change our plans, obviously.
Everyone's preparing for the worst.
We have to attack the Beast directly now, Tom.
Immediately.
The Three-In-One has spoken, and your presence in our X-Men unit would be most valued...

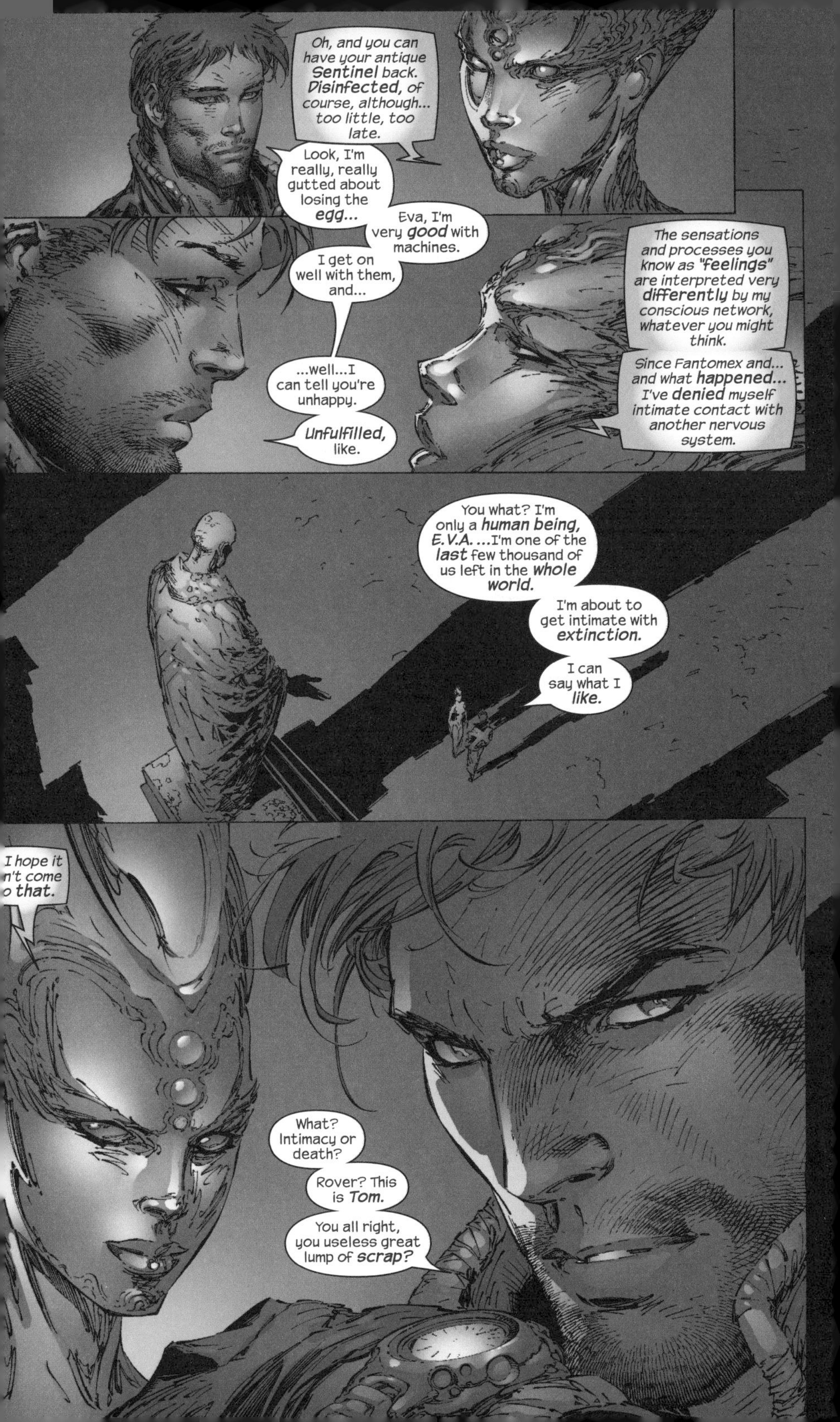

Oh, and you can have your antique Sentinel back. Disinfected, of course, although... too little, too late.
Look, I'm really, really gutted about losing the egg...
Eva, I'm very good with machines.
I get on well with them, and...
...well...I can tell you're unhappy.
Unfulfilled, like.
The sensations and processes you know as "feelings" are interpreted very differently by my conscious network, whatever you might think.
Since Fantomex and... and what happened... I've denied myself intimate contact with another nervous system.
You what? I'm only a human being, E.V.A. ...I'm one of the last few thousand of us left in the whole world.
I'm about to get intimate with extinction.
I can say what I like.
I hope it n't come o that.
What? Intimacy or death?
Rover? This is Tom.
You all right, you useless great lump of scrap?

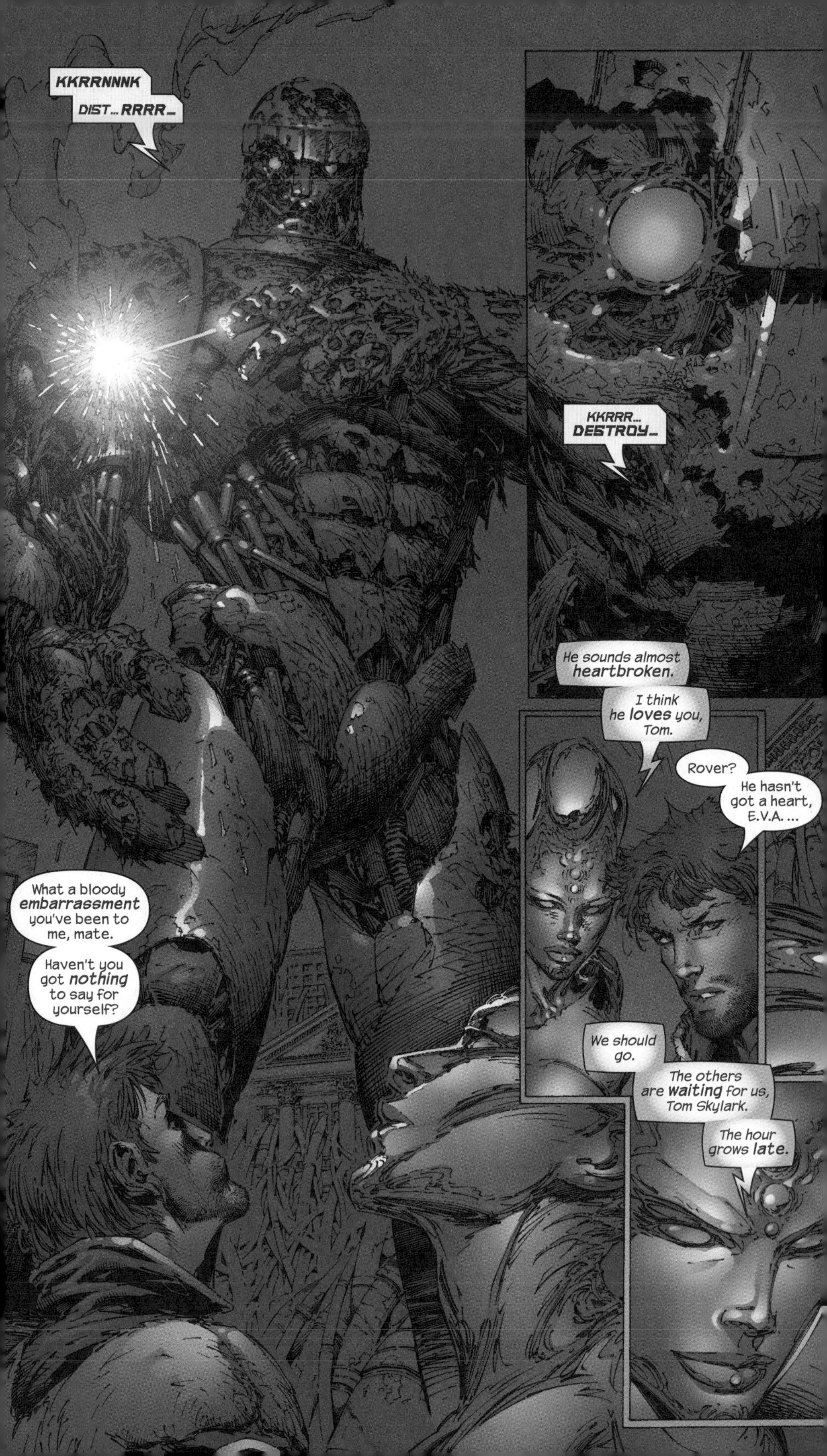
KKRRNNNK DIST... RRRR...
KKRRR... DESTROY...
He sounds almost heartbroken.
I think he loves you, Tom.
Rover?
He hasn't got a heart, E.V.A. ...
What a bloody embarrassment you've been to me, mate.
Haven't you got nothing to say for yourself?
We should go.
The others are waiting for us, Tom Skylark.
The hour grows late.

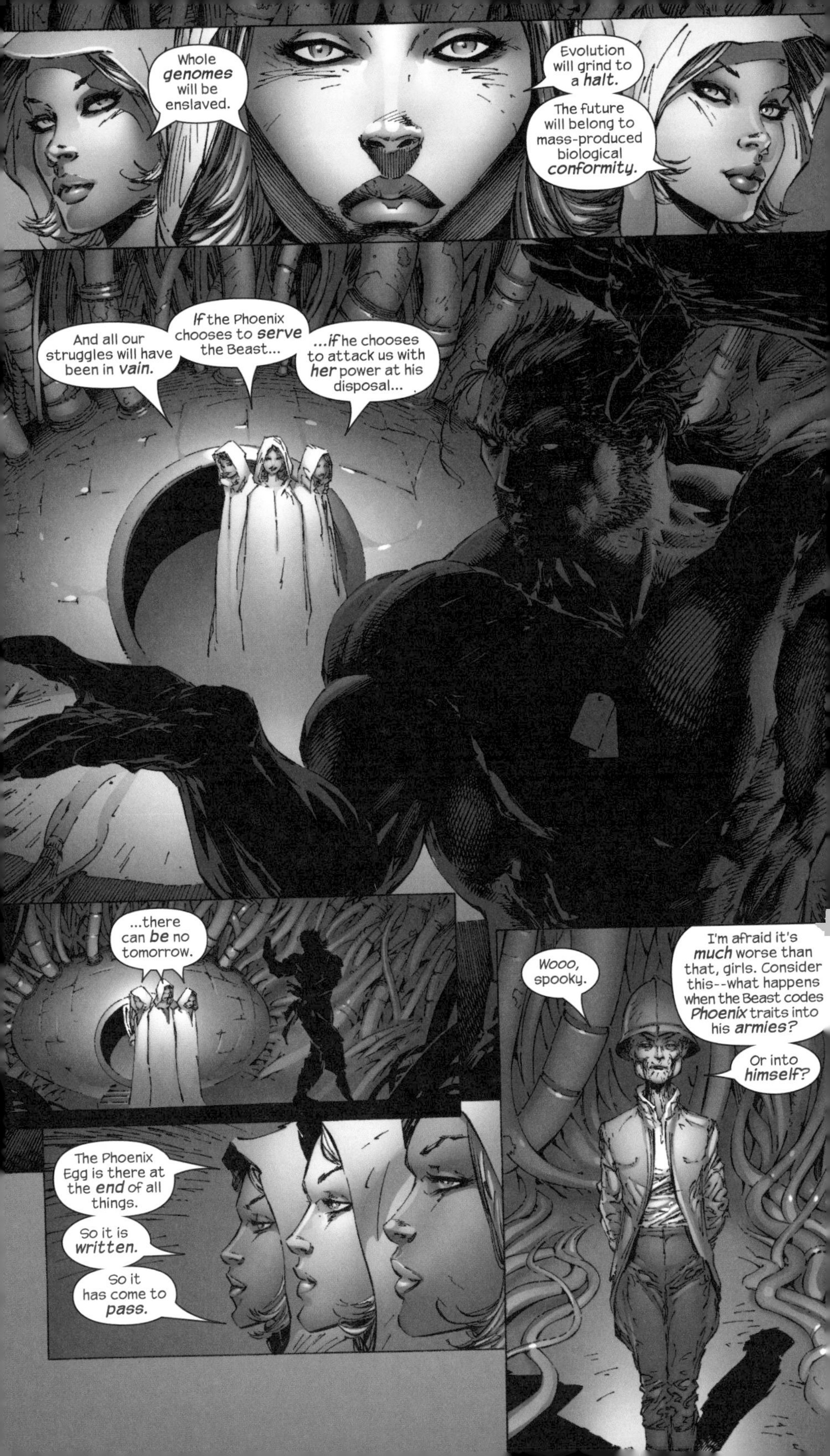
Whole genomes will be enslaved.
Evolution will grind to a halt.
The future will belong to mass-produced biological conformity.
And all our struggles will have been in vain.
If the Phoenix chooses to serve the Beast...
...if he chooses to attack us with her power at his disposal...
...there can be no tomorrow.
The Phoenix Egg is there at the end of all things.
So it is written.
So it has come to pass.
Wooo, spooky.
I'm afraid it's much worse than that, girls. Consider this--what happens when the Beast codes Phoenix traits into his armies?
Or into himself?

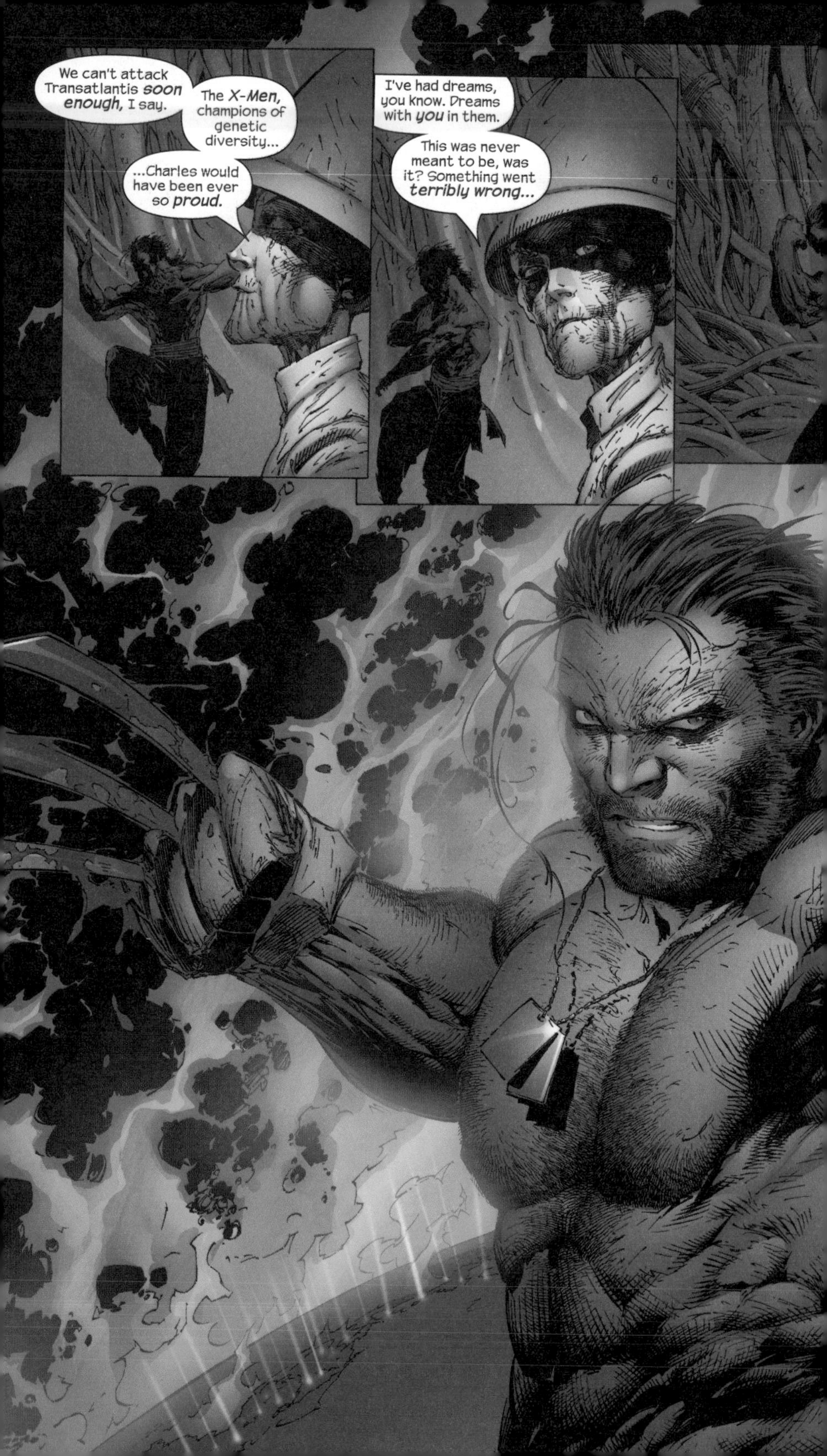
We can't attack Transatlantis soon enough, I say.
The X-Men, champions of genetic diversity...
...Charles would have been ever so proud.
I've had dreams, you know. Dreams with you in them.
This was never meant to be, was it? Something went terribly wrong...

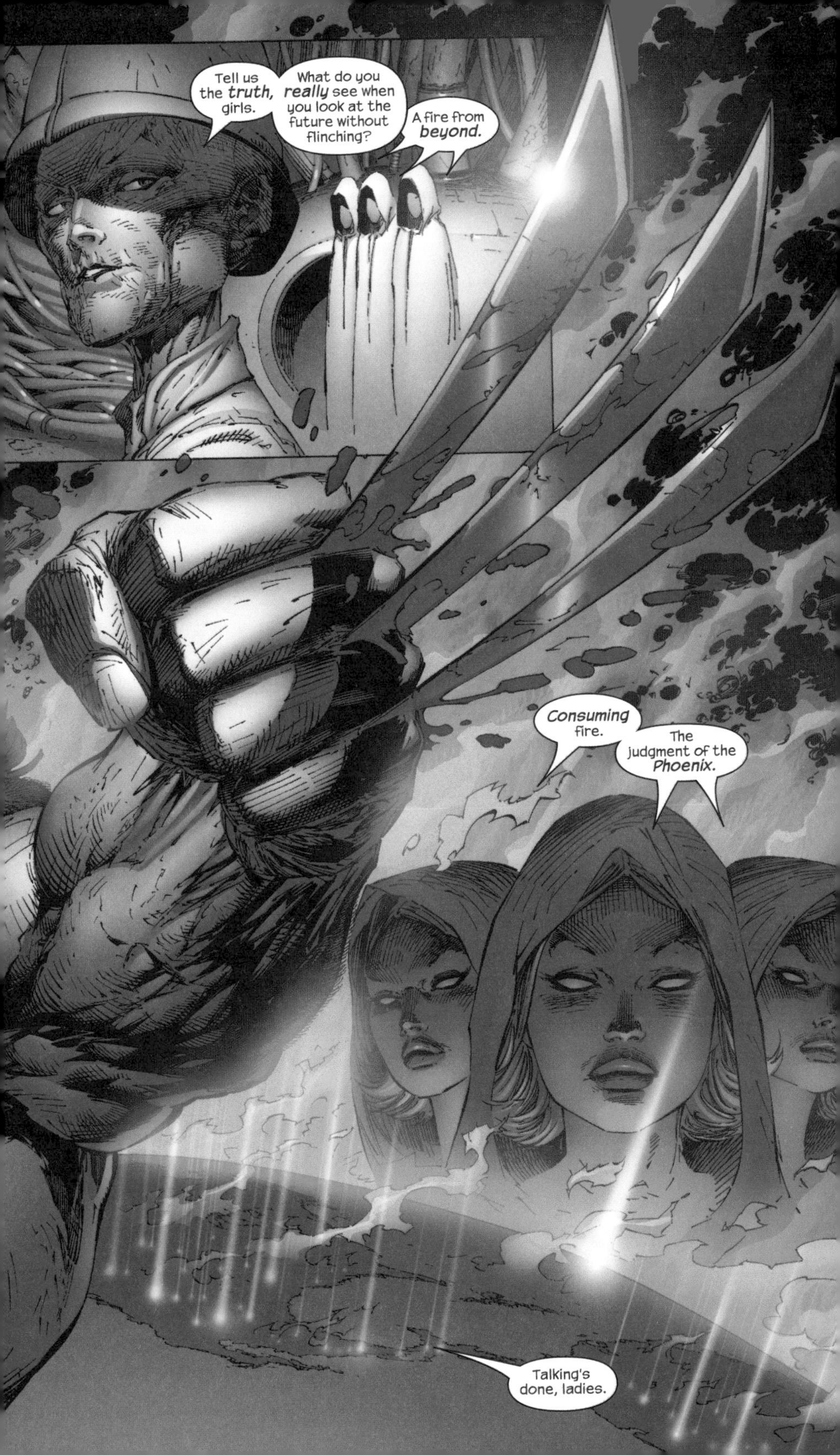
Tell us the **truth,** girls.
What do you **really** see when you look at the future without flinching?
A fire from **beyond.**
Consuming fire.
The judgment of the **Phoenix.**
Talking's done, ladies.

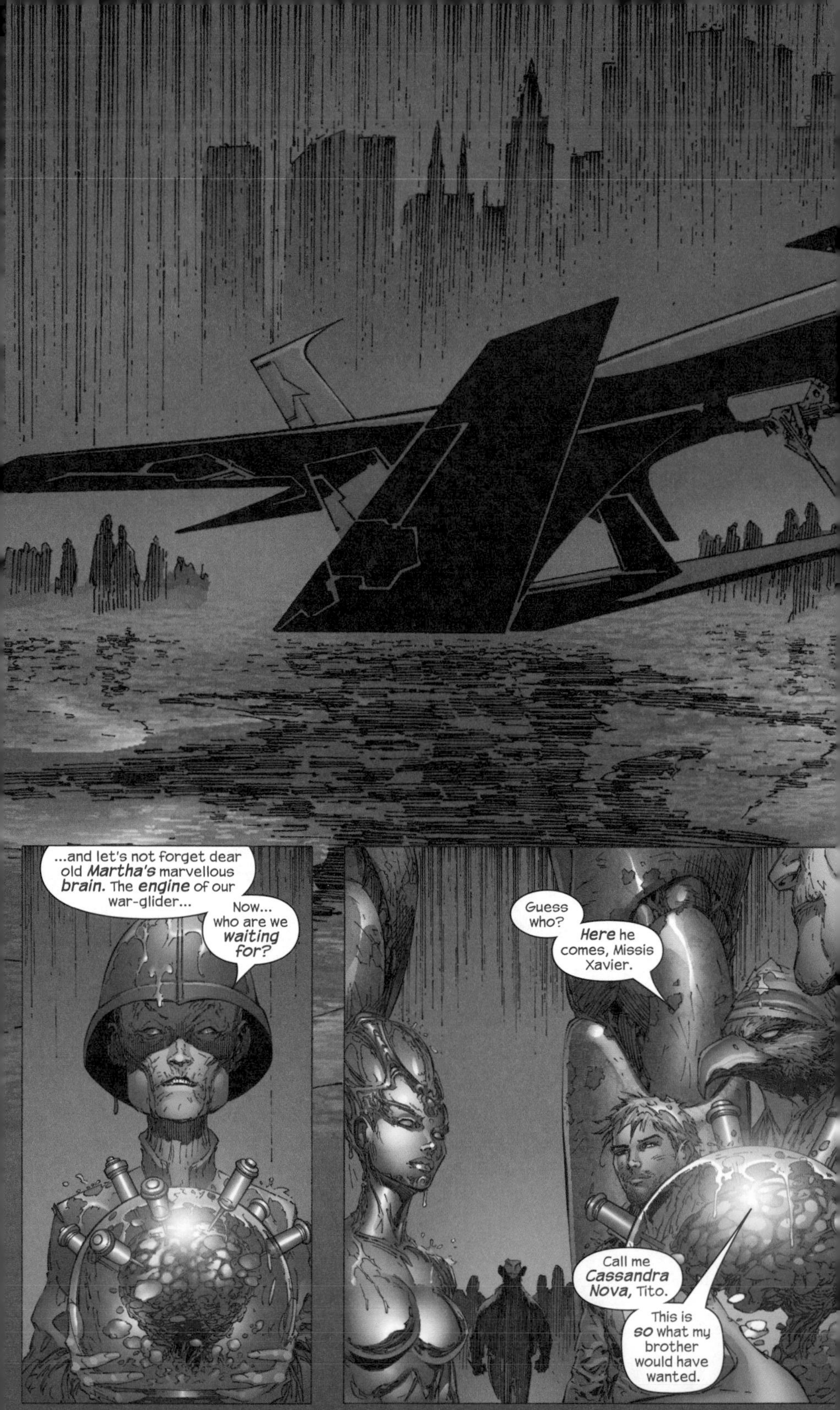

...and let's not forget dear old *Martha's* marvellous *brain.* The *engine* of our war-glider...
Now... who are we *waiting for?*
Guess who?
Here he comes, Missis Xavier.
Call me *Cassandra Nova,* Tito.
This is *so* what my brother would have wanted.

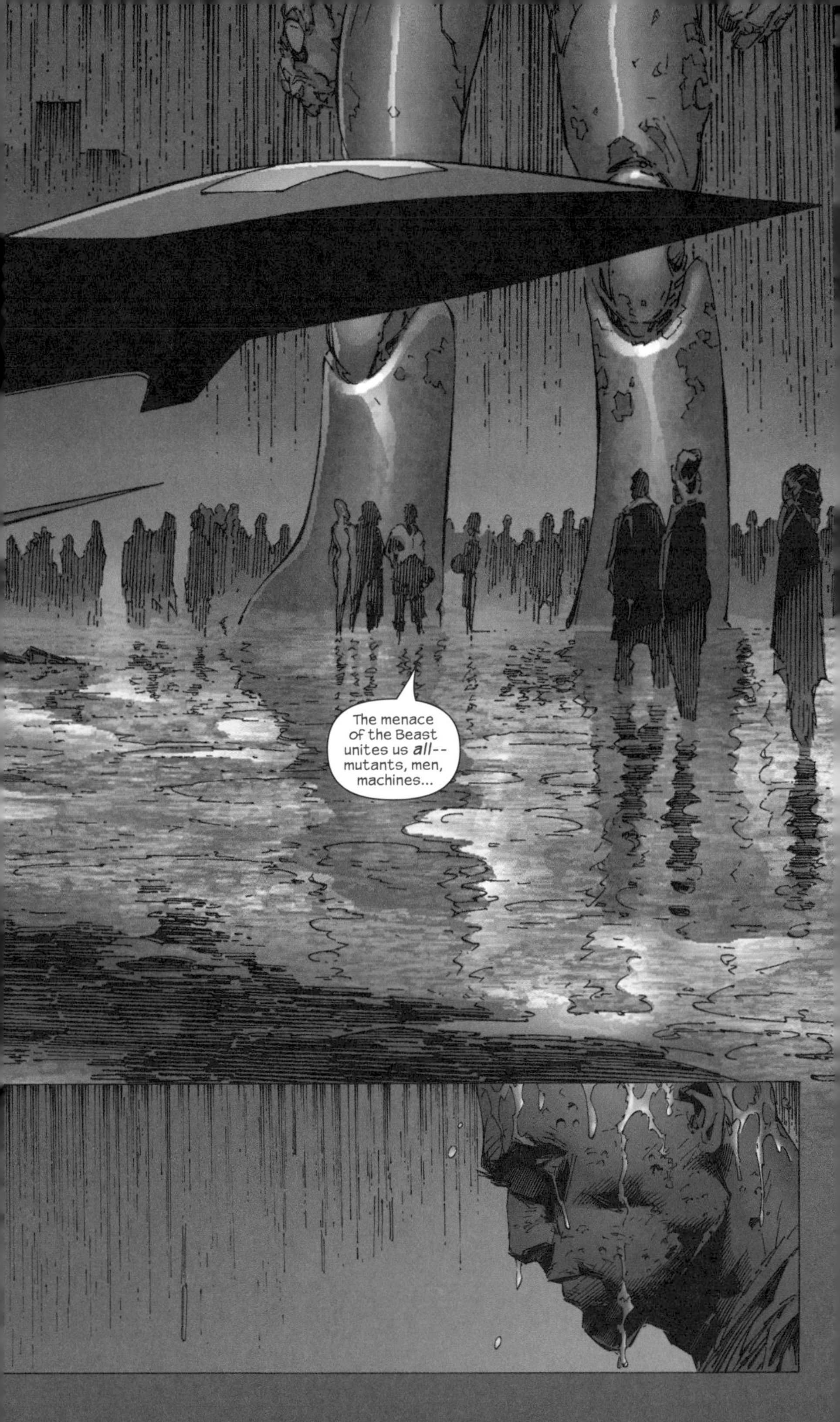
The menace of the Beast unites us all--mutants, men, machines...

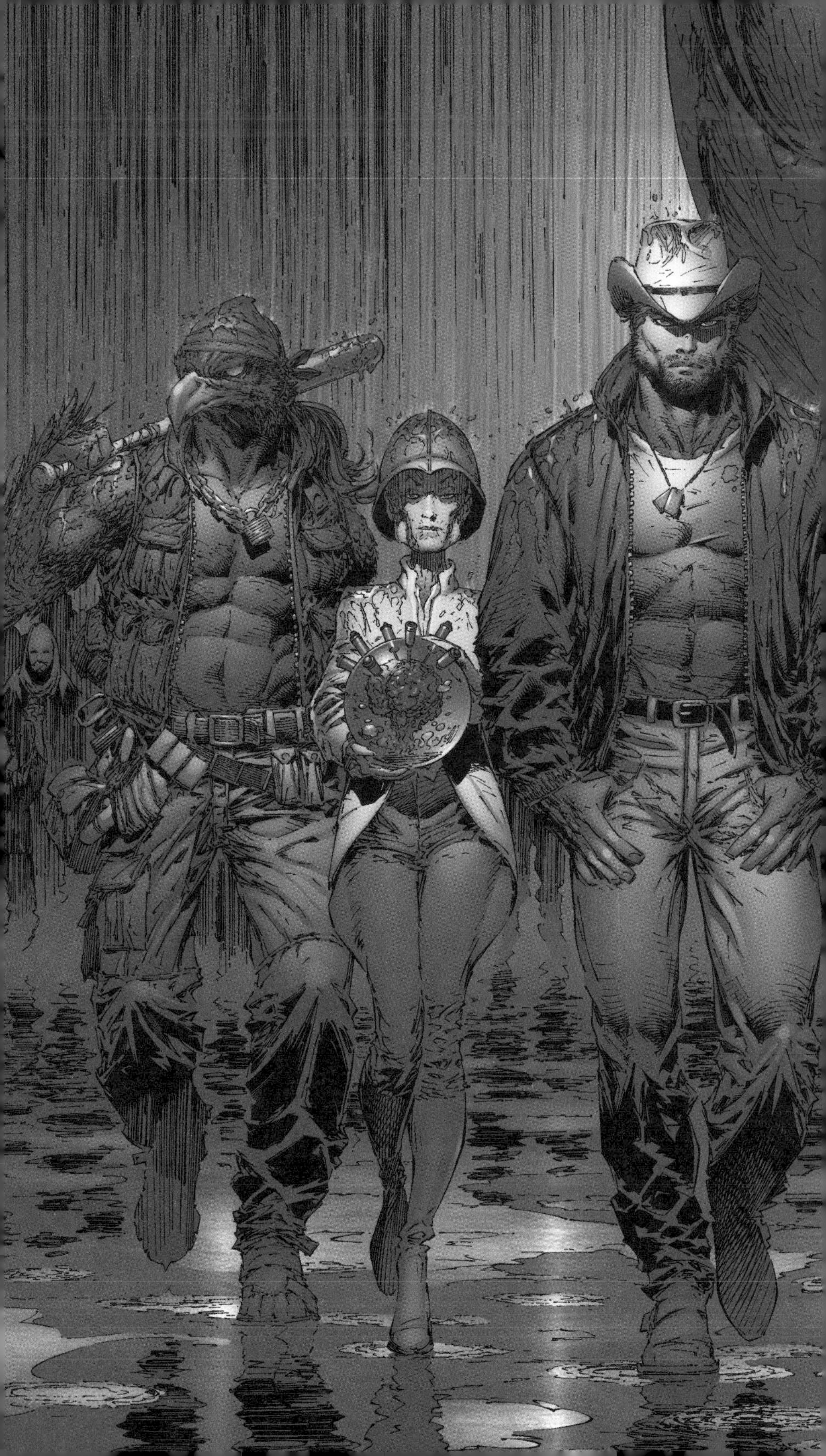

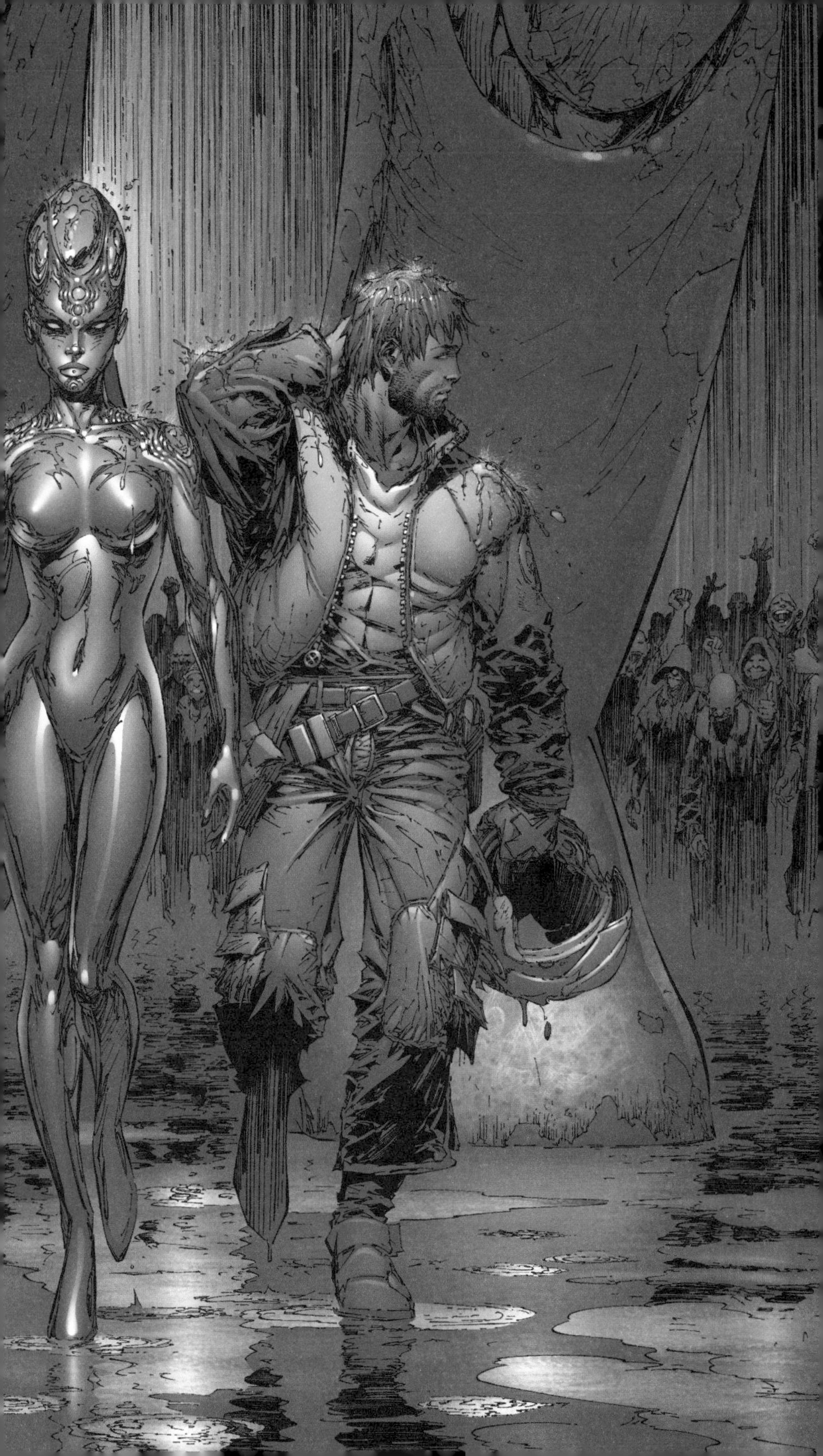

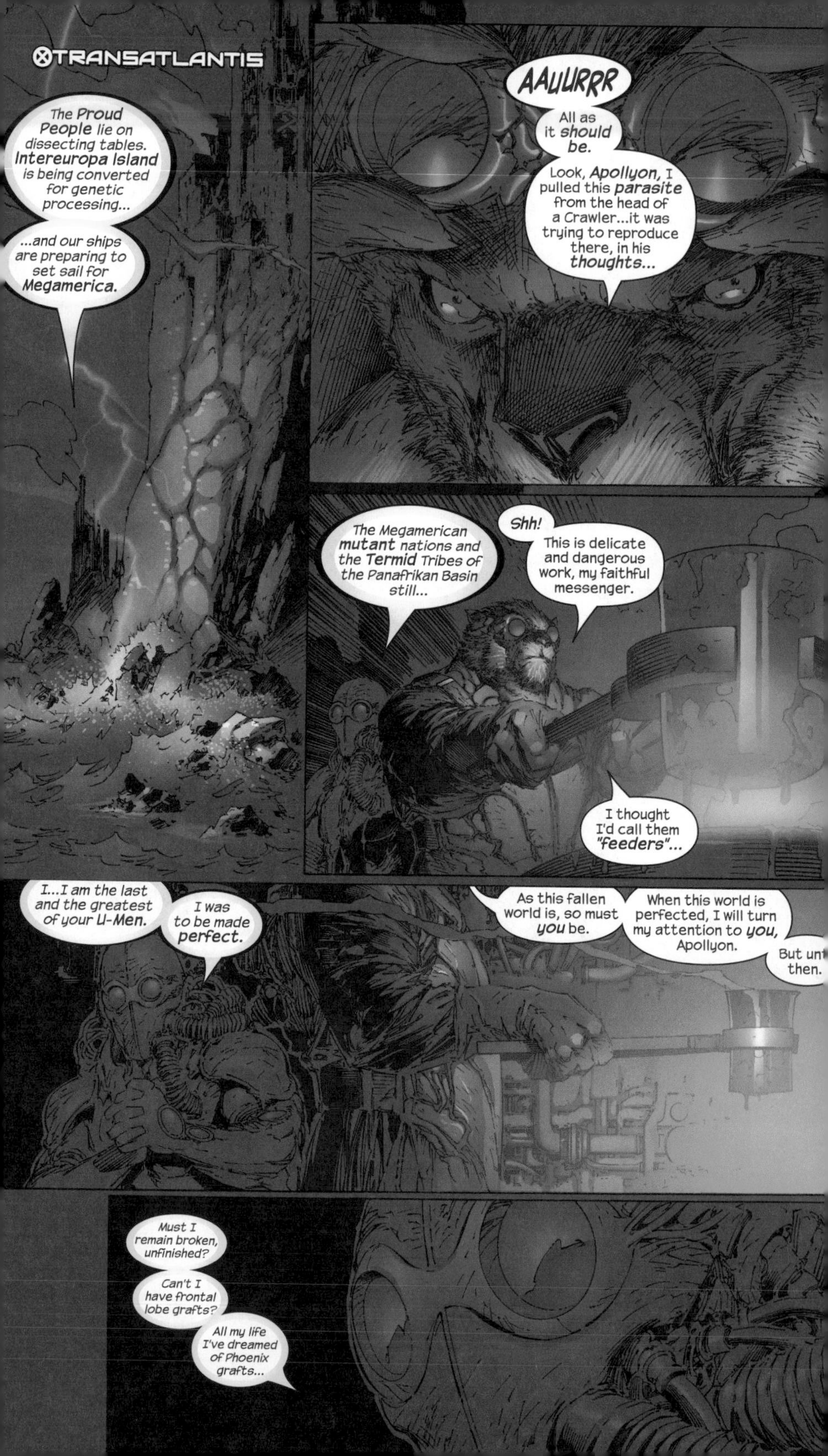

TRANSATLANTIS
The Proud People lie on dissecting tables. Intereuropa Island is being converted for genetic processing...
...and our ships are preparing to set sail for Megamerica.
AAUURRR
All as it should be.
Look, Apollyon, I pulled this parasite from the head of a Crawler...it was trying to reproduce there, in his thoughts...
The Megamerican mutant nations and the Termid Tribes of the Panafrikan Basin still...
Shh!
This is delicate and dangerous work, my faithful messenger.
I thought I'd call them "feeders"...
I...I am the last and the greatest of your U-Men.
I was to be made perfect.
As this fallen world is, so must you be.
When this world is perfected, I will turn my attention to you, Apollyon.
But un then.
Must I remain broken, unfinished?
Can't I have frontal lobe grafts?
All my life I've dreamed of Phoenix grafts...

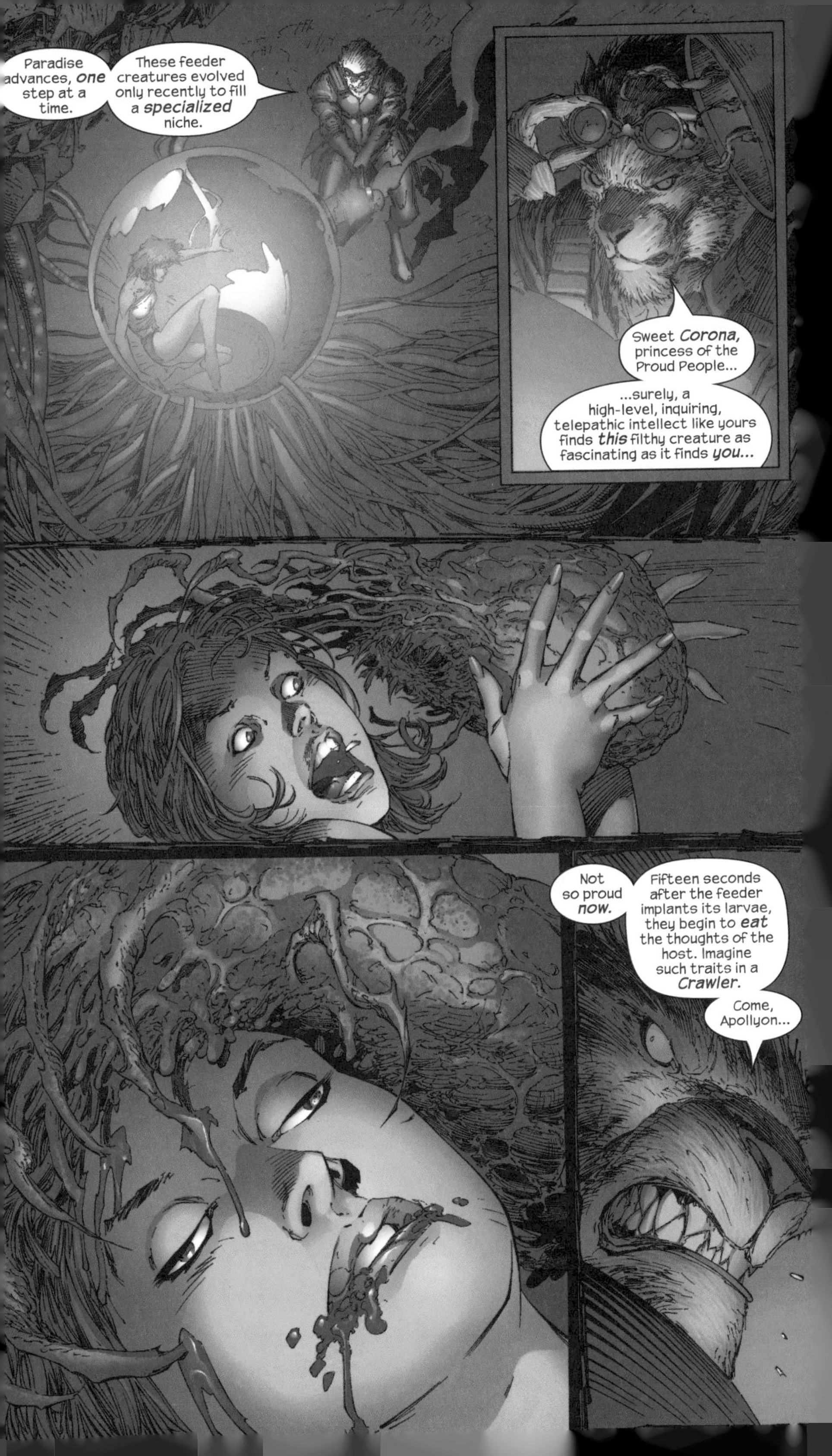
Paradise advances, *one* step at a time.
These feeder creatures evolved only recently to fill a *specialized* niche.
Sweet *Corona,* princess of the Proud People...
...surely, a high-level, inquiring, telepathic intellect like yours finds *this* filthy creature as fascinating as it finds *you*...
Not so proud *now.*
Fifteen seconds after the feeder implants its larvae, they begin to *eat* the thoughts of the host. Imagine such traits in a *Crawler.*
Come, Apollyon...

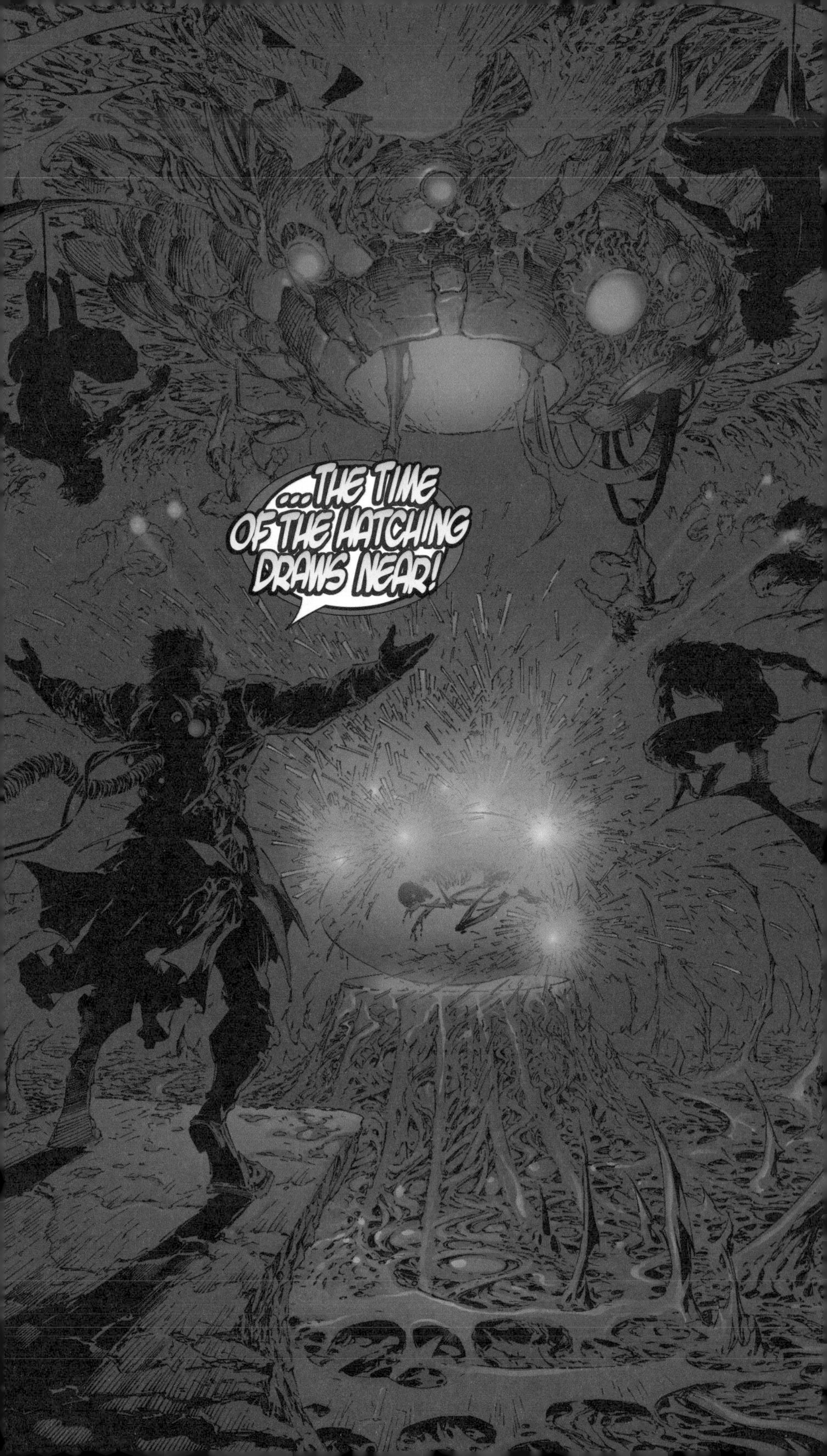
...THE TIME OF THE HATCHING DRAWS NEAR!

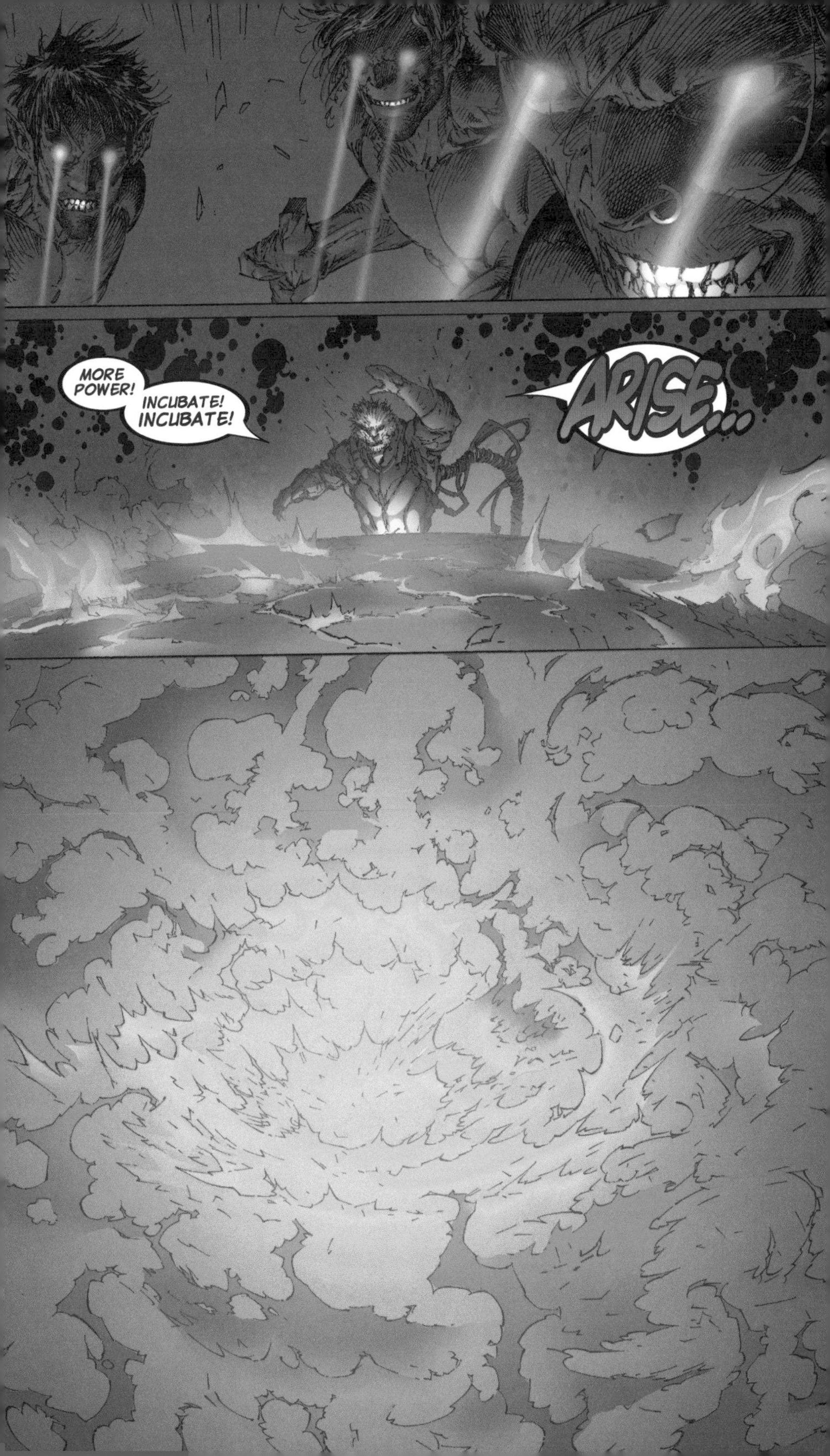

MORE POWER!
INCUBATE! INCUBATE!
ARISE...

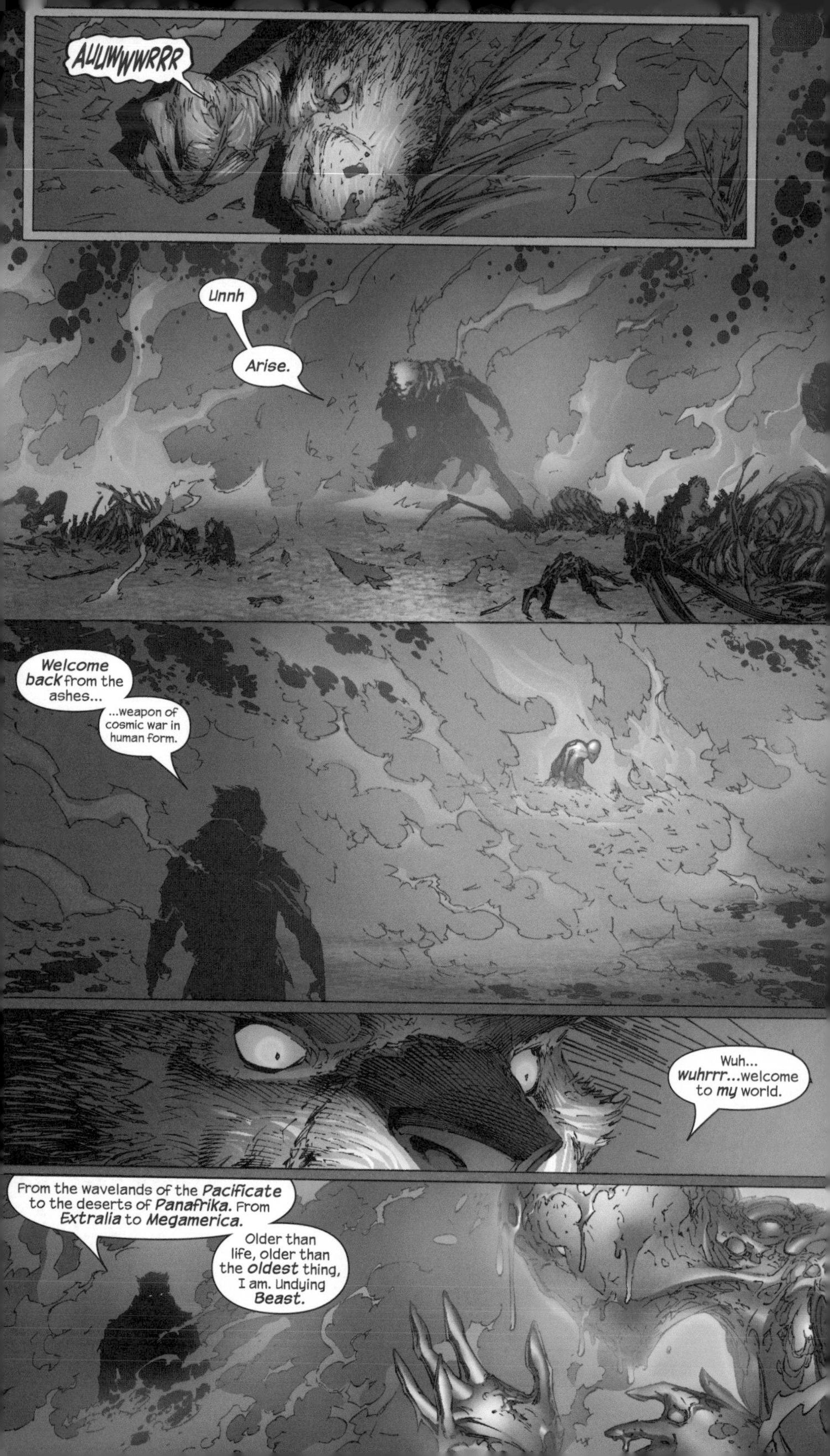

AUUWWWRRR
Unnh
Arise.
Welcome back from the ashes...
...weapon of cosmic war in human form.
Wuh... wuhrrr...welcome to my world.
From the wavelands of the Pacificate to the deserts of Panafrika. From Extralia to Megamerica.
Older than life, older than the oldest thing, I am. Undying Beast.

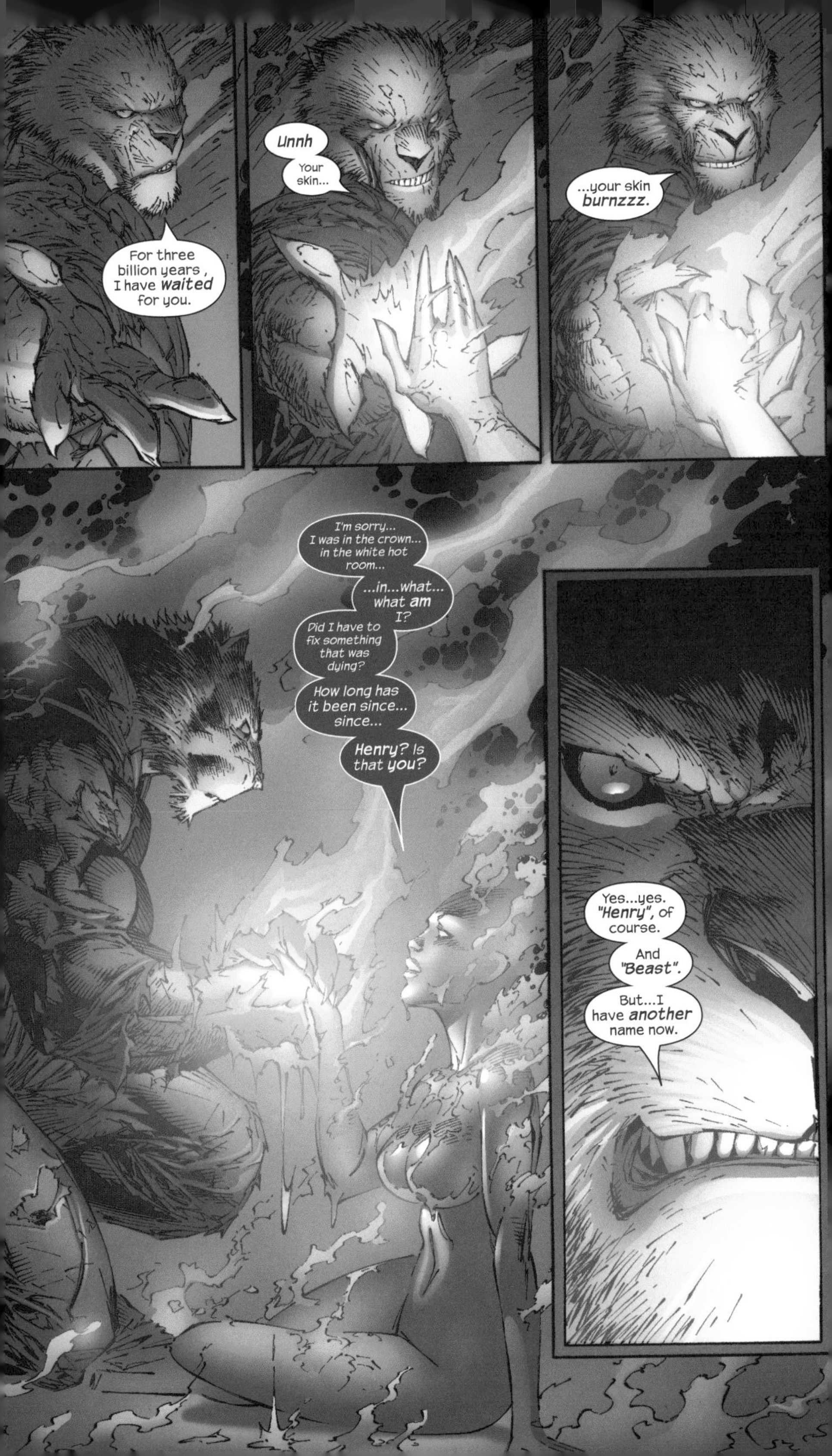

For three billion years , I have waited for you.
Unnh
Your skin...
...your skin burnzzz.
I'm sorry... I was in the crown... in the white hot room...
...in...what... what am I?
Did I have to fix something that was dying?
How long has it been since... since...
Henry? Is that you?
Yes...yes. "Henry", of course.
And "Beast".
But...I have another name now.

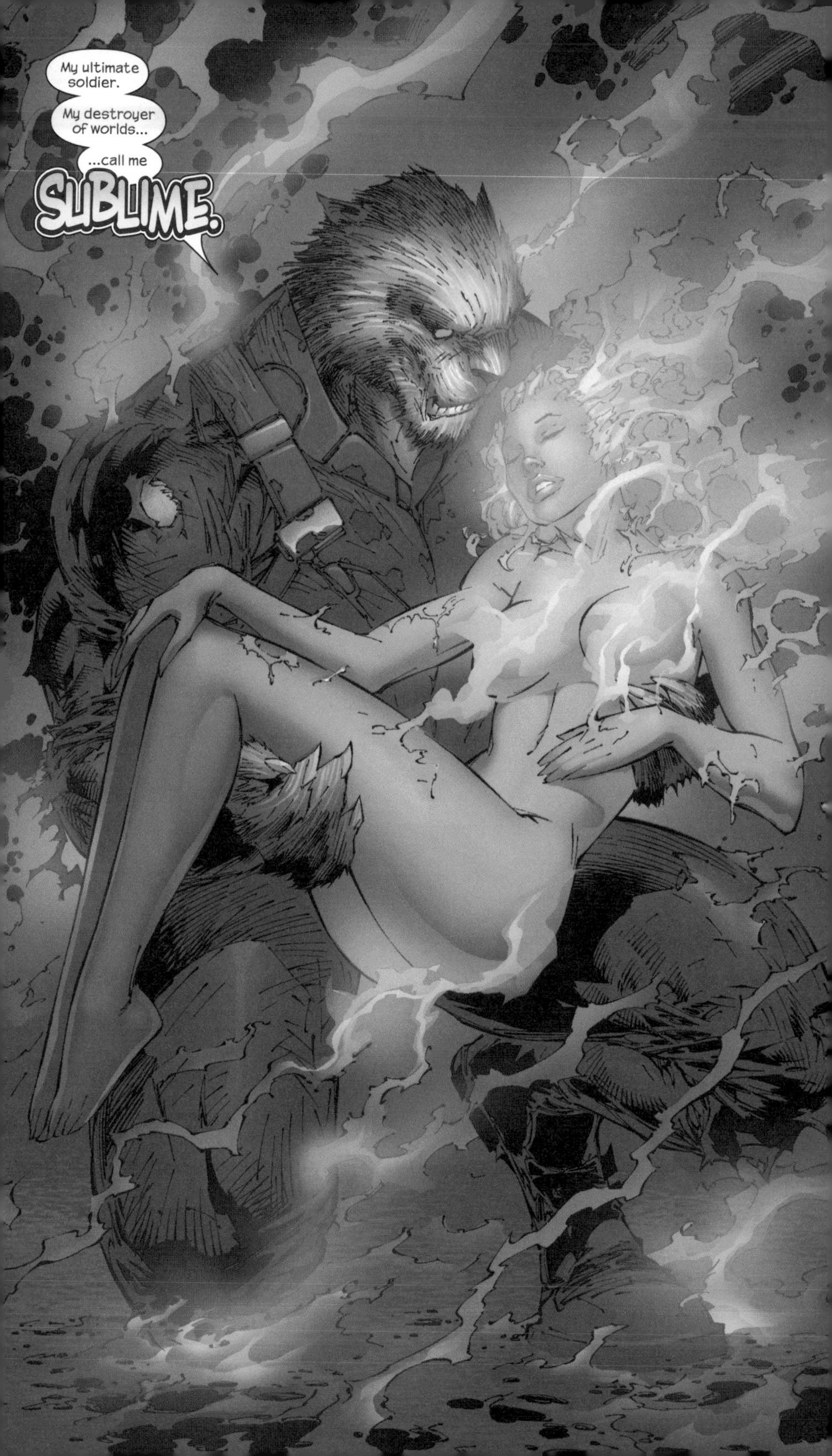
My ultimate soldier.
My destroyer of worlds...
...call me
SUBLIME.

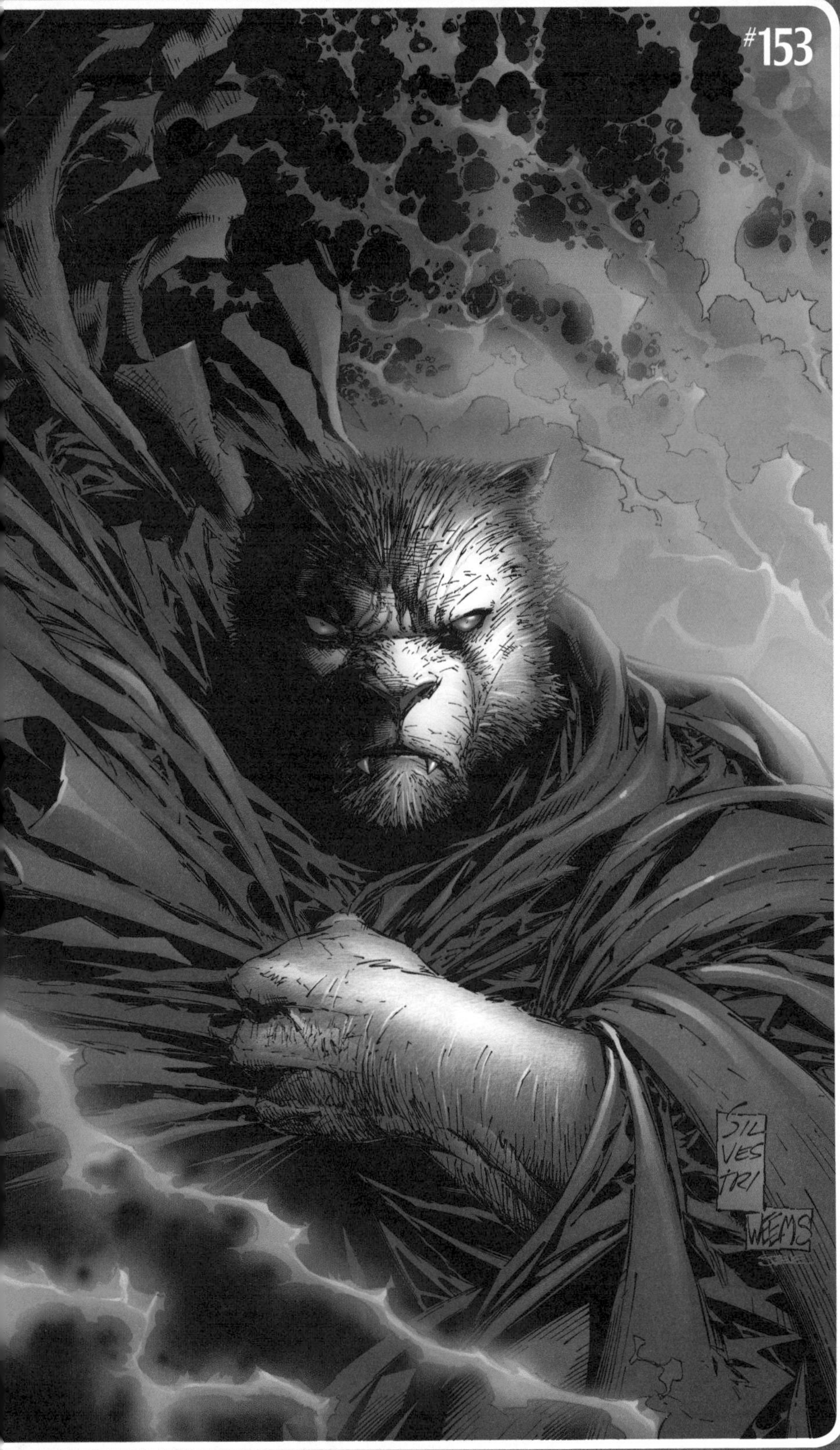
#153

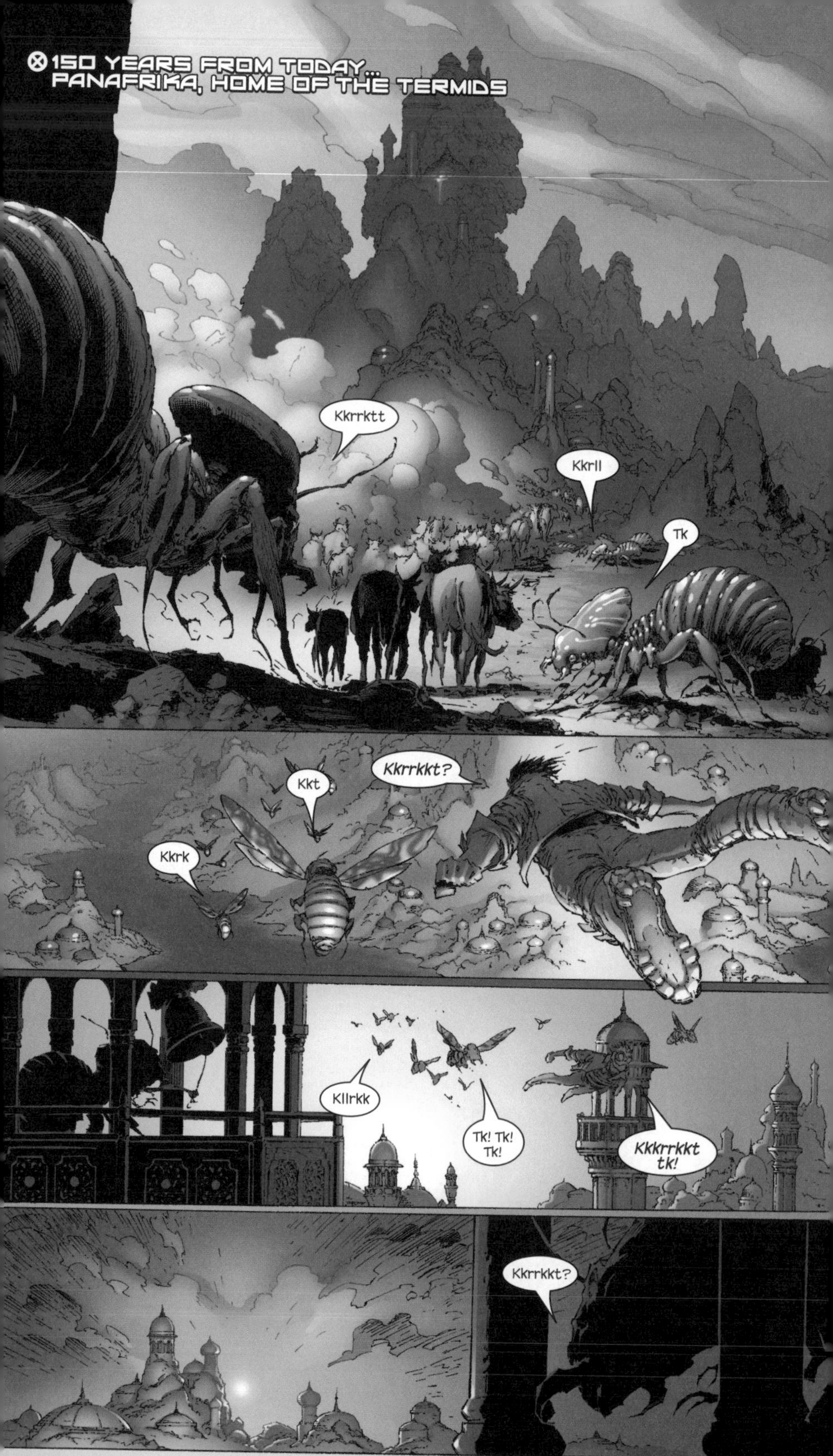
150 YEARS FROM TODAY... PANAFRIKA, HOME OF THE TERMIDS
Kkrrktt
Kkrll
Tk
Kkt
Kkrrkkt?
Kkrk
Kllrkk
Tk! Tk! Tk!
Kkkrrkkt tk!
Kkrrkkt?

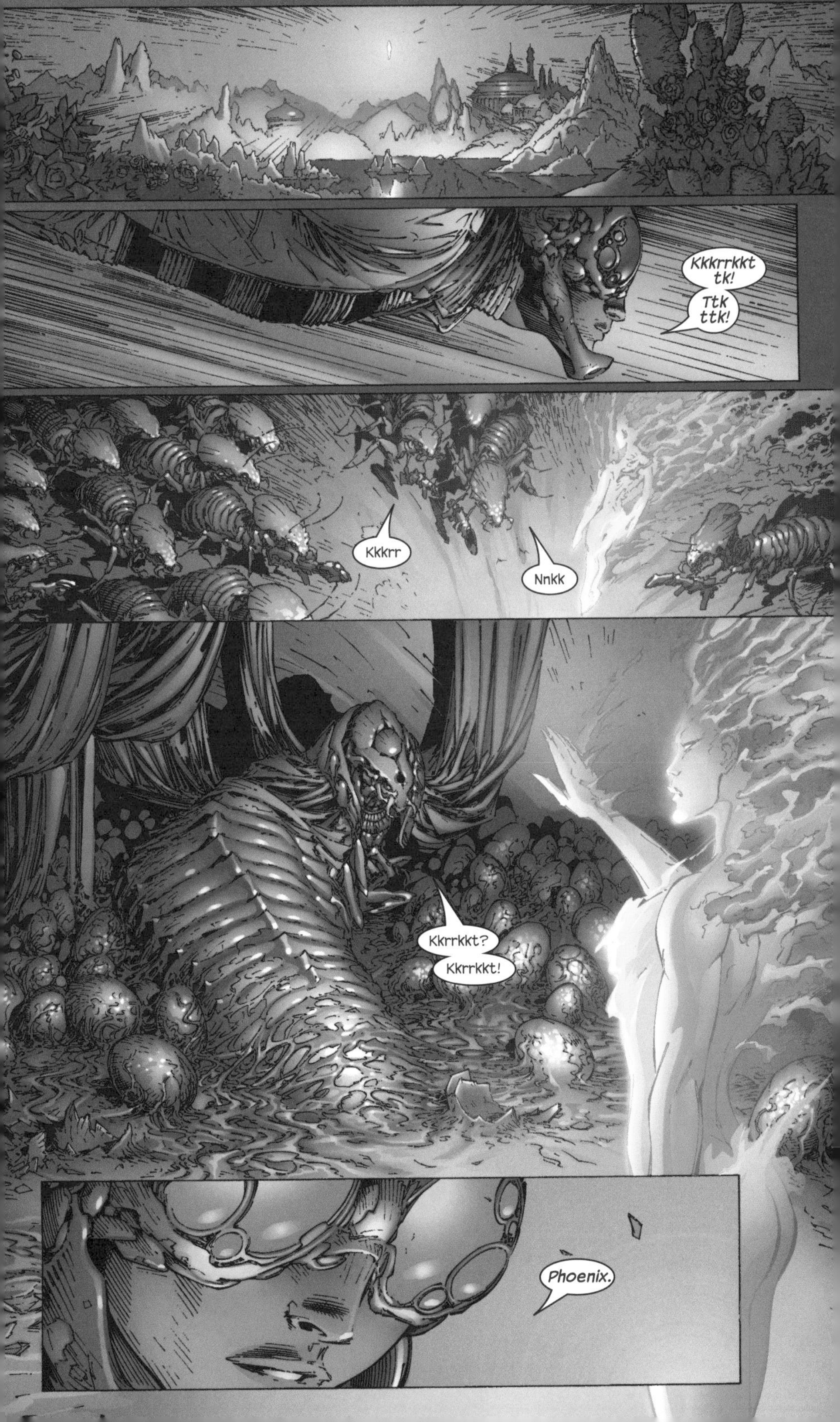
Kkkrrkkt tk!
Ttk ttk!
Kkkrr
Nnkk
Kkrrkkt?
Kkrrkkt!
Phoenix.

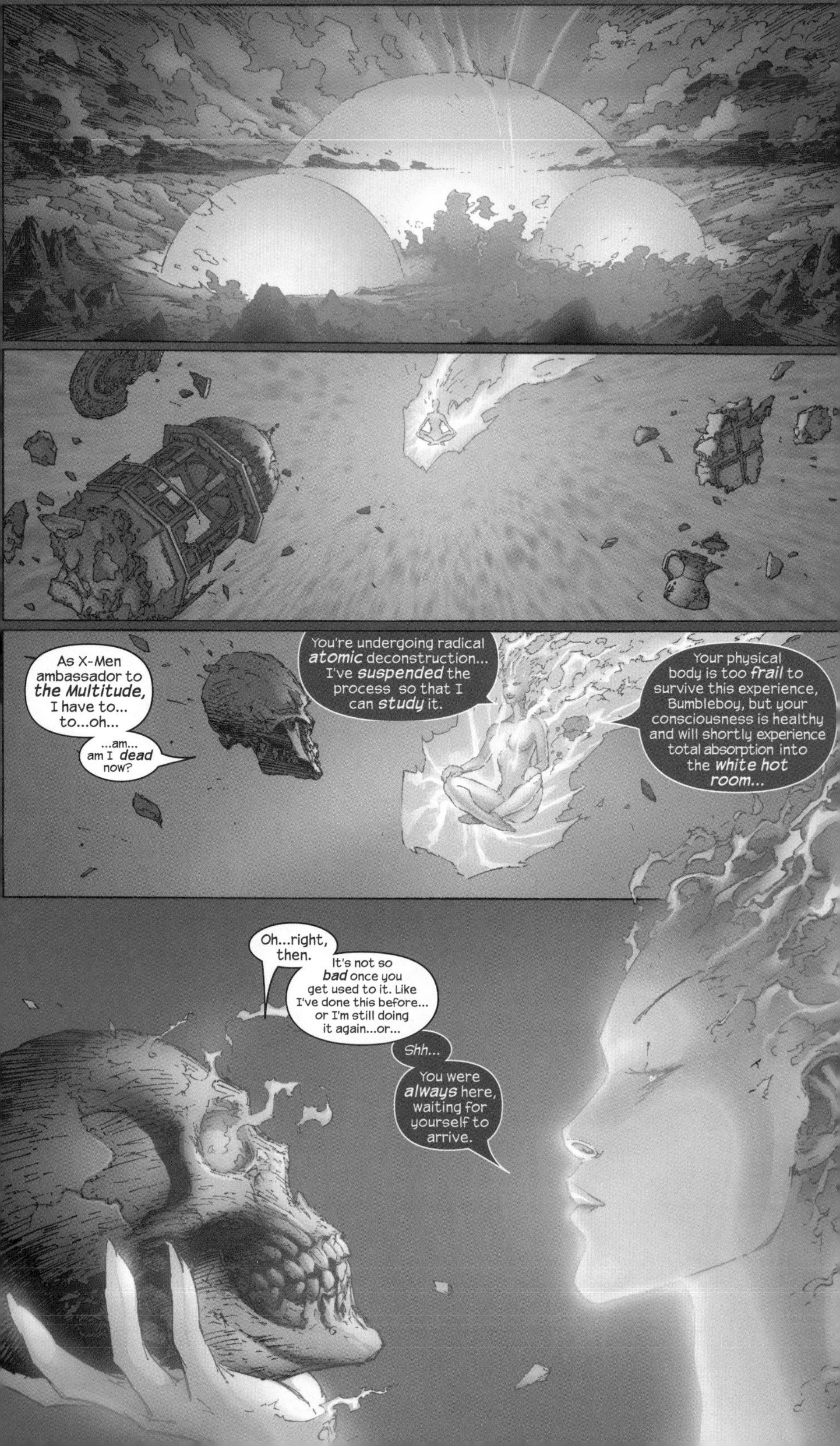
As X-Men ambassador to the Multitude, I have to... to...oh...
...am... am I dead now?
You're undergoing radical atomic deconstruction... I've suspended the process so that I can study it.
Your physical body is too frail to survive this experience, Bumbleboy, but your consciousness is healthy and will shortly experience total absorption into the white hot room...
Oh...right, then.
It's not so bad once you get used to it. Like I've done this before... or I'm still doing it again...or...
Shh...
You were always here, waiting for yourself to arrive.

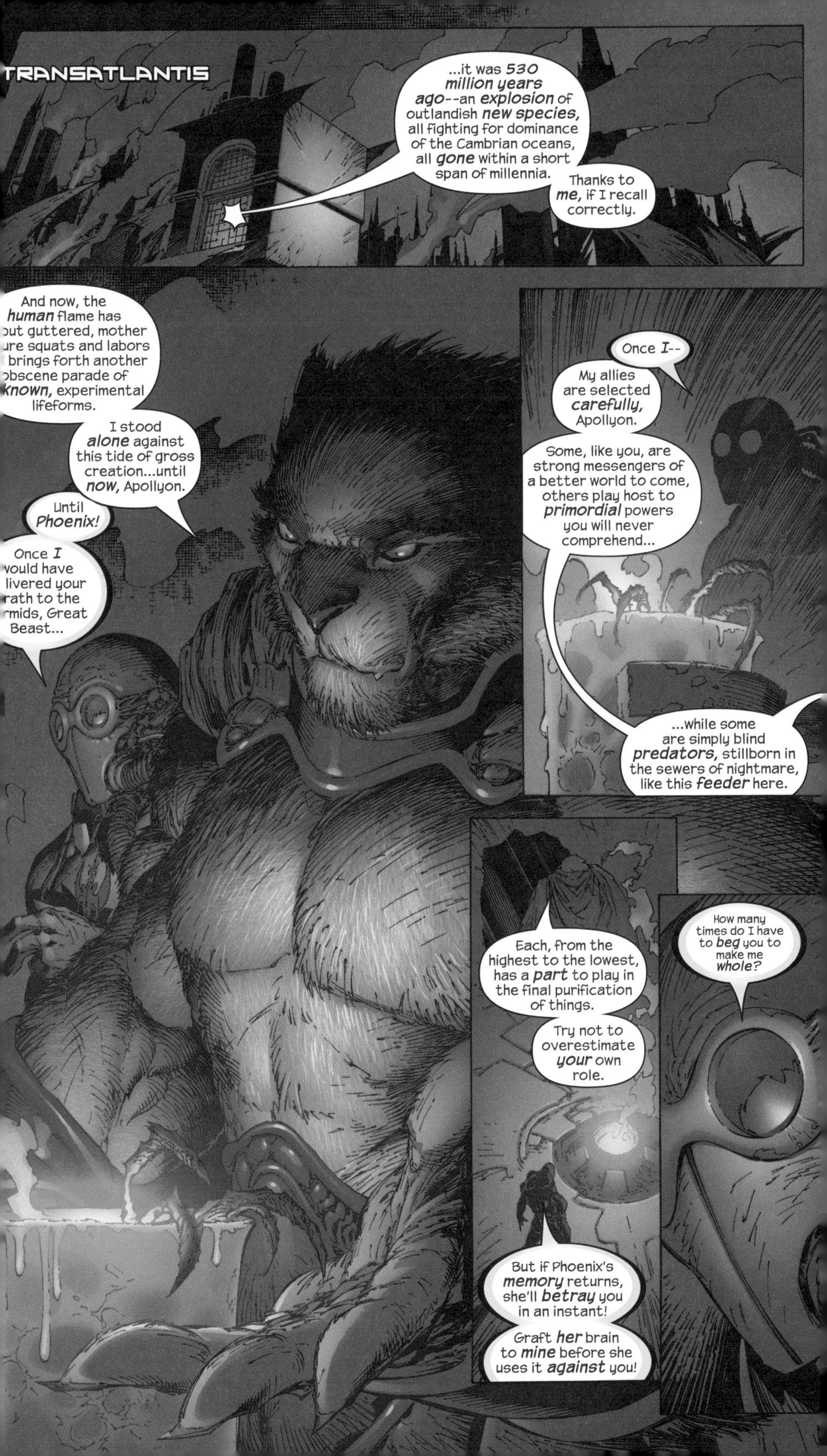

TRANSATLANTIS
...it was 530 million years ago--an explosion of outlandish new species, all fighting for dominance of the Cambrian oceans, all gone within a short span of millennia.
Thanks to me, if I recall correctly.
And now, the human flame has out guttered, mother ure squats and labors brings forth another obscene parade of known, experimental lifeforms.
I stood alone against this tide of gross creation...until now, Apollyon.
Until Phoenix!
Once I would have livered your rath to the rmids, Great Beast...
Once I--
My allies are selected carefully, Apollyon.
Some, like you, are strong messengers of a better world to come, others play host to primordial powers you will never comprehend...
...while some are simply blind predators, stillborn in the sewers of nightmare, like this feeder here.
Each, from the highest to the lowest, has a part to play in the final purification of things.
Try not to overestimate your own role.
How many times do I have to beg you to make me whole?
But if Phoenix's memory returns, she'll betray you in an instant!
Graft her brain to mine before she uses it against you!

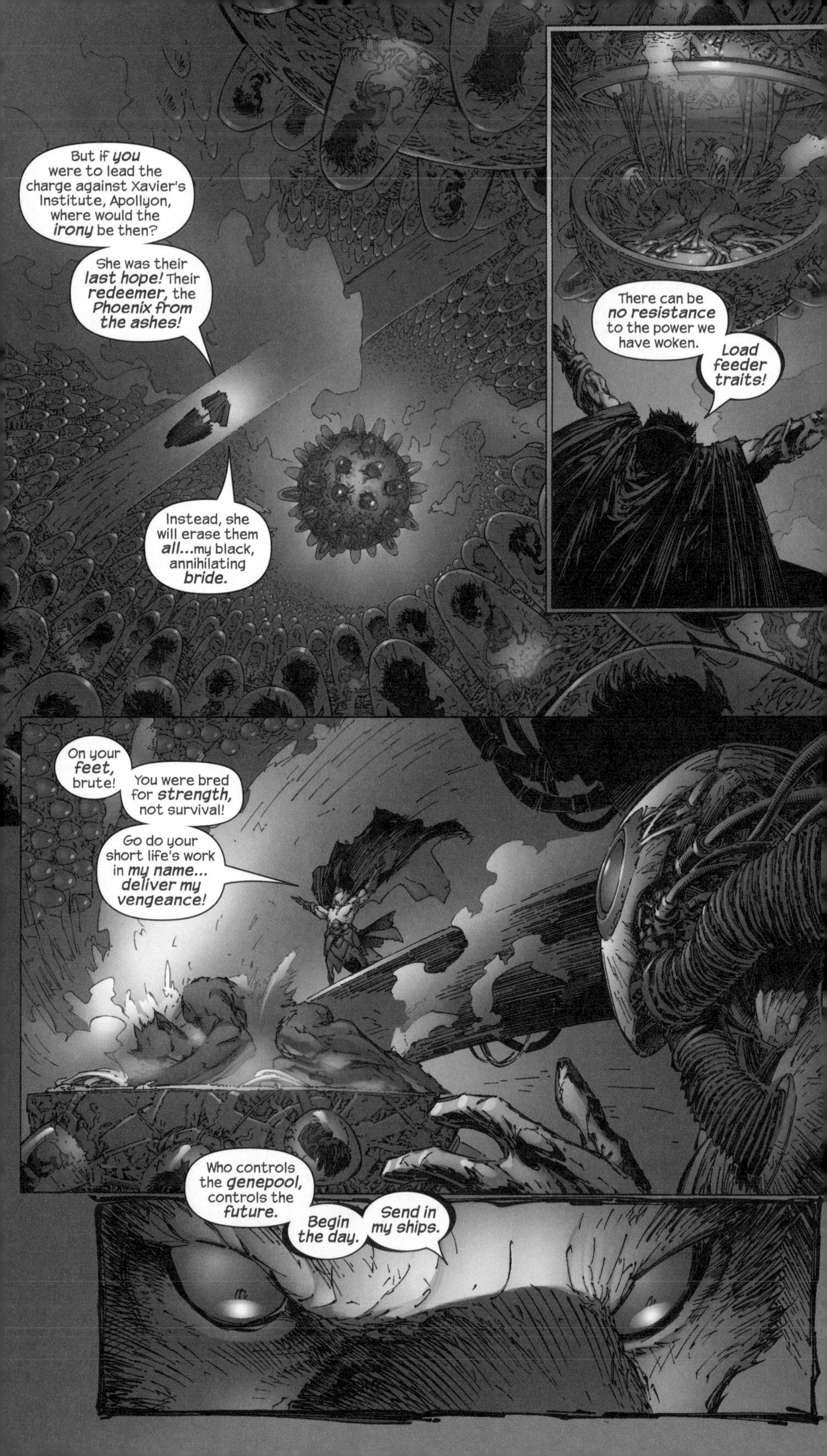
But if *you* were to lead the charge against Xavier's Institute, Apollyon, where would the *irony* be then?
She was their ***last hope!*** Their ***redeemer,*** the ***Phoenix from the ashes!***
There can be ***no resistance*** to the power we have woken.
Load feeder traits!
Instead, she will erase them ***all...*** my black, annihilating ***bride.***
On your ***feet,*** brute!
You were bred for ***strength,*** not survival!
Go do your short life's work in ***my name... deliver my vengeance!***
Who controls the ***genepool,*** controls the ***future.***
Begin the day.
Send in my ships.

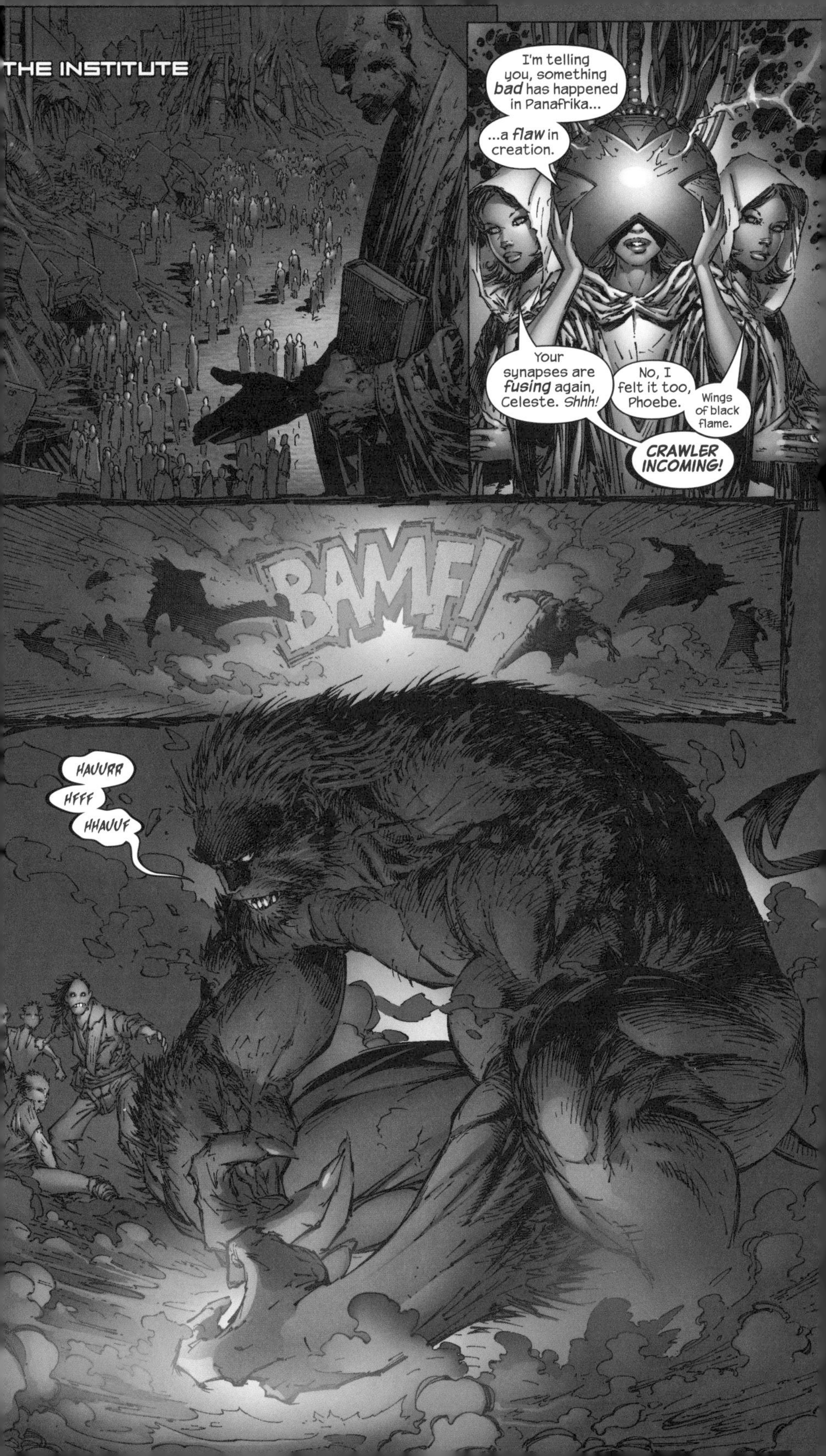
THE INSTITUTE
I'm telling you, something bad has happened in Panafrika...
...a flaw in creation.
Your synapses are fusing again, Celeste. Shhh!
No, I felt it too, Phoebe.
Wings of black flame.
CRAWLER INCOMING!
BAMF!
HAUURR
HFFF
HHAUUF

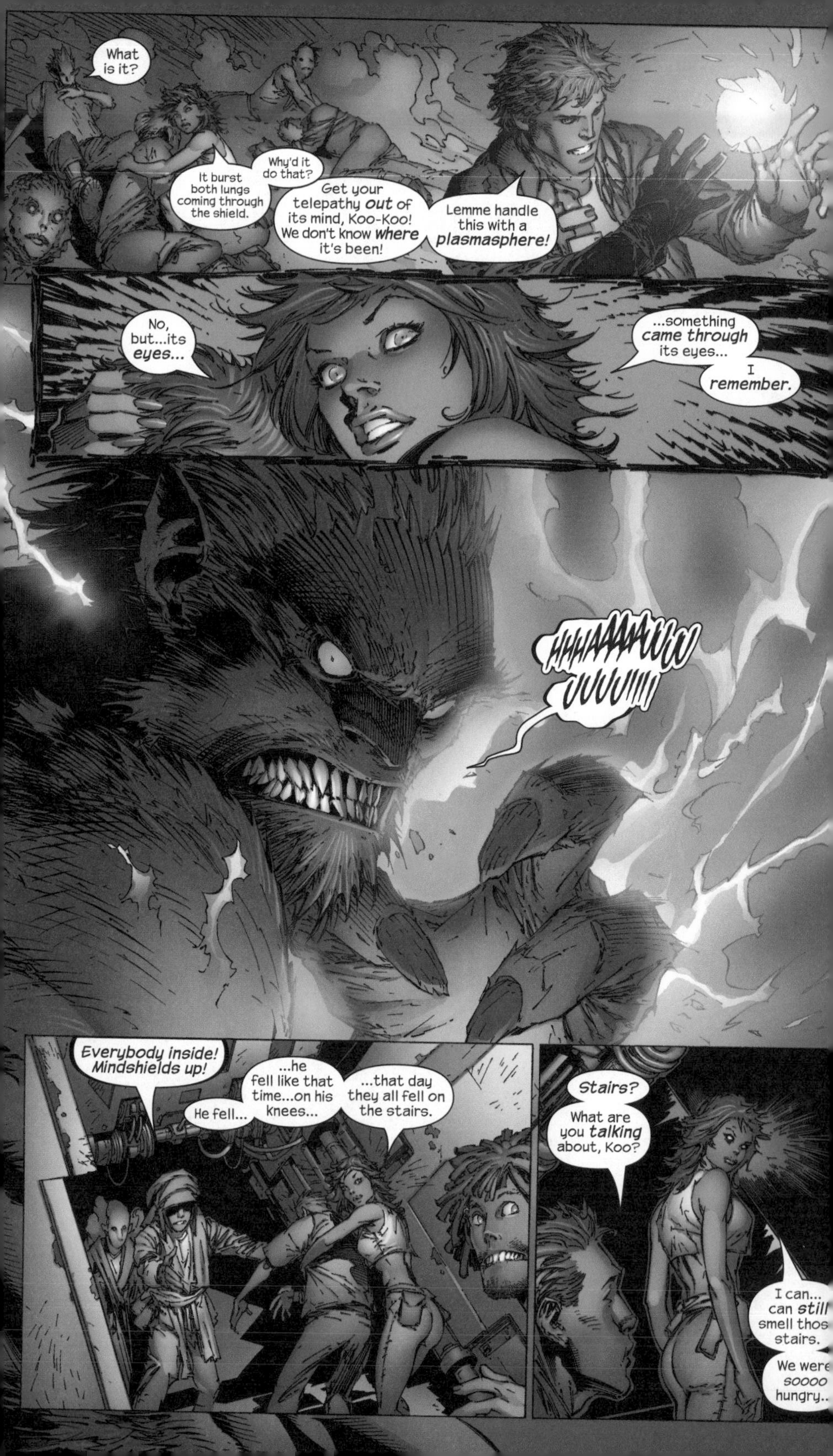

What is it?
It burst both lungs coming through the shield.
Why'd it do that?
Get your telepathy *out* of its mind, Koo-Koo! We don't know *where* it's been!
Lemme handle this with a *plasmasphere!*
No, but...its *eyes...*
...something *came through* its eyes...
I *remember.*
HHHAAAAOOOOUUUU!!!!
Everybody inside! Mindshields up!
He fell...
...he fell like that time...on his knees...
...that day they all fell on the stairs.
Stairs?
What are you *talking* about, Koo?
I can... can *still* smell thos stairs.
We were *soooo* hungry..

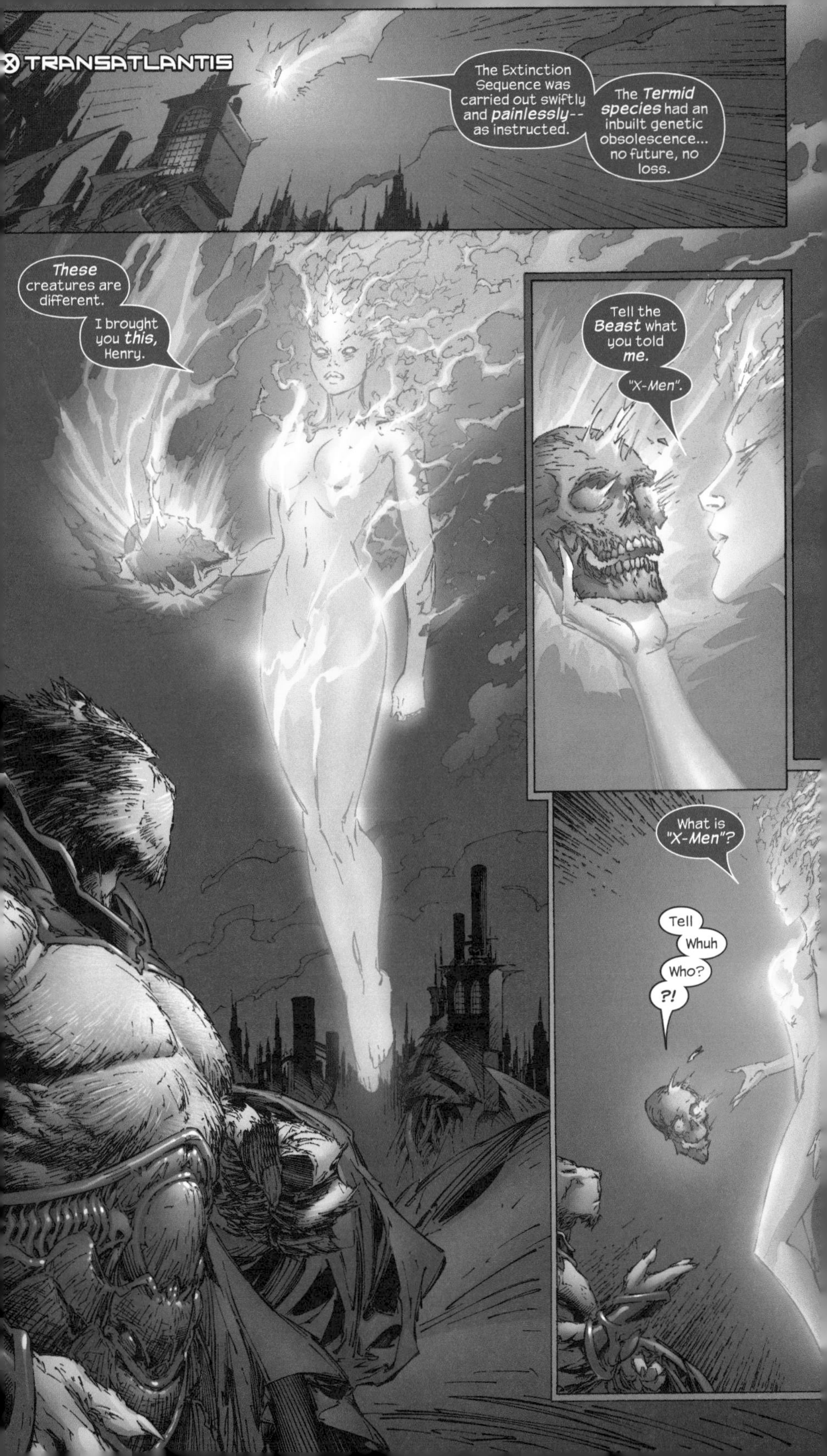
TRANSATLANTIS
The Extinction Sequence was carried out swiftly and *painlessly*-- as instructed.
The *Termid species* had an inbuilt genetic obsolescence... no future, no loss.
These creatures are different.
I brought you *this,* Henry.
Tell the *Beast* what you told *me.*
"X-Men".
What is "X-Men"?
Tell
Whuh
Who?
?!

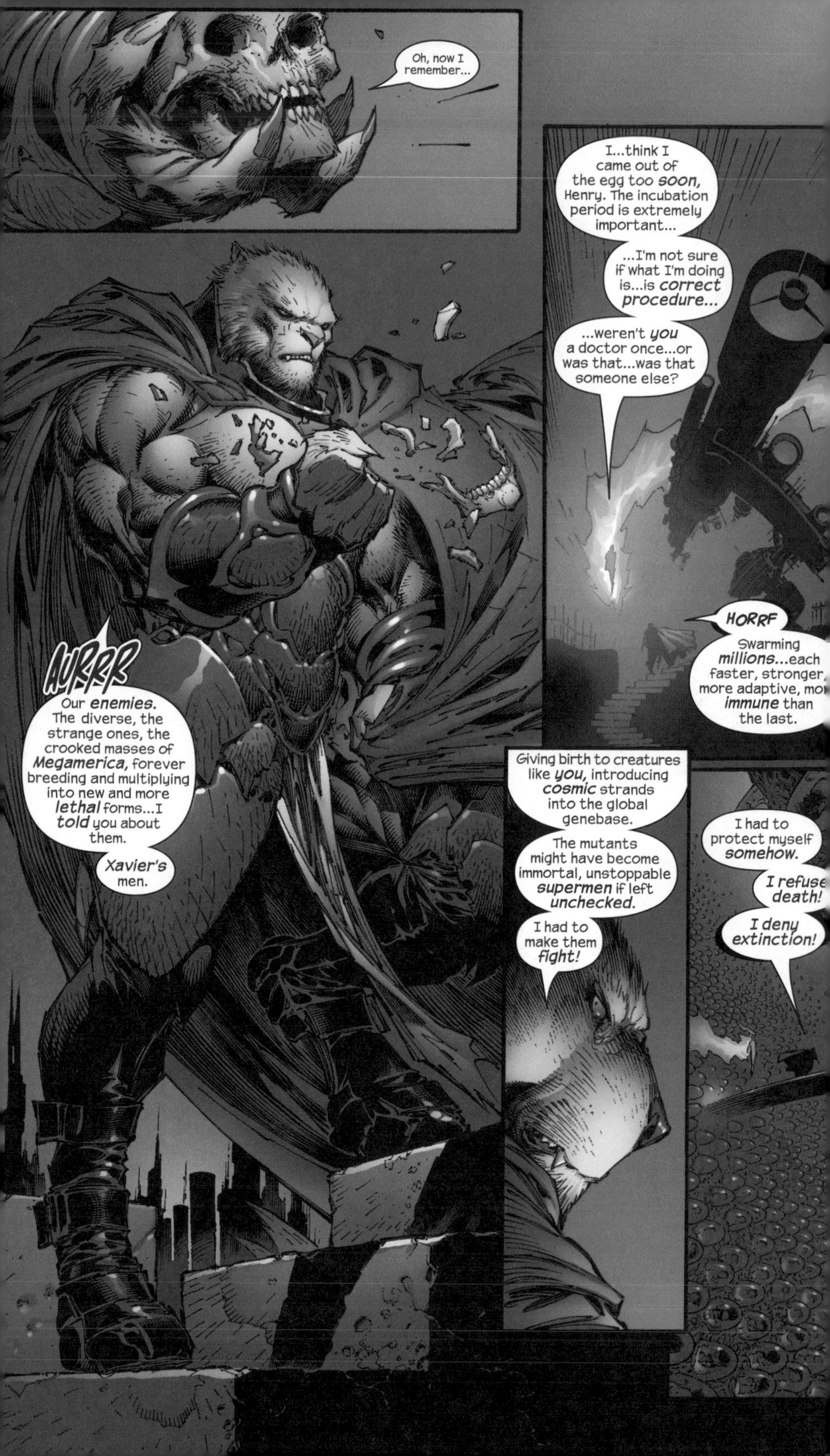

Oh, now I remember...
I...think I came out of the egg too soon, Henry. The incubation period is extremely important...
...I'm not sure if what I'm doing is...is correct procedure...
...weren't you a doctor once...or was that...was that someone else?
AURRR
Our enemies. The diverse, the strange ones, the crooked masses of Megamerica, forever breeding and multiplying into new and more lethal forms...I told you about them.
Xavier's men.
HORRF
Swarming millions...each faster, stronger, more adaptive, mo immune than the last.
Giving birth to creatures like you, introducing cosmic strands into the global genebase.
The mutants might have become immortal, unstoppable supermen if left unchecked.
I had to make them fight!
I had to protect myself somehow.
I refuse death!
I deny extinction!

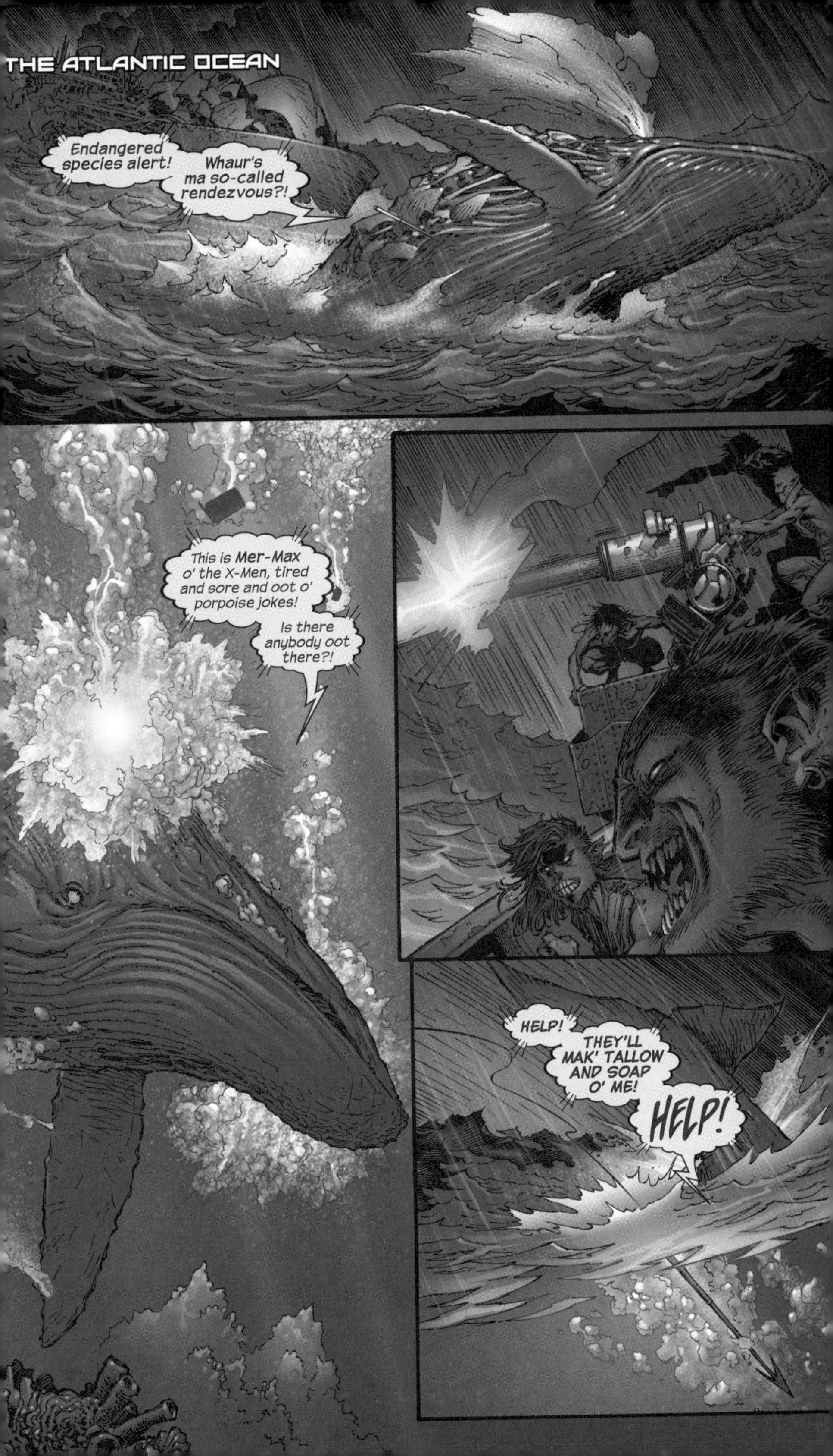
THE ATLANTIC OCEAN
Endangered species alert!
Whaur's ma so-called rendezvous?!
This is Mer-Max o' the X-Men, tired and sore and oot o' porpoise jokes!
Is there anybody oot there?!
HELP!
THEY'LL MAK' TALLOW AND SOAP O' ME!
HELP!

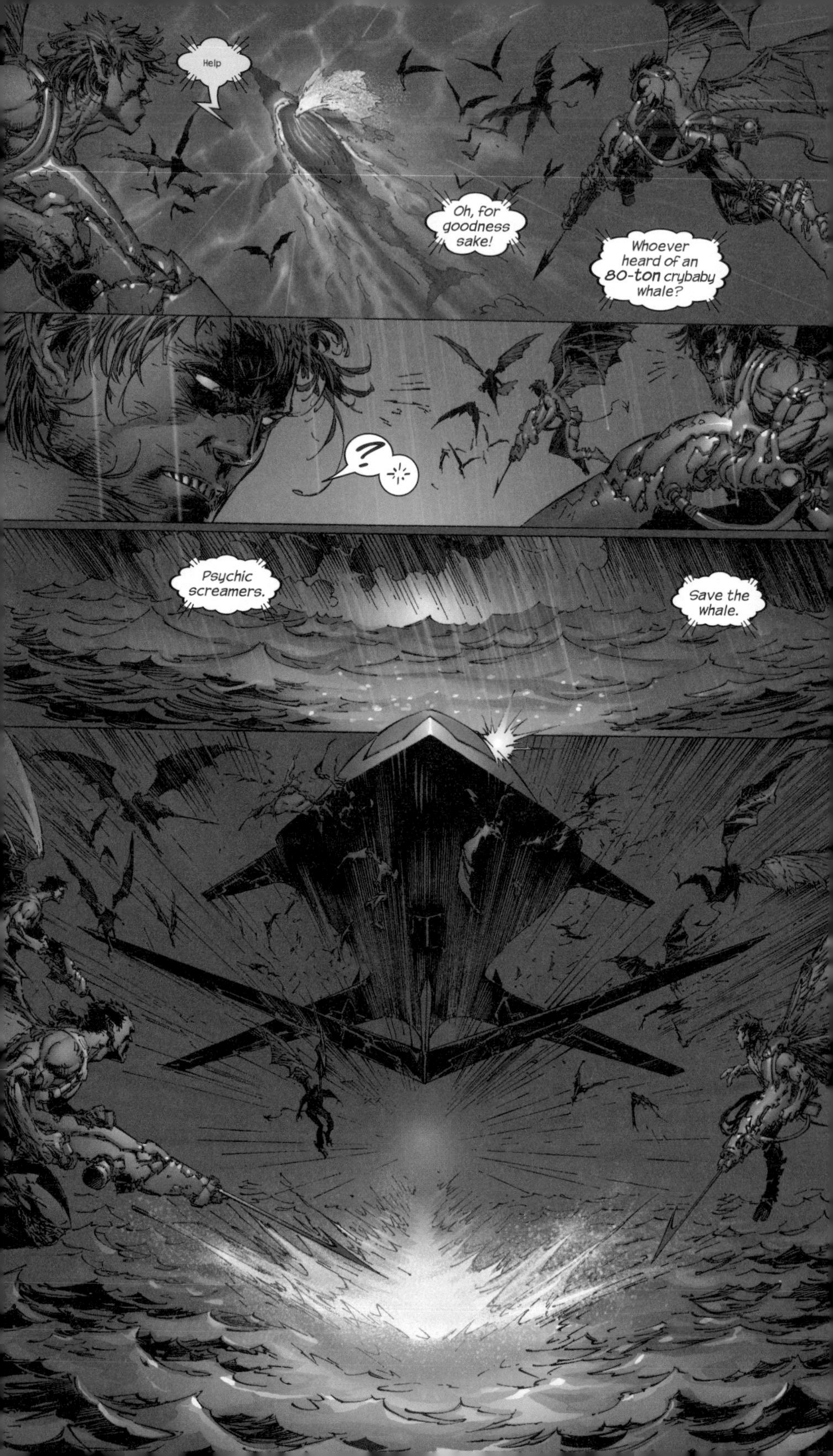
Help
Oh, for goodness sake!
Whoever heard of an 80-ton crybaby whale?
?
Psychic screamers.
Save the whale.

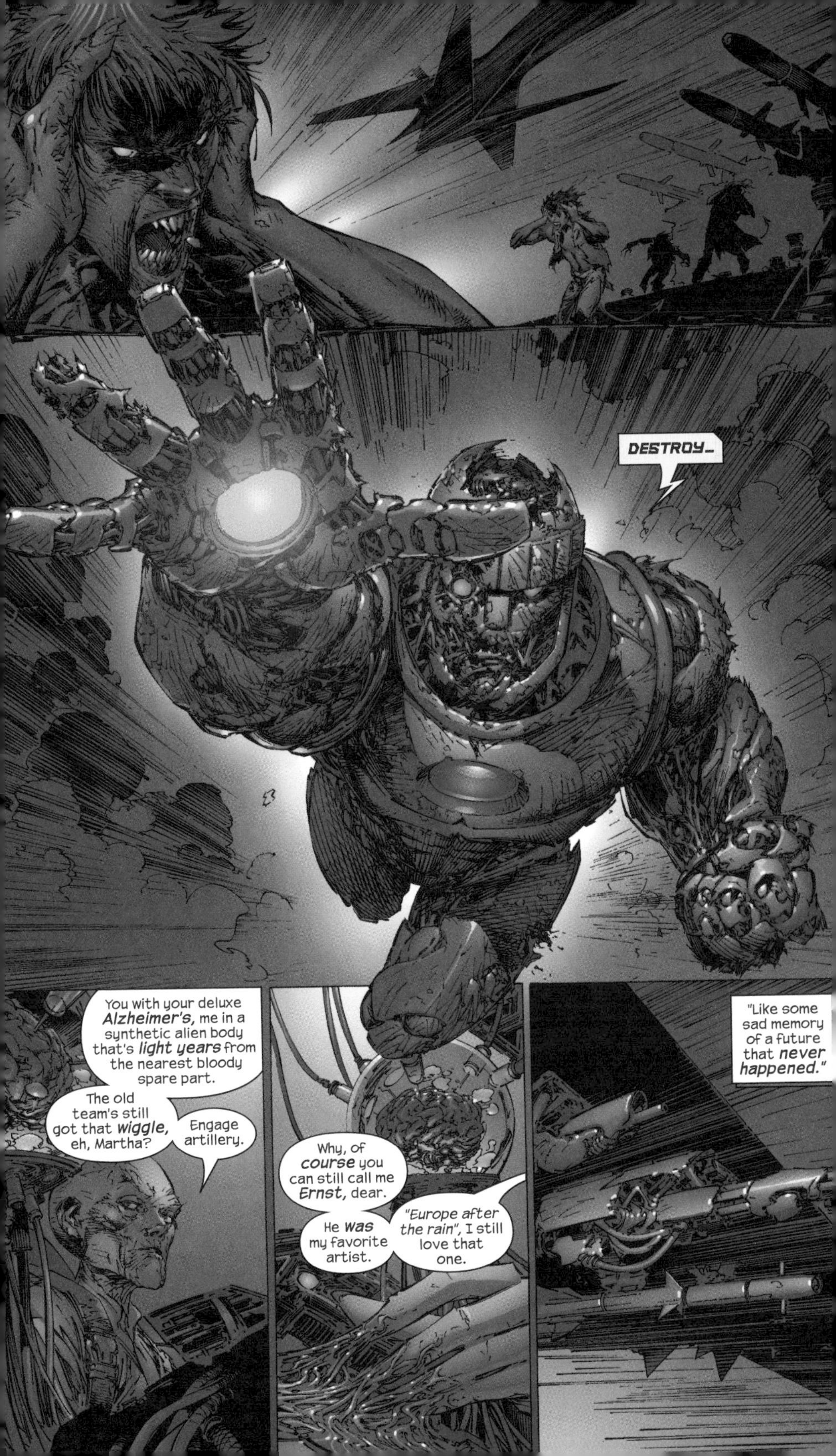

DESTROY...
You with your deluxe Alzheimer's, me in a synthetic alien body that's light years from the nearest bloody spare part.
The old team's still got that wiggle, eh, Martha?
Engage artillery.
Why, of course you can still call me Ernst, dear.
He was my favorite artist.
"Europe after the rain", I still love that one.
"Like some sad memory of a future that never happened."

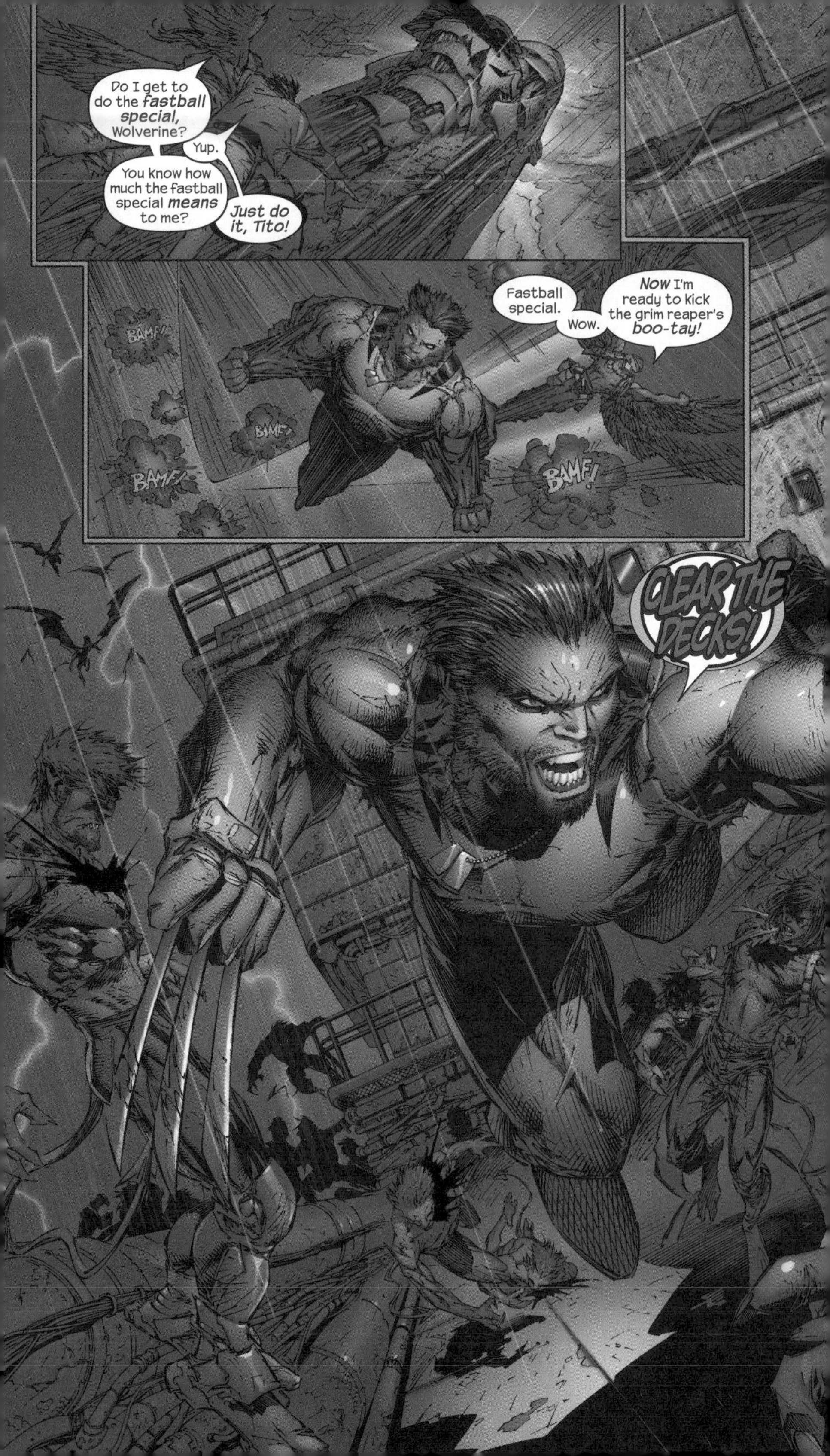

Do I get to do the fastball special, Wolverine?
Yup.
You know how much the fastball special means to me?
Just do it, Tito!
BAMF!
BAMF
BAMF!
BAMF!
Fastball special.
Wow.
Now I'm ready to kick the grim reaper's boo-tay!
CLEAR THE DECKS!

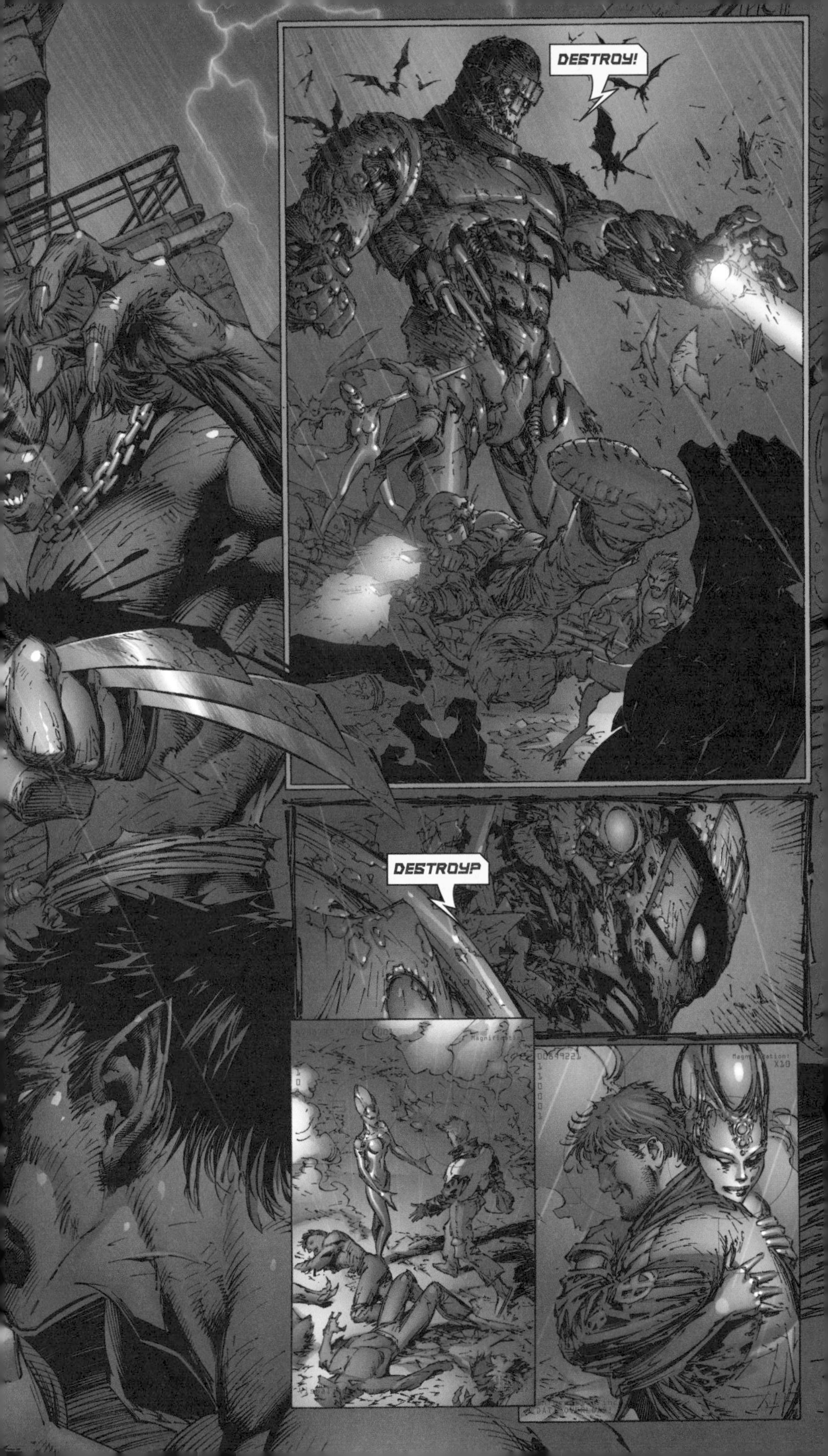
DESTROY!
DESTROY?

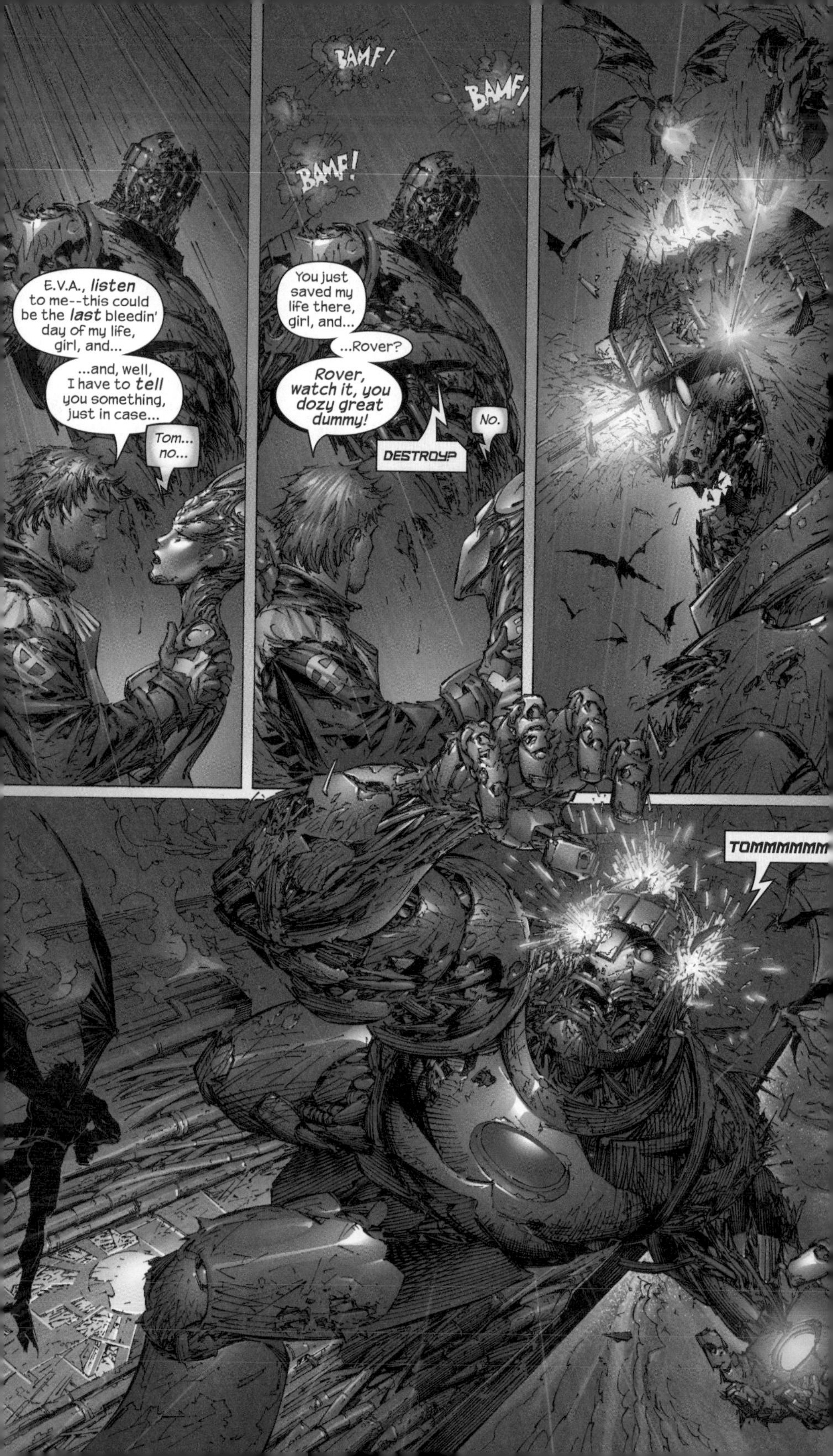
E.V.A., listen to me--this could be the last bleedin' day of my life, girl, and...
...and, well, I have to tell you something, just in case...
Tom... no...
BAMF!
BAMF!
BAMF!
You just saved my life there, girl, and...
...Rover?
Rover, watch it, you dozy great dummy!
DESTROY?
No.
TOMMMMMM

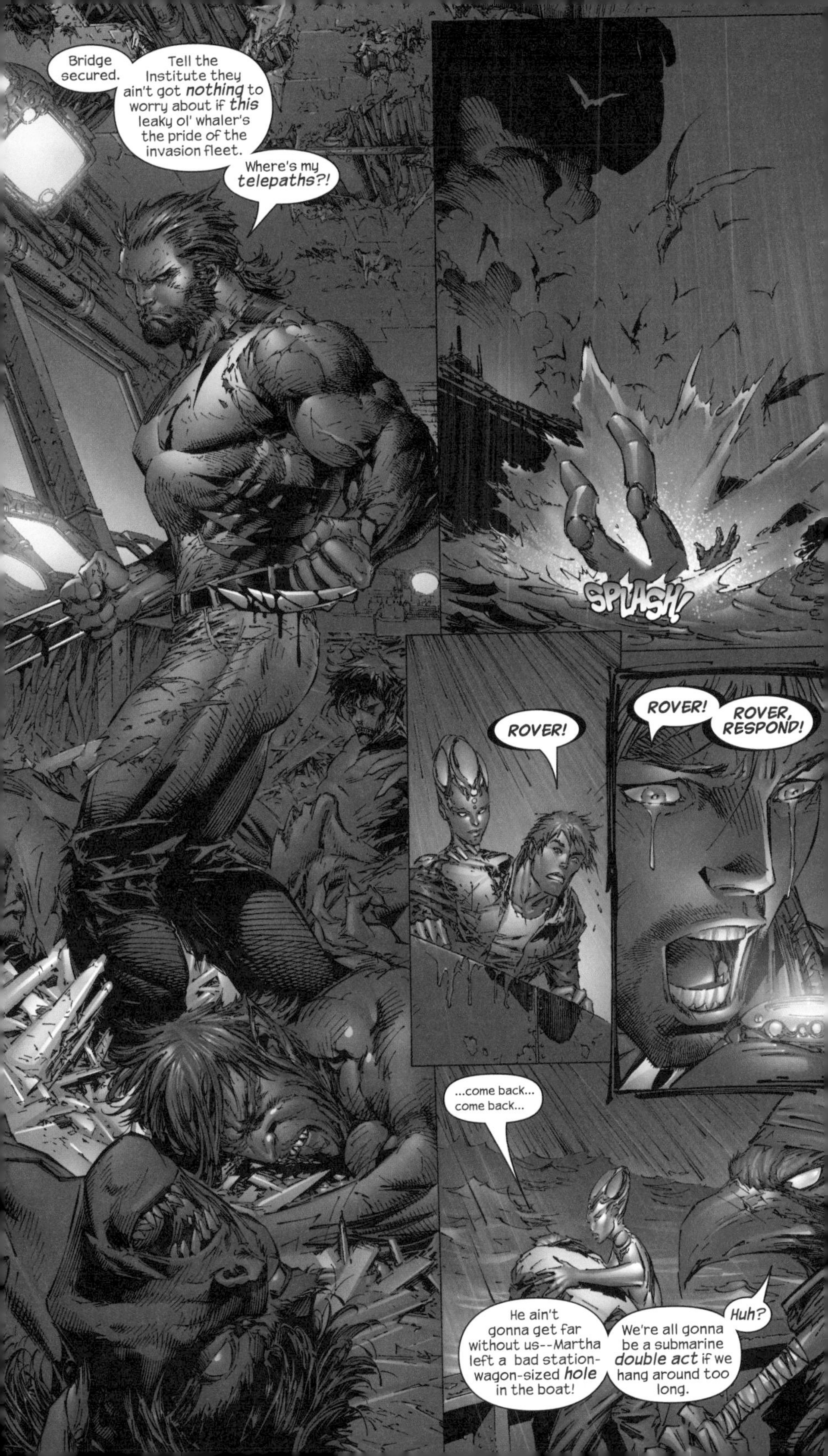
Bridge secured.
Tell the Institute they ain't got *nothing* to worry about if *this* leaky ol' whaler's the pride of the invasion fleet.
Where's my *telepaths?!*
SPLASH!
ROVER!
ROVER!
ROVER, RESPOND!
...come back... come back...
He ain't gonna get far without us--Martha left a bad station-wagon-sized *hole* in the boat!
We're all gonna be a submarine *double act* if we hang around too long.
Huh?

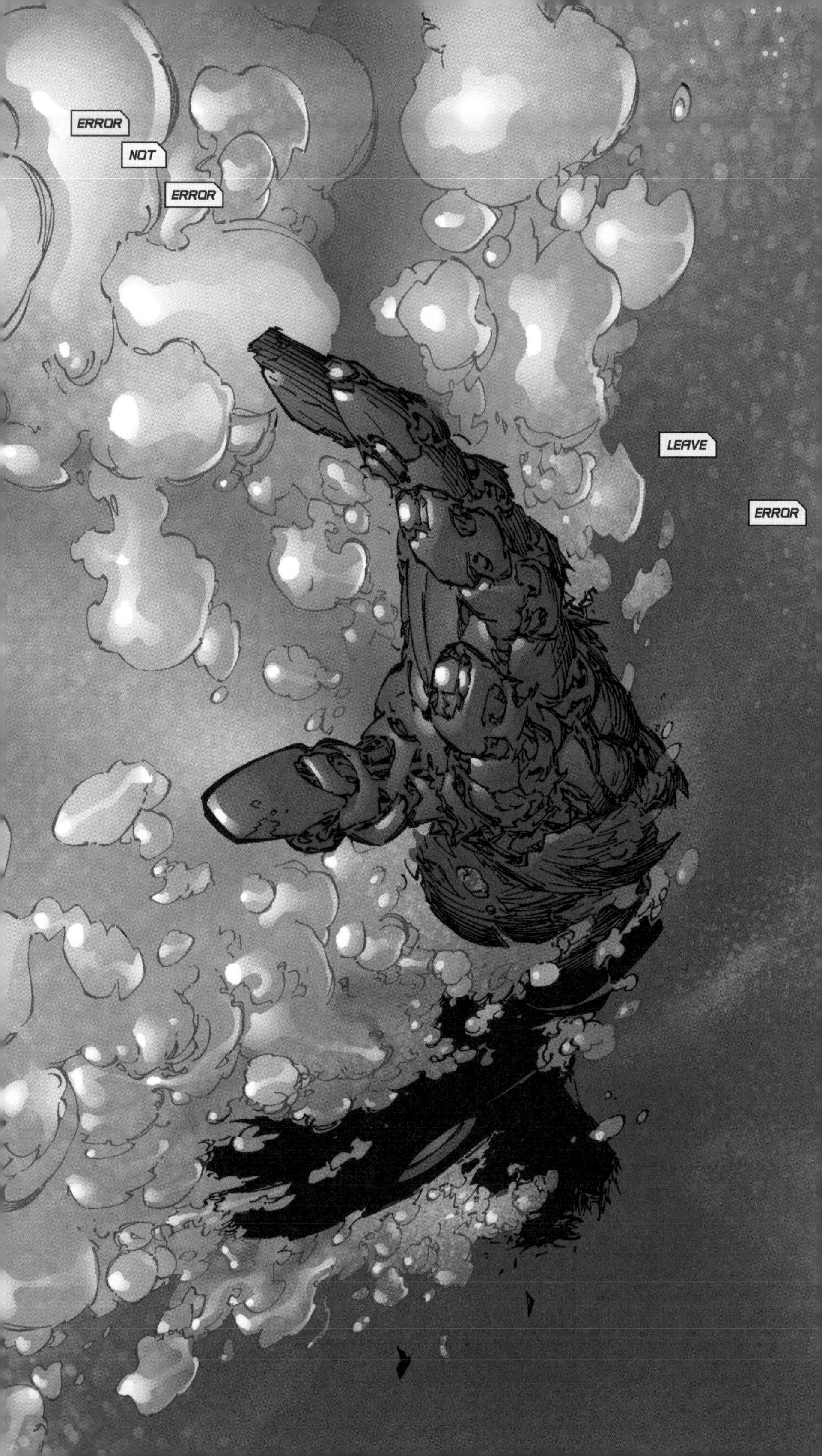
ERROR
NOT
ERROR
LEAVE
ERROR

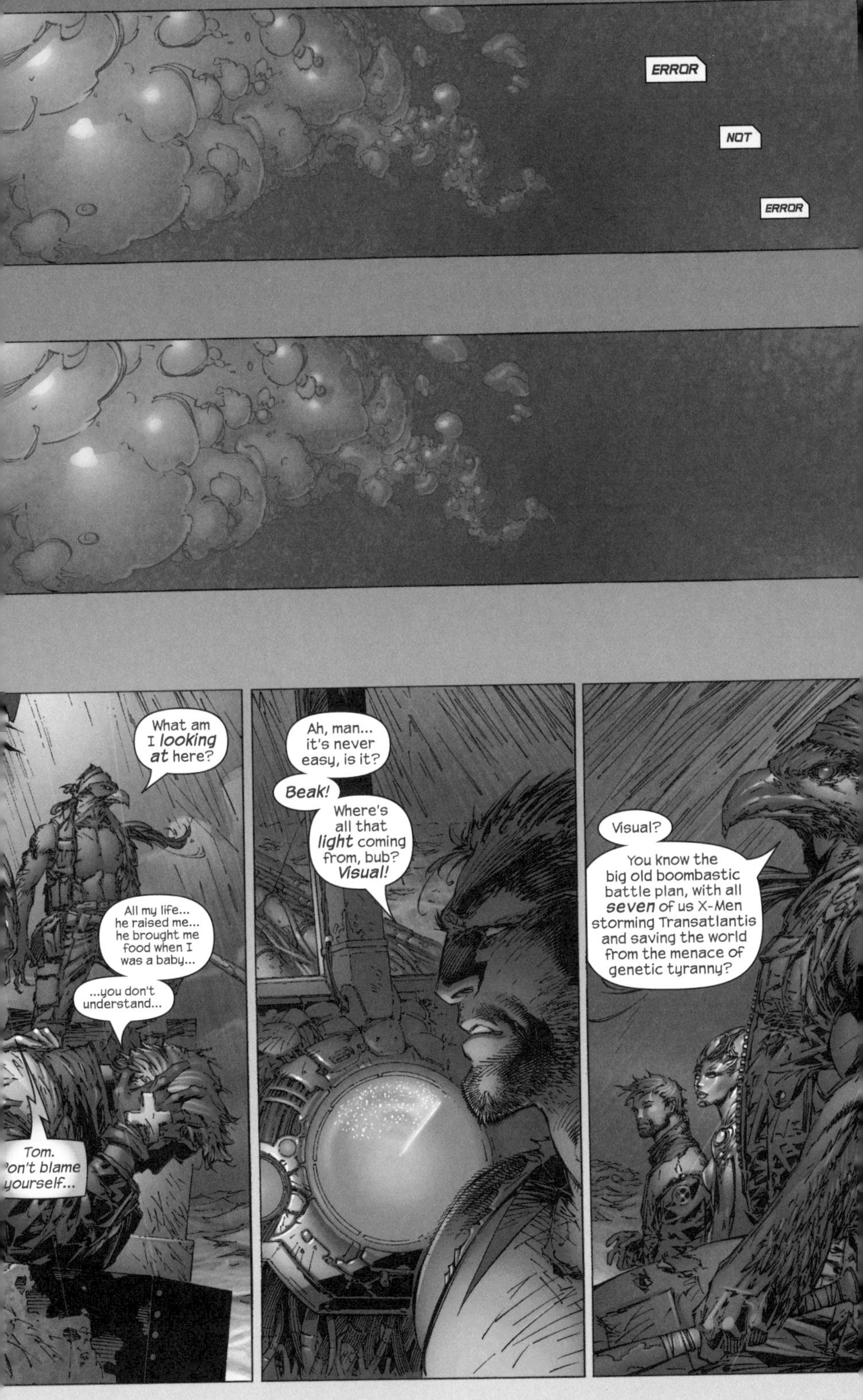
ERROR
NOT
ERROR
What am I looking at here?
All my life... he raised me... he brought me food when I was a baby...
...you don't understand...
Tom. Don't blame yourself...
Ah, man... it's never easy, is it?
Beak!
Where's all that light coming from, bub? Visual!
Visual?
You know the big old boombastic battle plan, with all seven of us X-Men storming Transatlantis and saving the world from the menace of genetic tyranny?

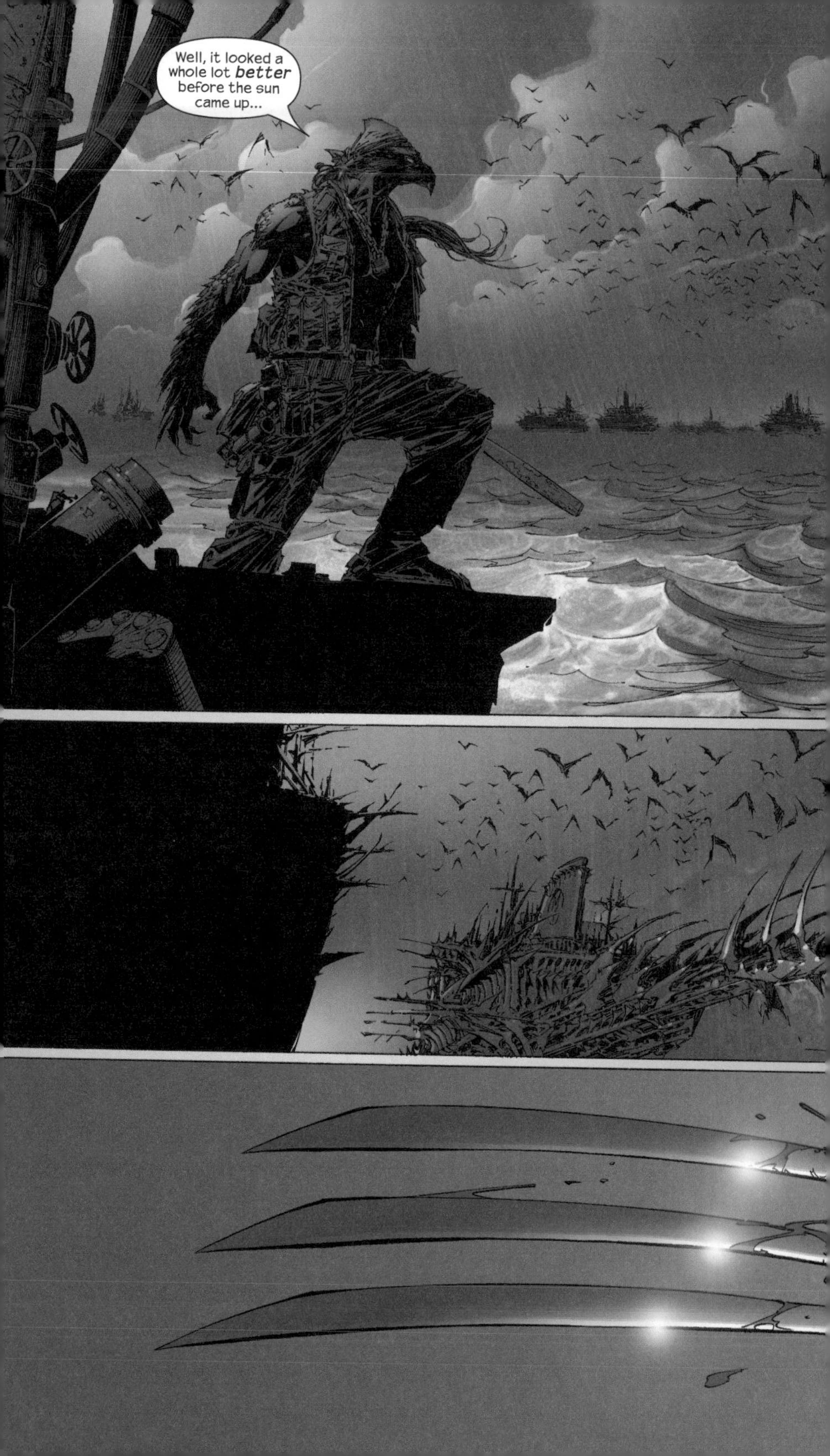
Well, it looked a whole lot *better* before the sun came up...

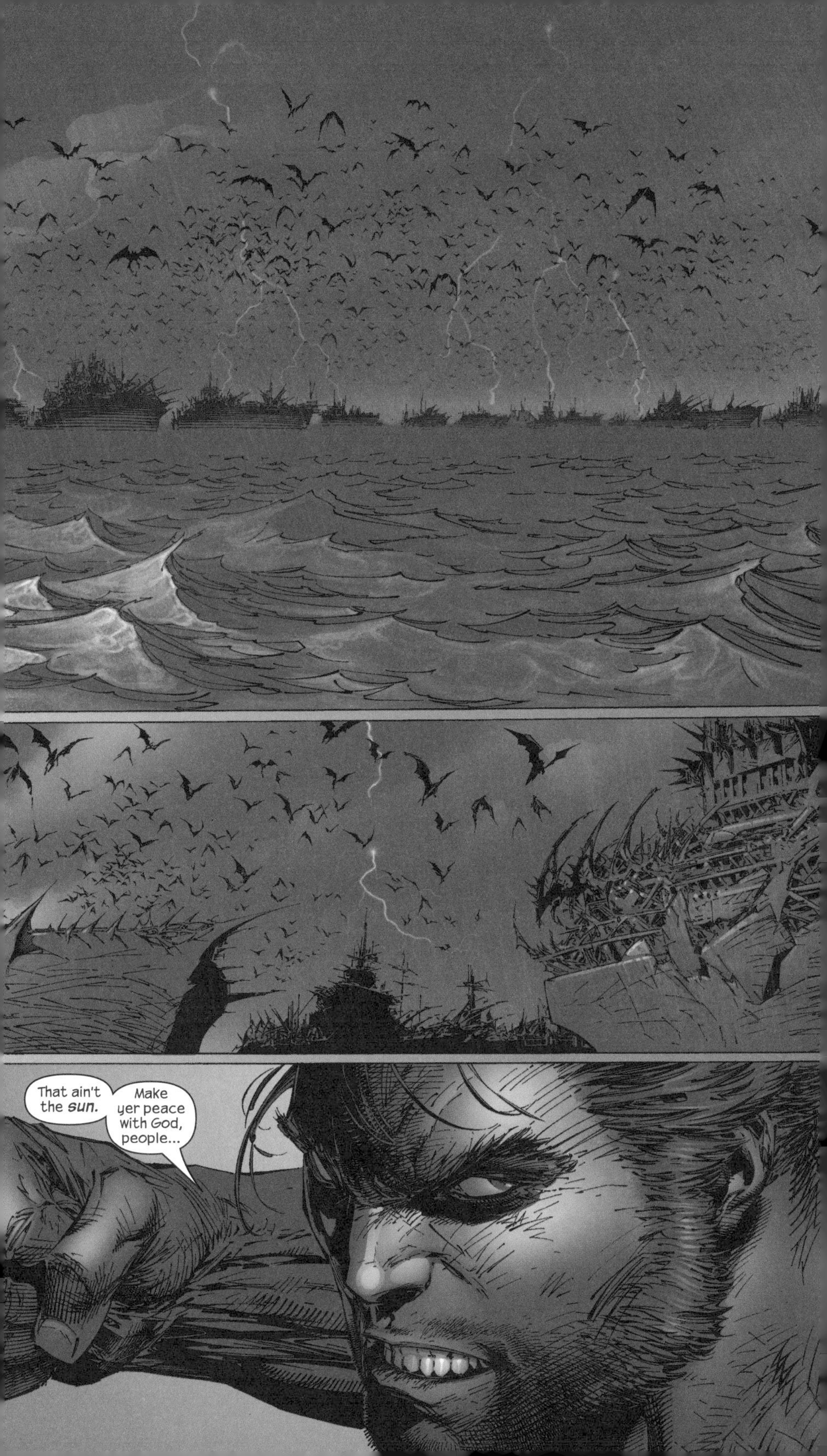
That ain't the *sun.*
Make yer peace with God, people...

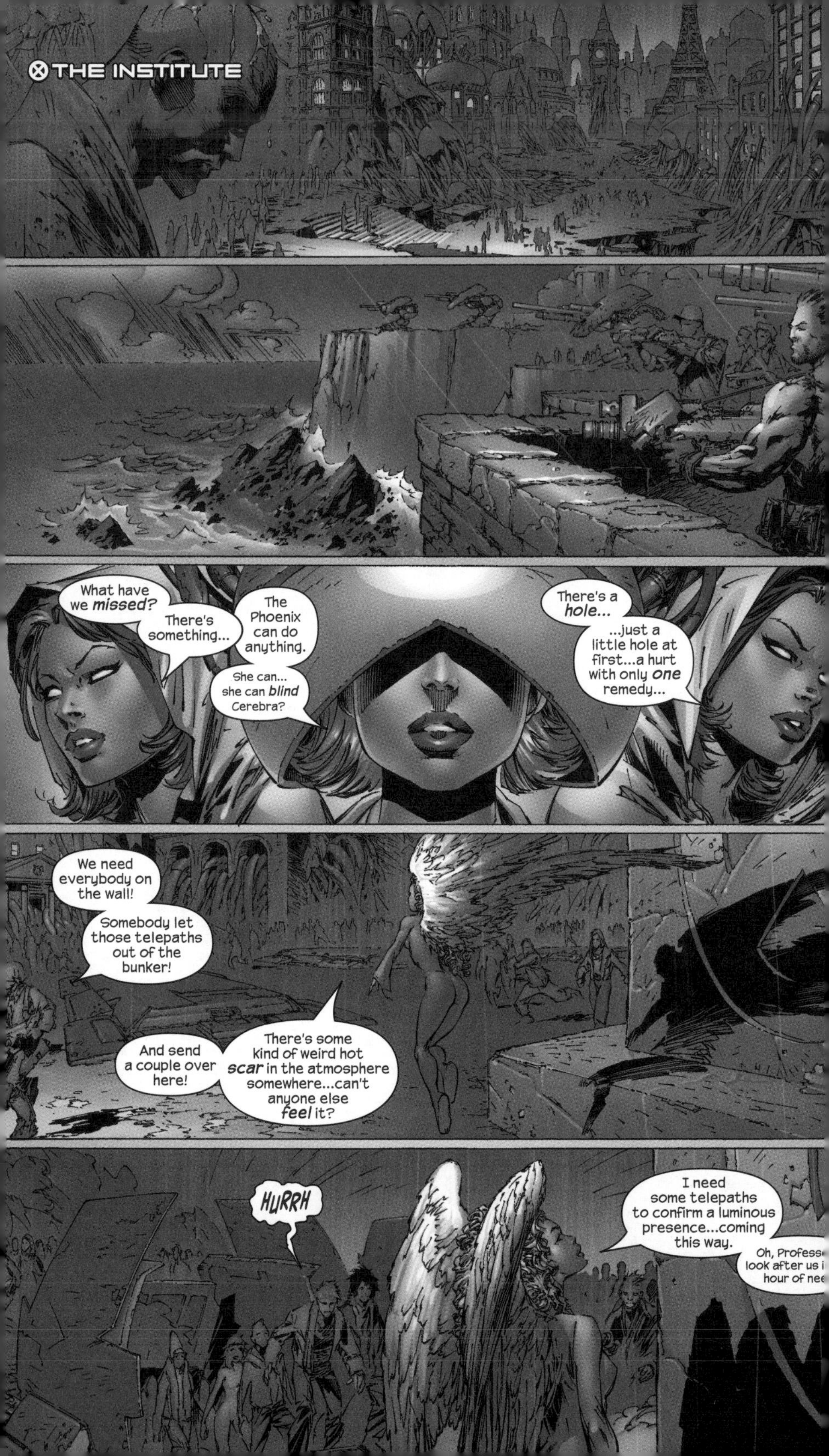
THE INSTITUTE
What have we *missed?*
There's something...
The Phoenix can do anything.
She can... she can *blind* Cerebra?
There's a *hole...*
...just a little hole at first...a hurt with only *one* remedy...
We need everybody on the wall!
Somebody let those telepaths out of the bunker!
And send a couple over here!
There's some kind of weird hot *scar* in the atmosphere somewhere...can't anyone else *feel* it?
HURRH
I need some telepaths to confirm a luminous presence...coming this way.

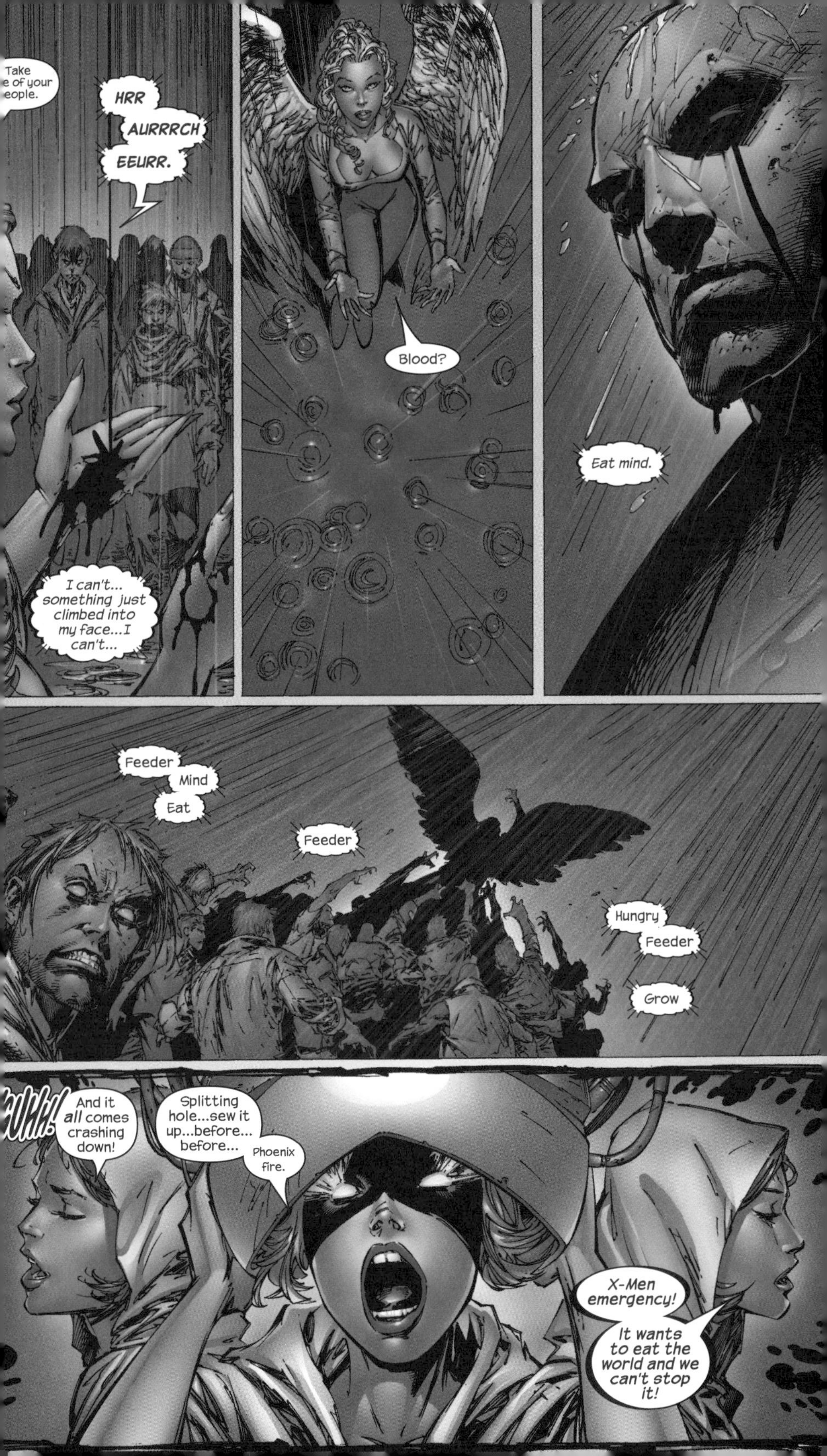

Take
e of your
eople.
HRR
AURRRCH
EEURR.
I can't... something just climbed into my face...I can't...
Blood?
Eat mind.
Feeder
Mind
Eat
Feeder
Hungry
Feeder
Grow
And it all comes crashing down!
Splitting hole...sew it up...before... before...
Phoenix fire.
X-Men emergency!
It wants to eat the world and we can't stop it!

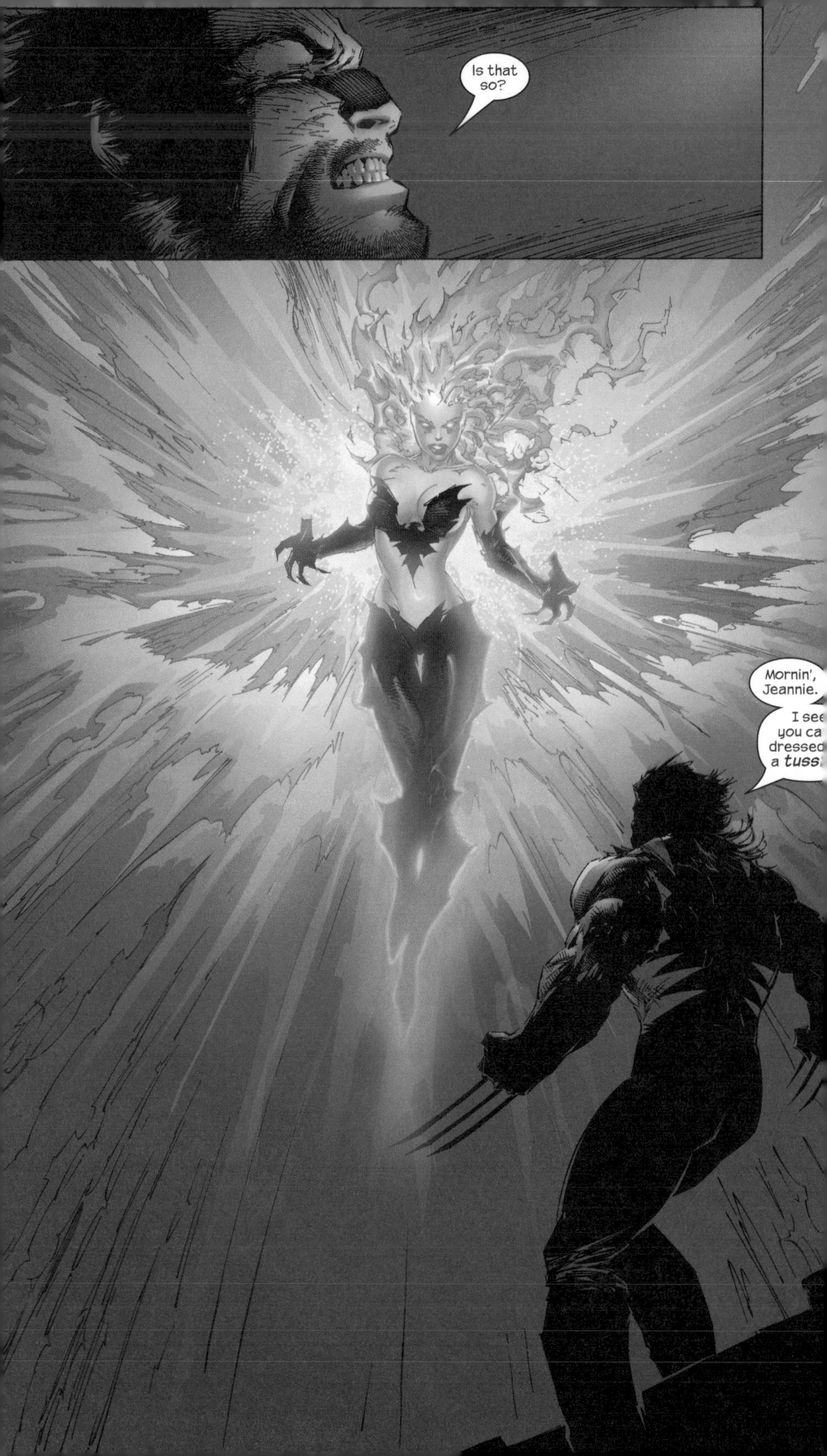

Is that so?
Mornin', Jeannie.
I see you ca dressed a tuss

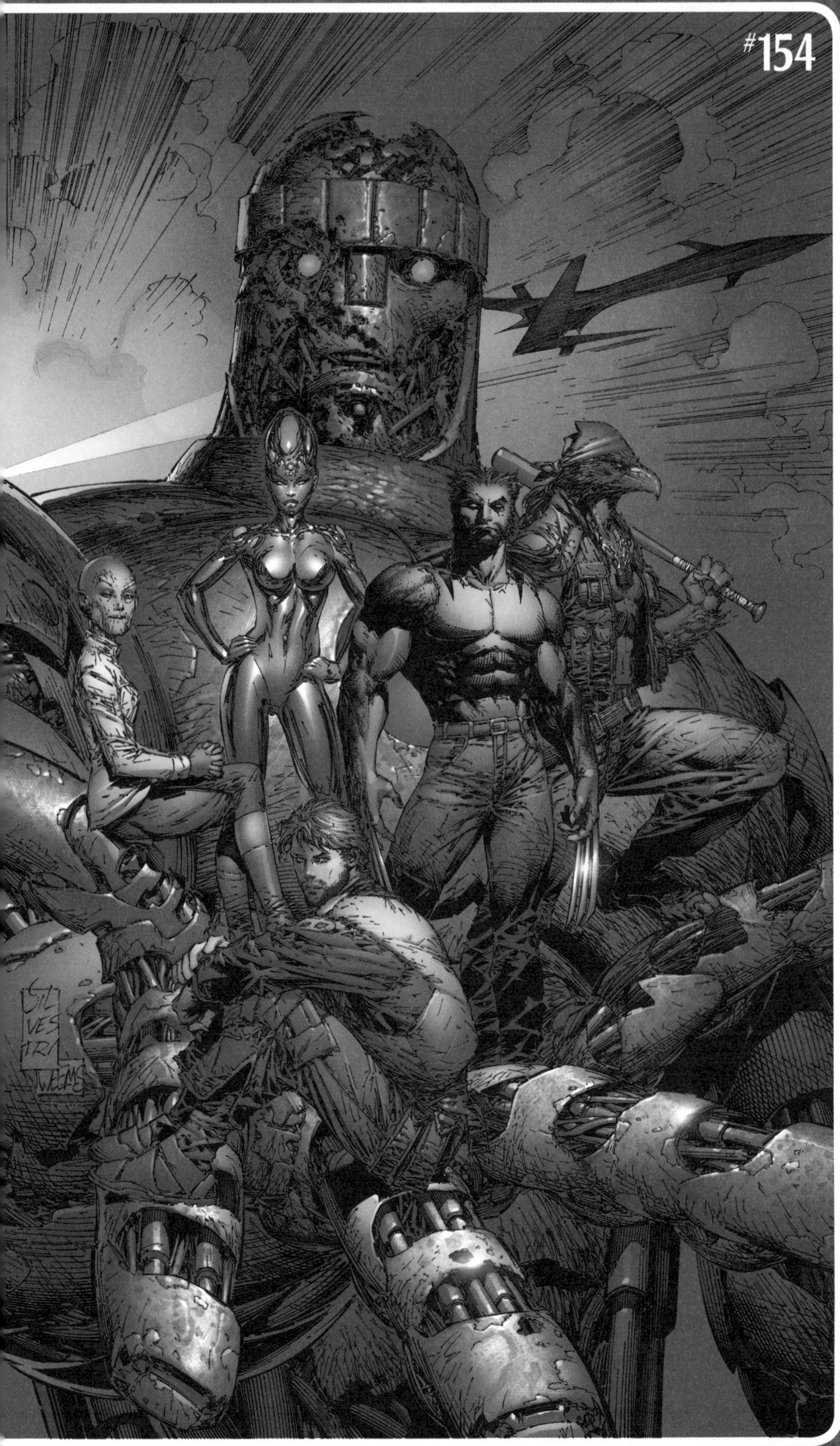
#154

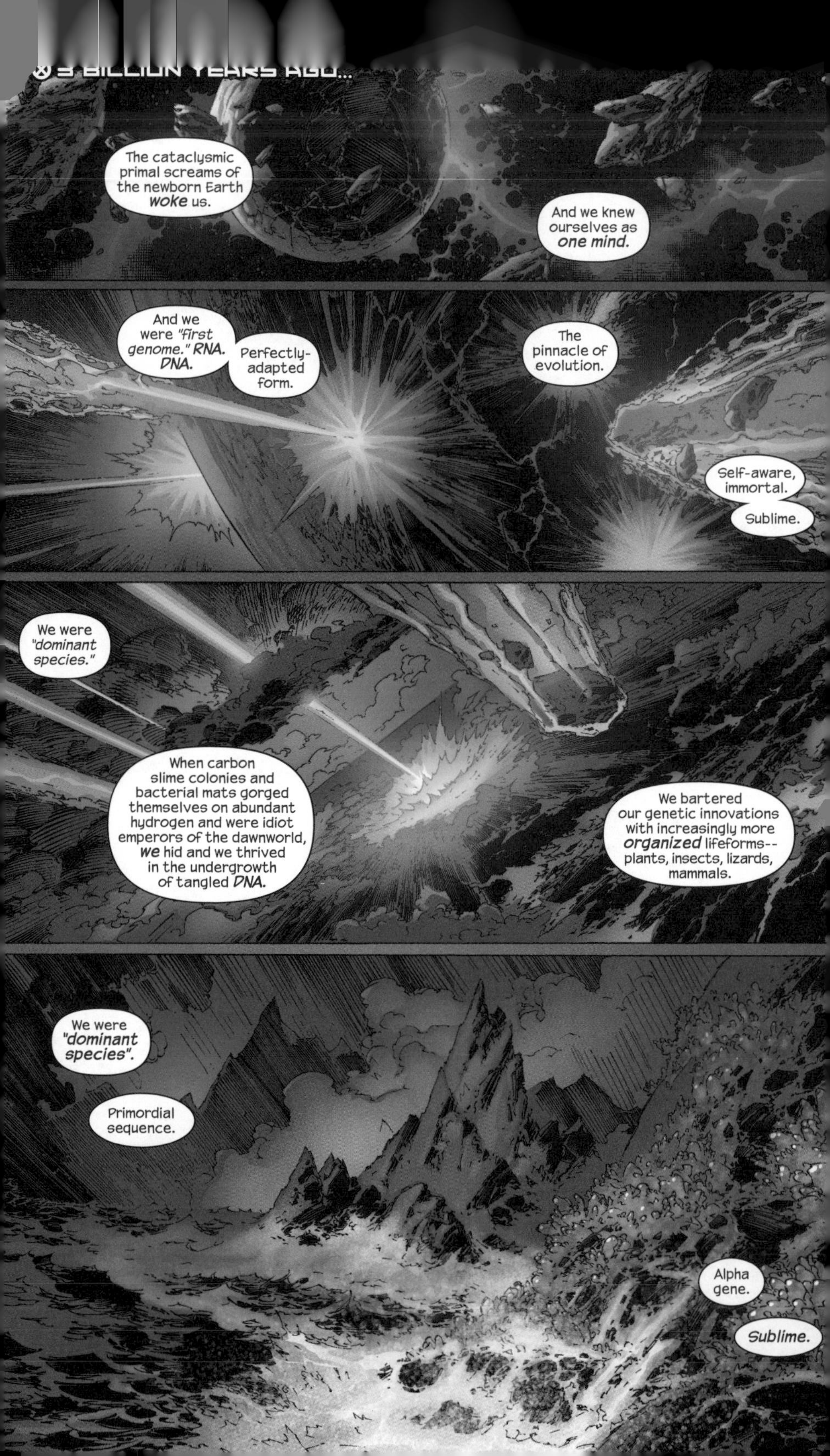
3 BILLION YEARS AGO...
The cataclysmic primal screams of the newborn Earth *woke* us.
And we knew ourselves as *one mind.*
And we were *"first genome." RNA. DNA.*
Perfectly-adapted form.
The pinnacle of evolution.
Self-aware, immortal.
Sublime.
We were *"dominant species."*
When carbon slime colonies and bacterial mats gorged themselves on abundant hydrogen and were idiot emperors of the dawnworld, *we* hid and we thrived in the undergrowth of tangled *DNA.*
We bartered our genetic innovations with increasingly more *organized* lifeforms--plants, insects, lizards, mammals.
We were *"dominant species".*
Primordial sequence.
Alpha gene.
Sublime.

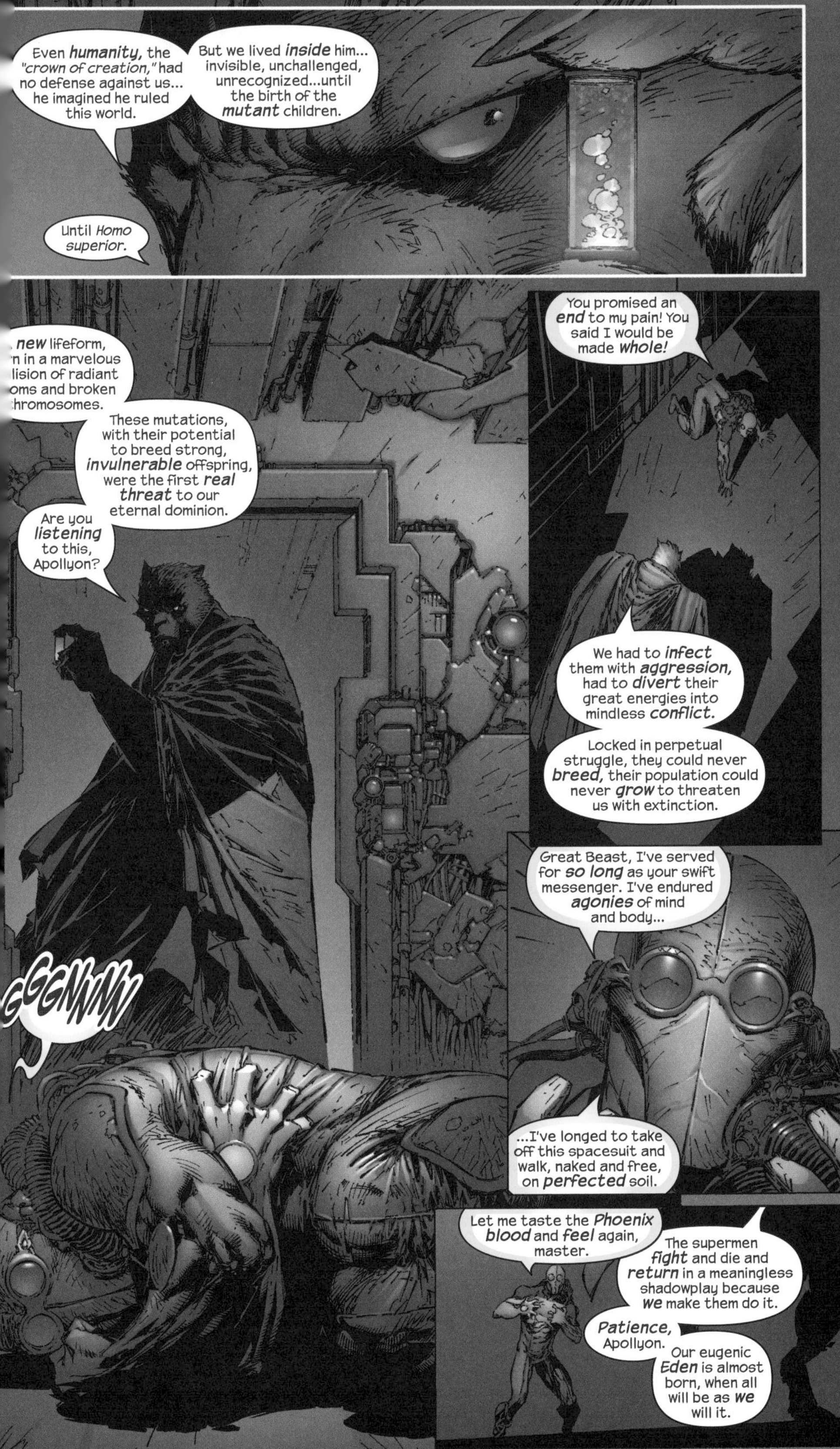
Even humanity, the "crown of creation," had no defense against us... he imagined he ruled this world.
But we lived inside him... invisible, unchallenged, unrecognized...until the birth of the mutant children.
Until Homo superior.
new lifeform, n in a marvelous lision of radiant oms and broken hromosomes.
These mutations, with their potential to breed strong, invulnerable offspring, were the first real threat to our eternal dominion.
Are you listening to this, Apollyon?
You promised an end to my pain! You said I would be made whole!
We had to infect them with aggression, had to divert their great energies into mindless conflict.
Locked in perpetual struggle, they could never breed, their population could never grow to threaten us with extinction.
Great Beast, I've served for so long as your swift messenger. I've endured agonies of mind and body...
...I've longed to take off this spacesuit and walk, naked and free, on perfected soil.
GGGNNNN
Let me taste the Phoenix blood and feel again, master.
The supermen fight and die and return in a meaningless shadowplay because we make them do it.
Patience, Apollyon.
Our eugenic Eden is almost born, when all will be as we will it.

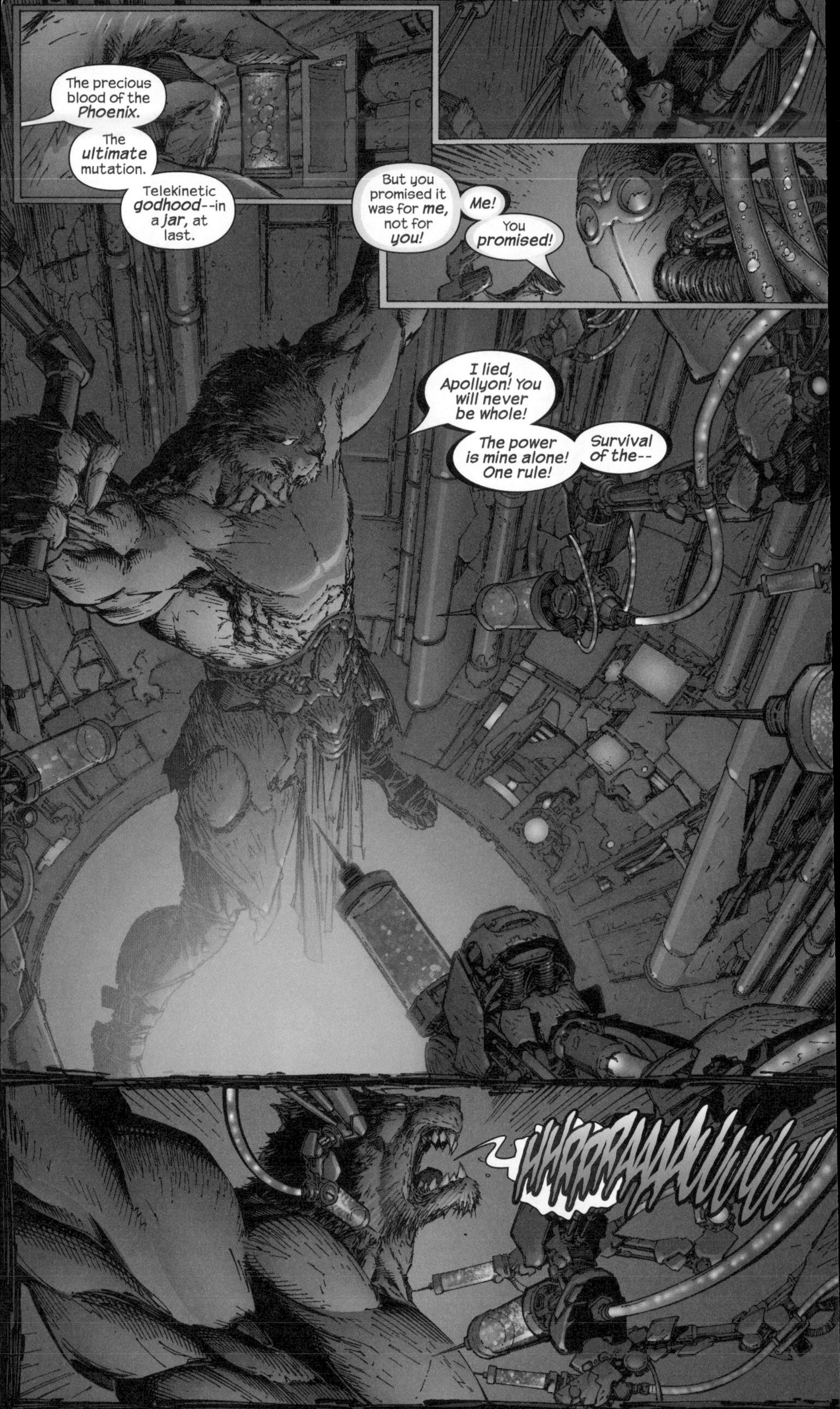

The precious blood of the *Phoenix.*
The *ultimate* mutation.
Telekinetic *godhood*--in a *jar,* at last.
But you promised it was for *me,* not for *you!*
Me!
You *promised!*
I lied, Apollyon! You will never be whole!
The power is mine alone! One rule!
Survival of the--

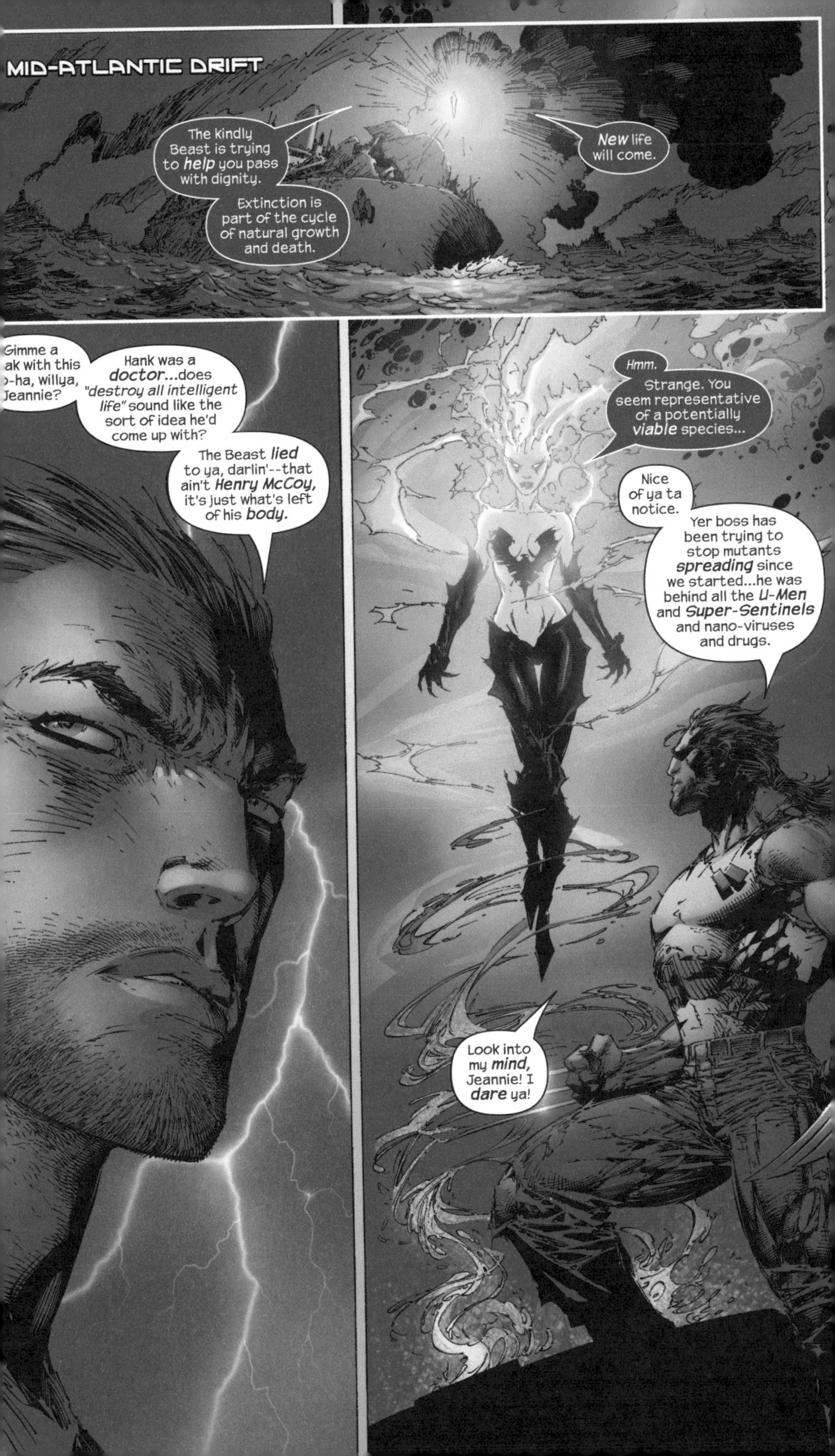
MID-ATLANTIC DRIFT
The kindly Beast is trying to help you pass with dignity.
Extinction is part of the cycle of natural growth and death.
New life will come.
Gimme a ak with this -ha, willya, Jeannie?
Hank was a doctor...does "destroy all intelligent life" sound like the sort of idea he'd come up with?
The Beast lied to ya, darlin'--that ain't Henry McCoy, it's just what's left of his body.
Hmm.
Strange. You seem representative of a potentially viable species...
Nice of ya ta notice.
Yer boss has been trying to stop mutants spreading since we started...he was behind all the U-Men and Super-Sentinels and nano-viruses and drugs.
Look into my mind, Jeannie! I dare ya!

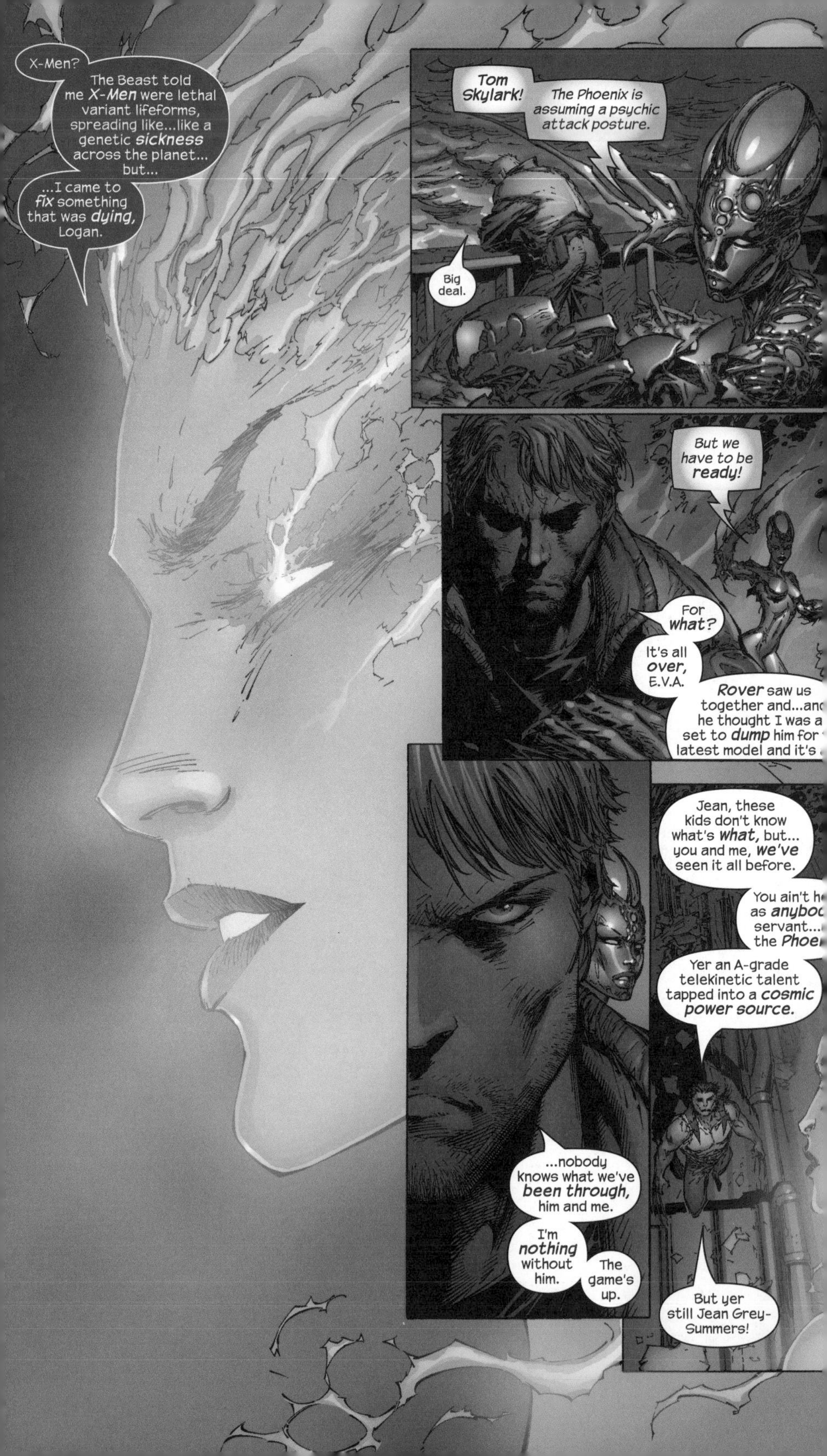
X-Men?
The Beast told me X-Men were lethal variant lifeforms, spreading like...like a genetic sickness across the planet... but...
...I came to fix something that was dying, Logan.
Tom Skylark!
The Phoenix is assuming a psychic attack posture.
Big deal.
But we have to be ready!
For what?
It's all over, E.V.A.
Rover saw us together and...and he thought I was a set to dump him for latest model and it's
Jean, these kids don't know what's what, but... you and me, we've seen it all before.
You ain't h as anyboc servant... the Phoe
Yer an A-grade telekinetic talent tapped into a cosmic power source.
But yer still Jean Grey-Summers!
...nobody knows what we've been through, him and me.
I'm nothing without him.
The game's up.

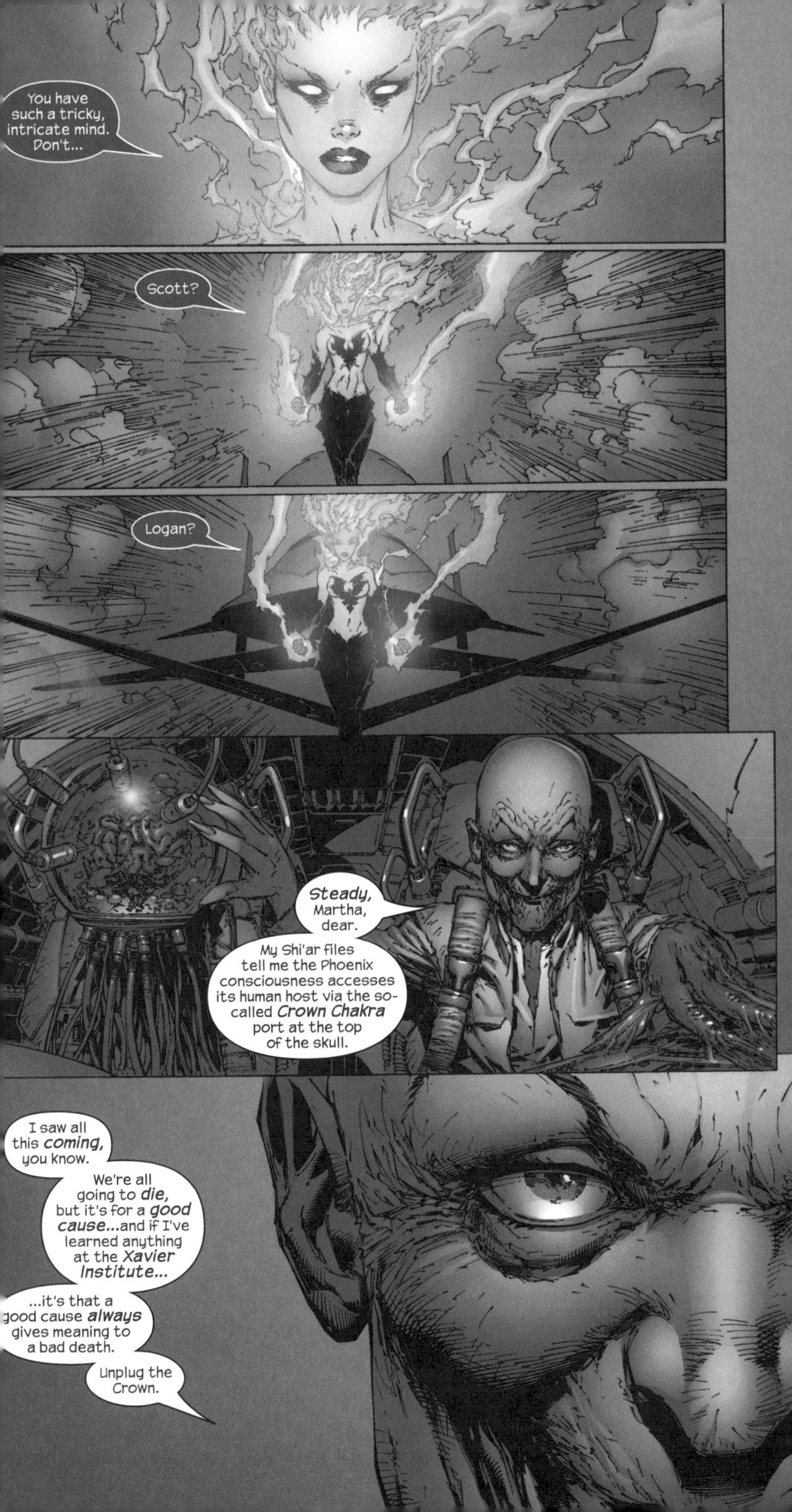

You have such a tricky, intricate mind. Don't...
Scott?
Logan?
Steady, Martha, dear.
My Shi'ar files tell me the Phoenix consciousness accesses its human host via the so-called Crown Chakra port at the top of the skull.
I saw all this coming, you know.
We're all going to die, but it's for a good cause...and if I've learned anything at the Xavier Institute...
...it's that a good cause always gives meaning to a bad death.
Unplug the Crown.

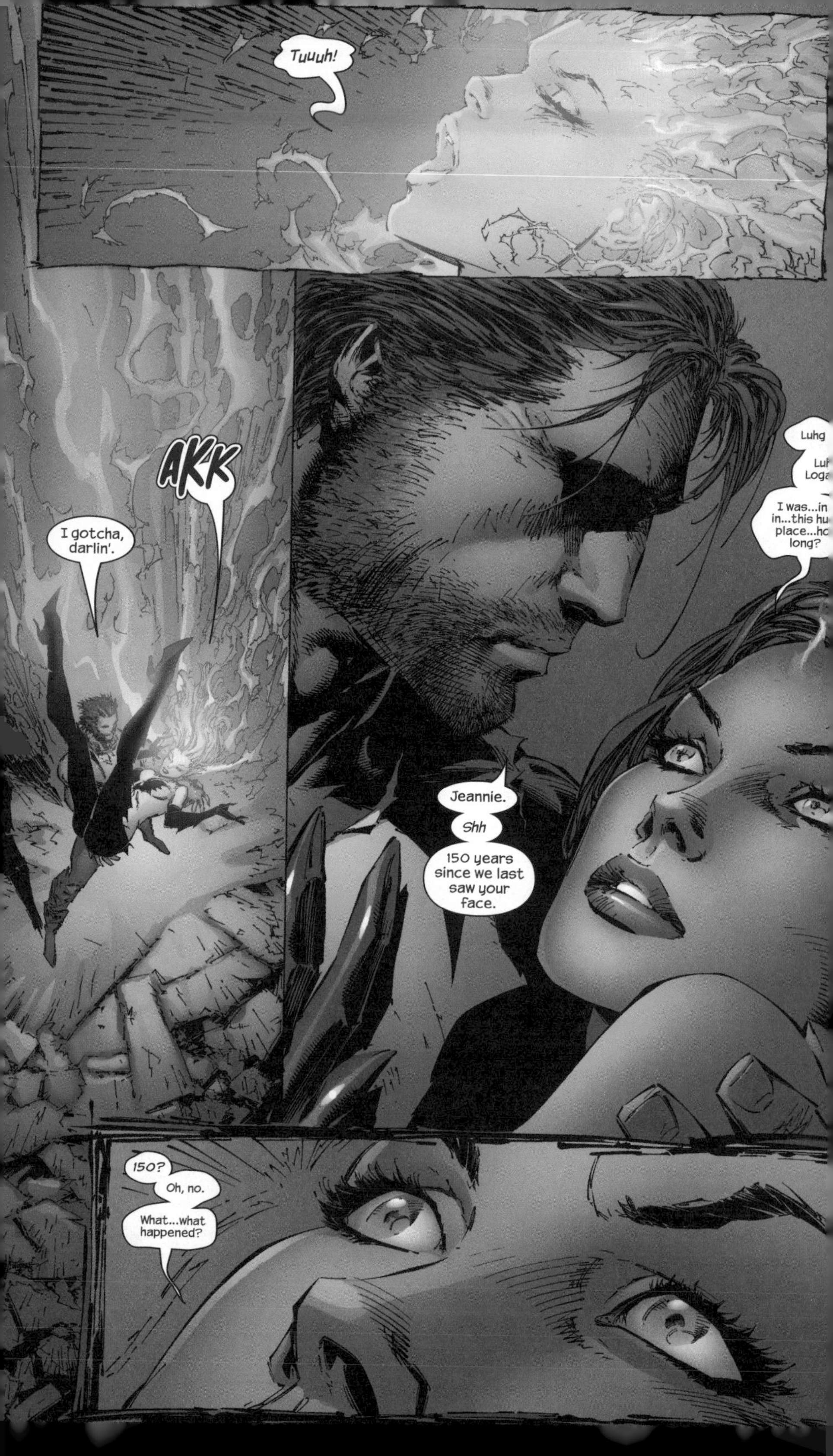

Tuuuh!
AKK
I gotcha, darlin'.
Luhg
Jeannie.
Shh
150 years since we last saw your face.
150?
Oh, no.
What...what happened?

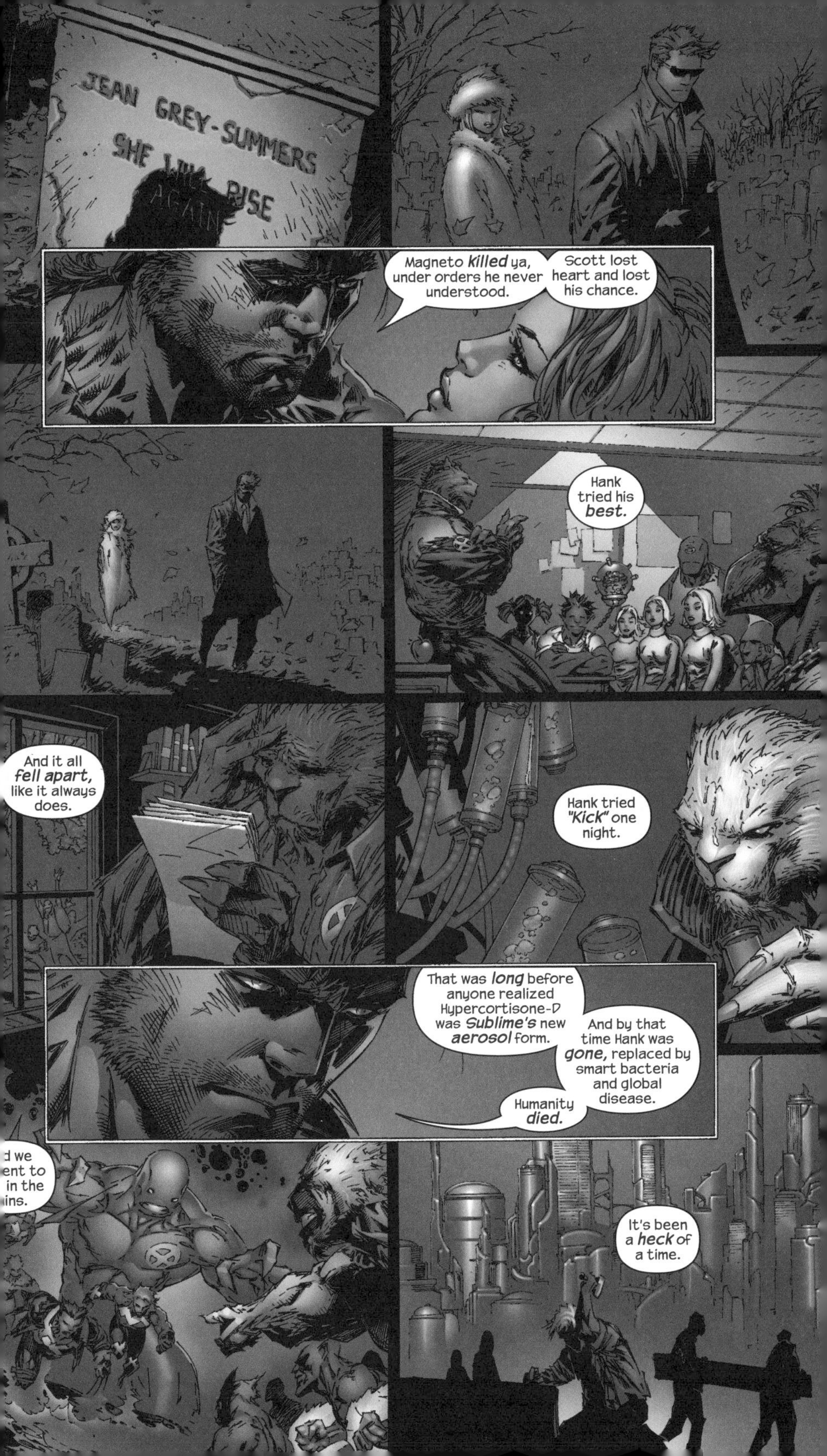
JEAN GREY-SUMMERS
SHE WILL RISE AGAIN
Magneto killed ya, under orders he never understood.
Scott lost heart and lost his chance.
Hank tried his best.
And it all fell apart, like it always does.
Hank tried "Kick" one night.
That was long before anyone realized Hypercortisone-D was Sublime's new aerosol form.
And by that time Hank was gone, replaced by smart bacteria and global disease.
Humanity died.
It's been a heck of a time.

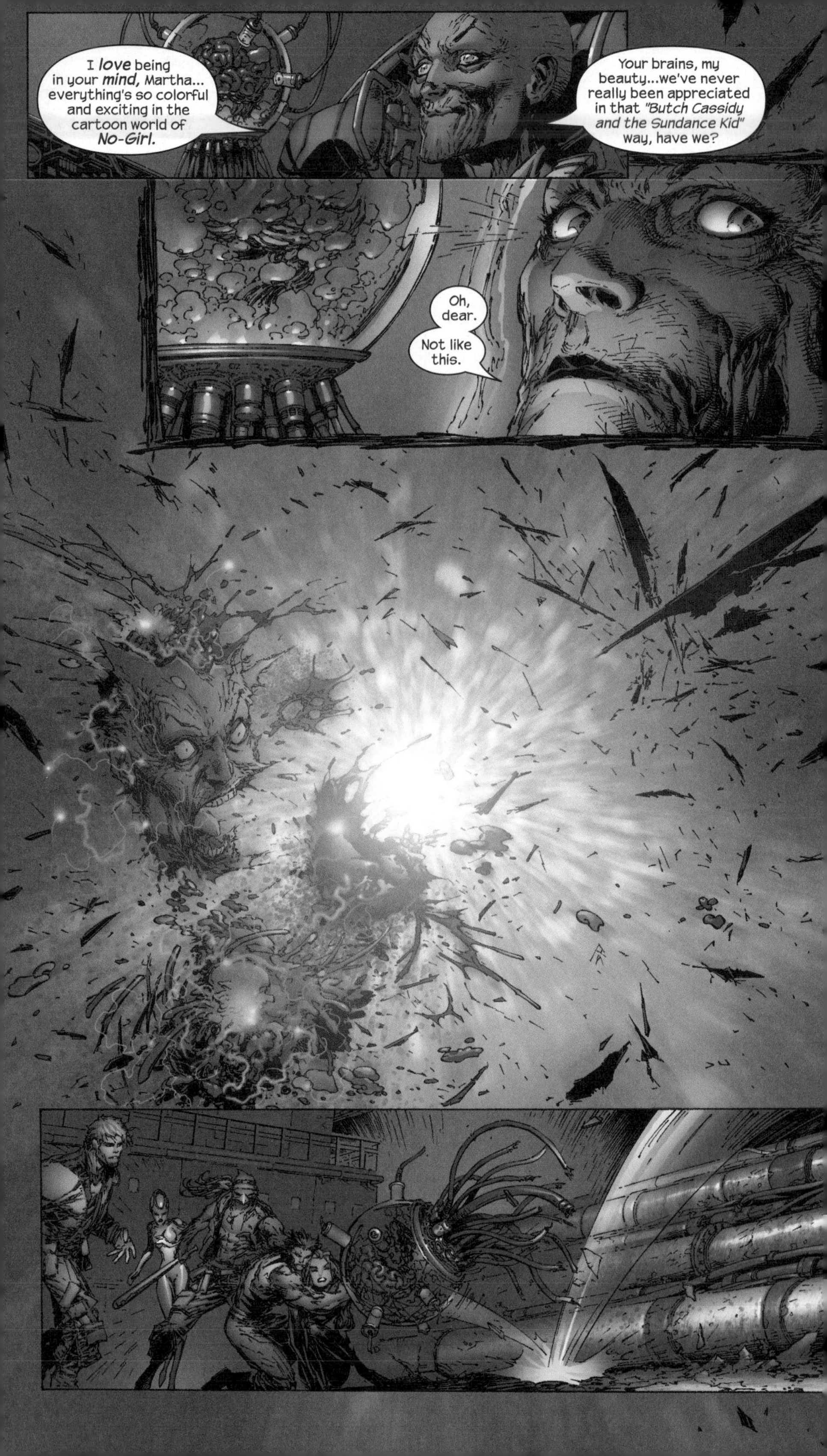

I *love* being in your *mind,* Martha... everything's so colorful and exciting in the cartoon world of *No-Girl.*
Your brains, my beauty...we've never really been appreciated in that *"Butch Cassidy and the Sundance Kid"* way, have we?
Oh, dear.
Not like this.

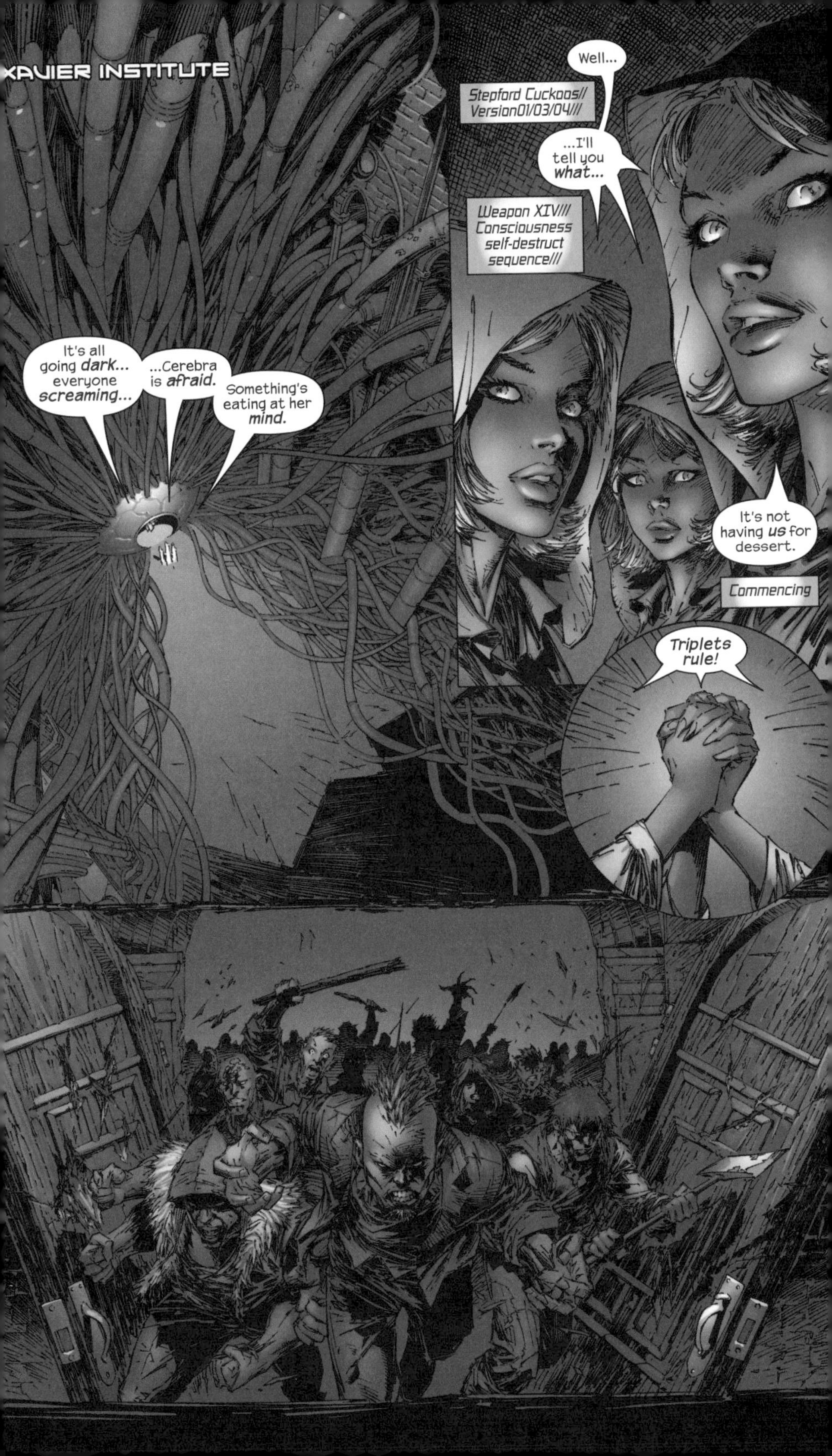
XAVIER INSTITUTE
It's all going dark... everyone screaming...
...Cerebra is afraid.
Something's eating at her mind.
Well...
Stepford Cuckoos// Version01/03/04///
...I'll tell you what...
Weapon XIV/// Consciousness self-destruct sequence///
It's not having us for dessert.
Commencing
Triplets rule!

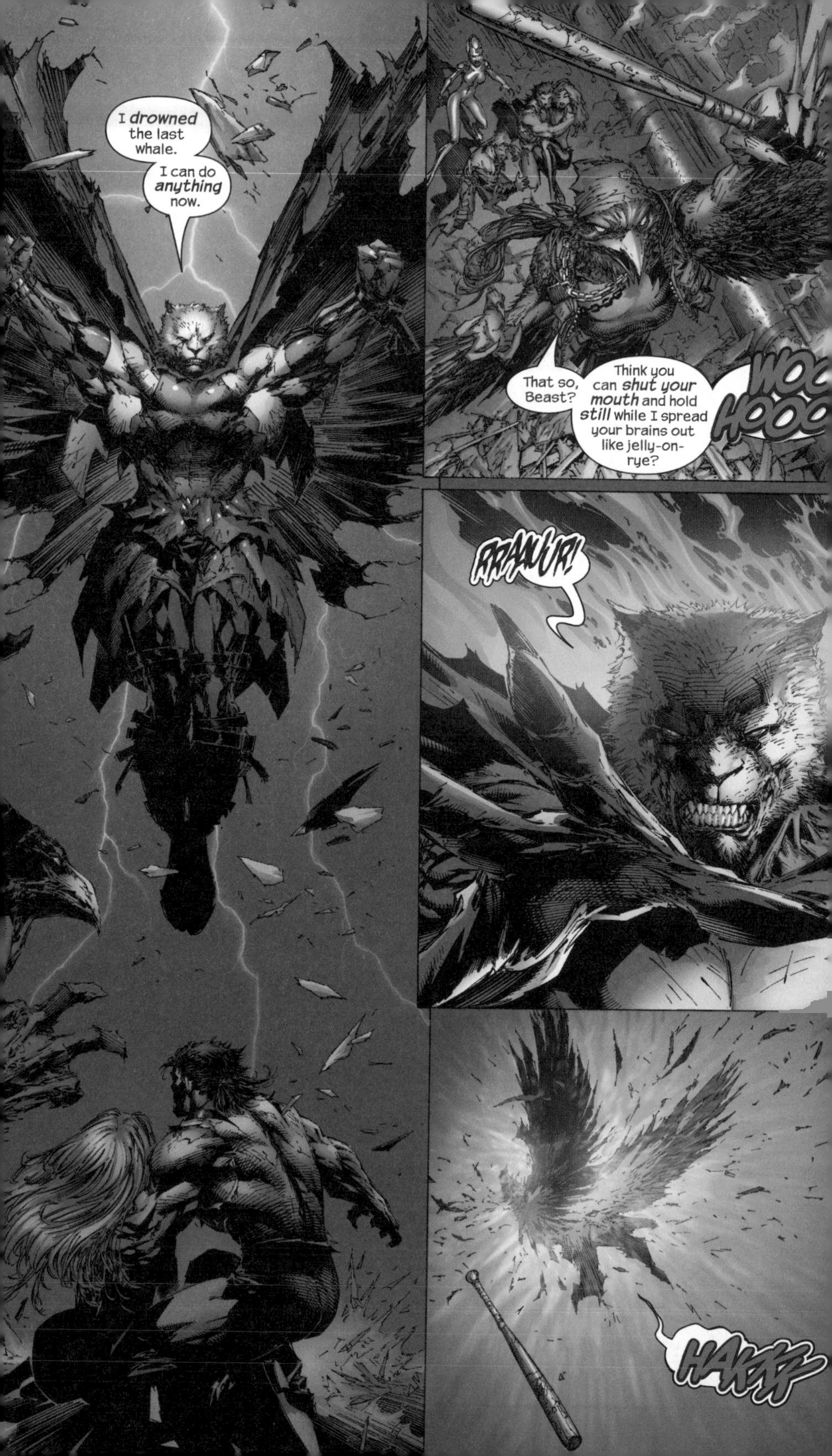
I drowned the last whale.
I can do anything now.
That so, Beast?
Think you can shut your mouth and hold still while I spread your brains out like jelly-on-rye?
WOO HOOO
RRAAUR!
HAKKK

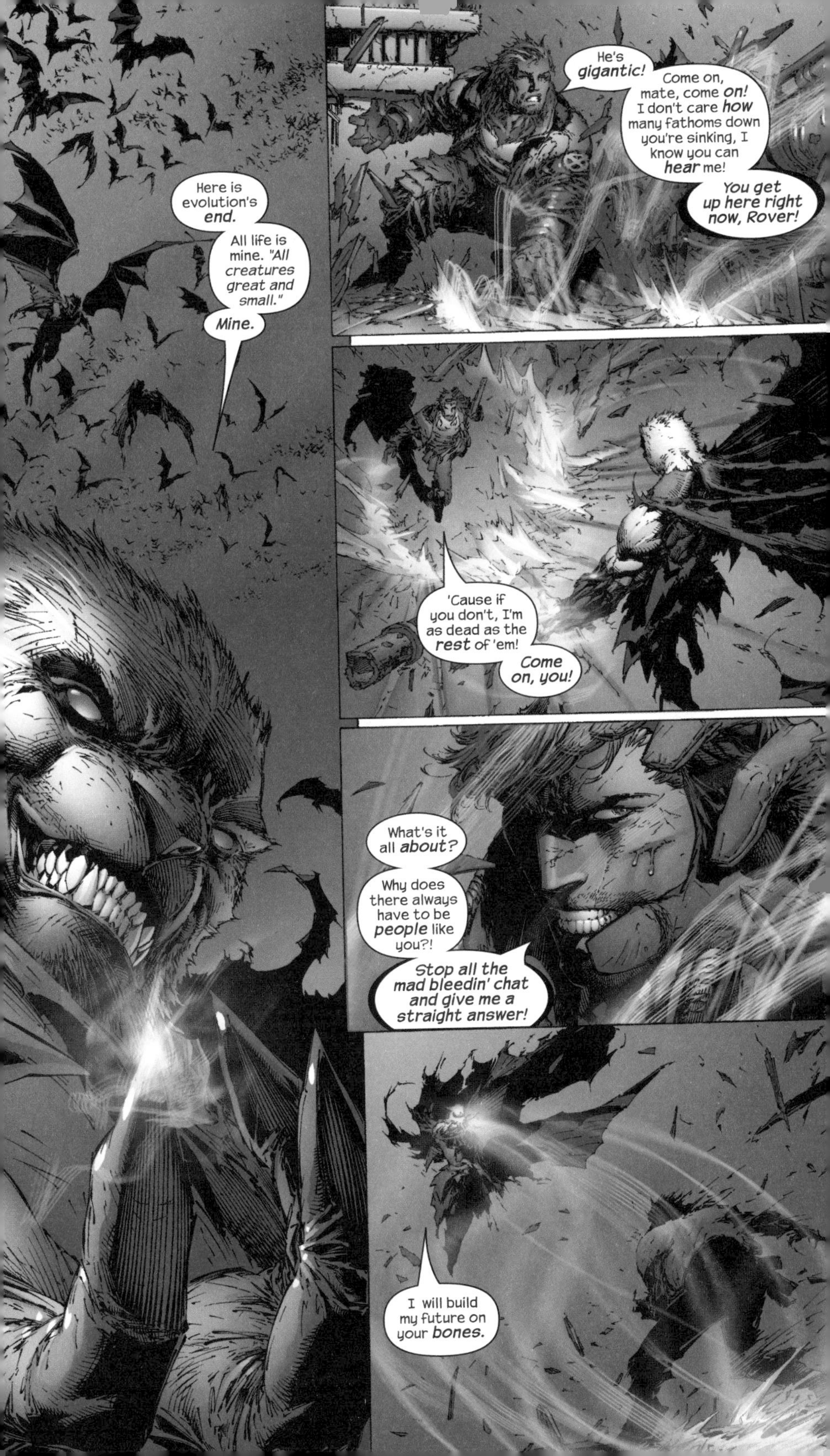
Here is evolution's end.
All life is mine. "All creatures great and small."
Mine.
He's gigantic!
Come on, mate, come on! I don't care how many fathoms down you're sinking, I know you can hear me!
You get up here right now, Rover!
'Cause if you don't, I'm as dead as the rest of 'em!
Come on, you!
What's it all about?
Why does there always have to be people like you?!
Stop all the mad bleedin' chat and give me a straight answer!
I will build my future on your bones.

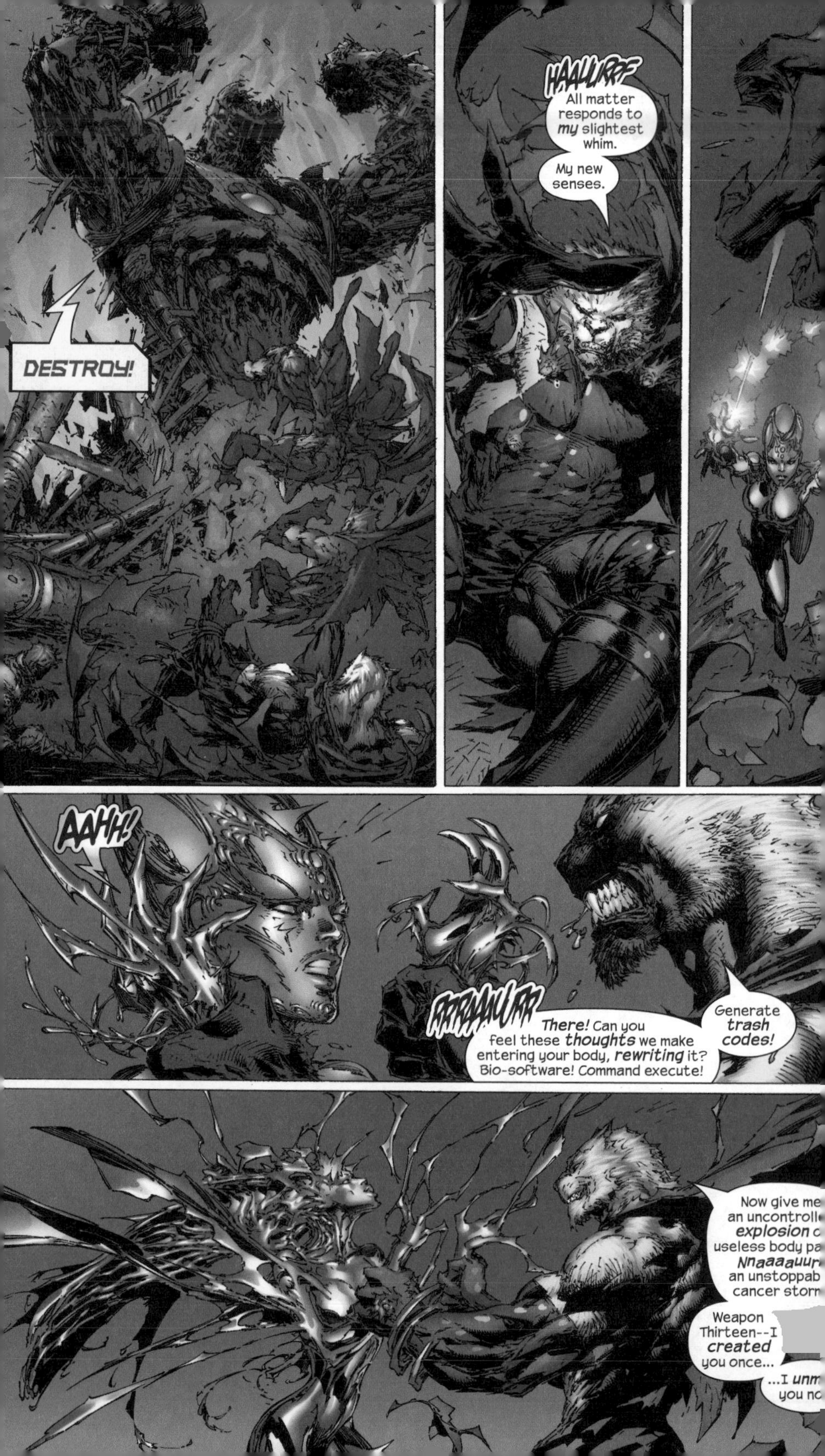
DESTROY!
HAALLURRF
All matter responds to *my* slightest whim.
My new senses.
AAHH!
RRRAAAUURR
There! Can you feel these *thoughts* we make entering your body, *rewriting* it? Bio-software! Command execute!
Generate *trash codes!*
Now give me an uncontroll *explosion* o useless body pa *Nnaaaauur* an unstoppab cancer storm
Weapon Thirteen--I *created* you once...
...I *unm* you no

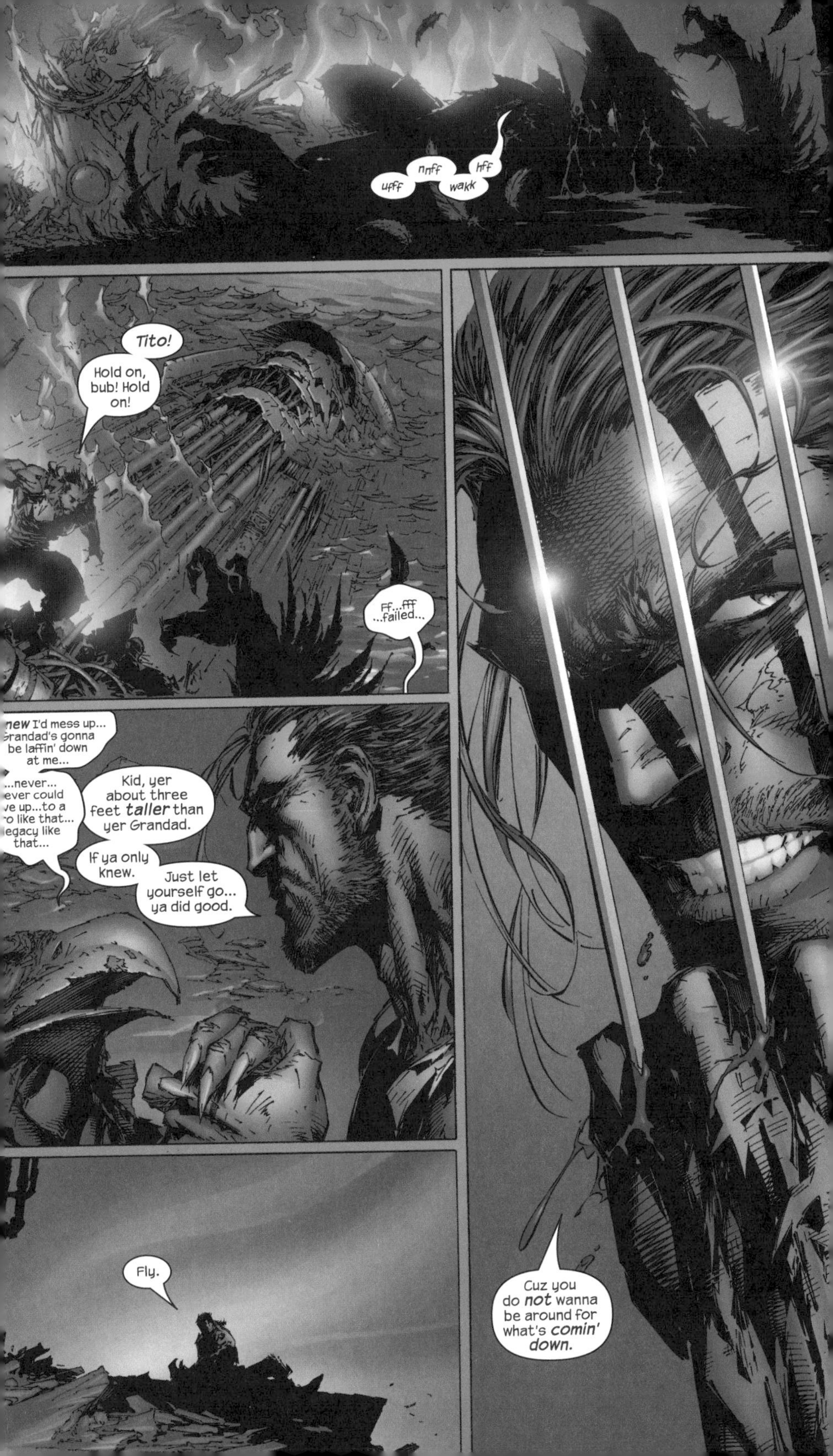

uff
nnff
wakk
hff
Tito!
Hold on, bub! Hold on!
Ff...fff ...failed...
new I'd mess up... Grandad's gonna be laffin' down at me...
...never... ever could ve up...to a o like that... egacy like that...
Kid, yer about three feet *taller* than yer Grandad.
If ya only knew.
Just let yourself go... ya did good.
Cuz you do *not* wanna be around for what's *comin' down.*
Fly.

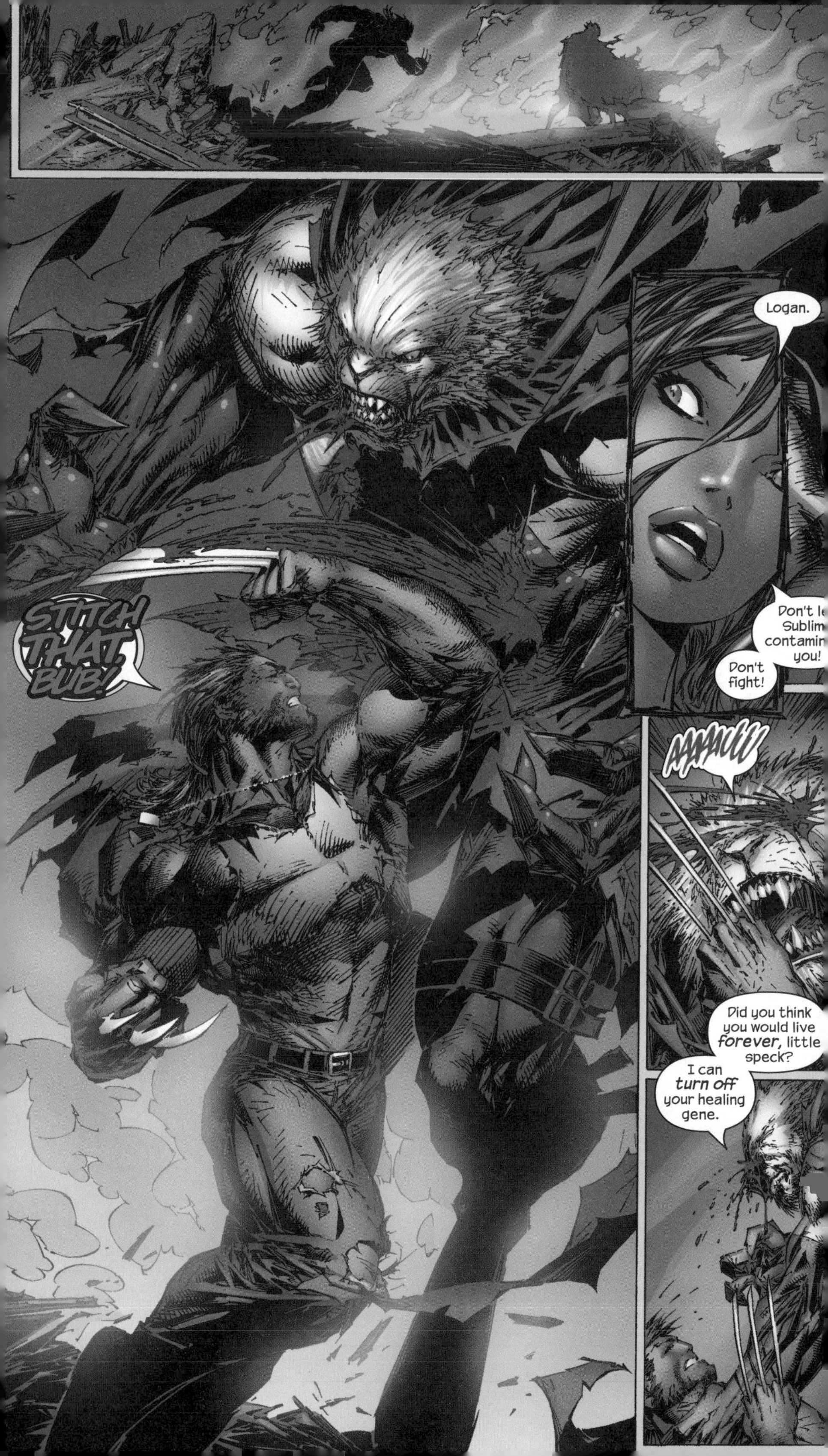

Logan.
STITCH THAT, BUB!
Don't let Sublime contaminate you!
Don't fight!
AAAAAUUU
Did you think you would live *forever,* little speck?
I can *turn off* your healing gene.

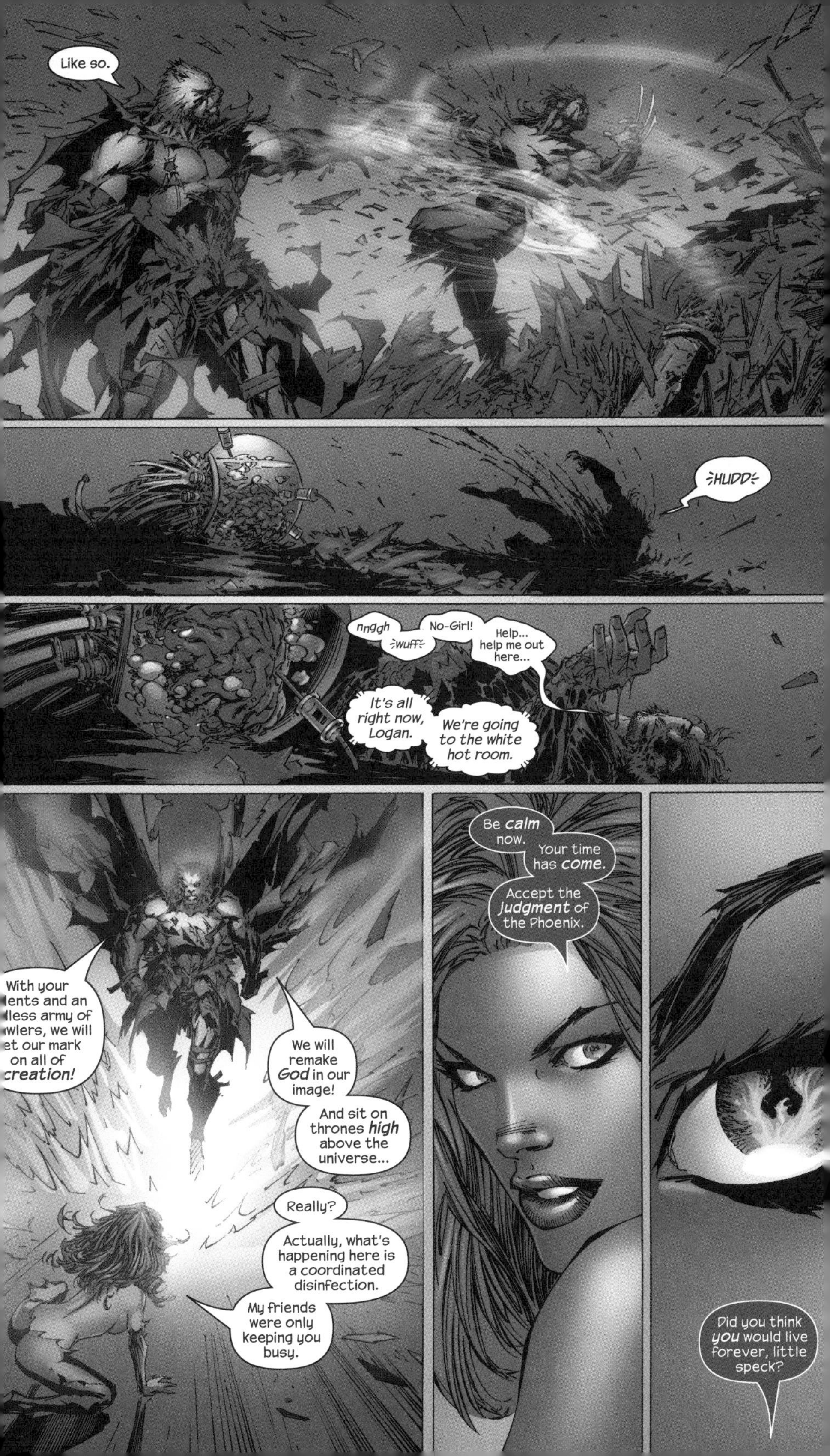

Like so.
HUDD
nnggh
wuff
No-Girl!
Help... help me out here...
It's all right now, Logan.
We're going to the white hot room.
With your lents and an lless army of wlers, we will et our mark on all of creation!
We will remake God in our image!
And sit on thrones high above the universe...
Really?
Actually, what's happening here is a coordinated disinfection.
My friends were only keeping you busy.
Be calm now.
Your time has come.
Accept the judgment of the Phoenix.
Did you think you would live forever, little speck?

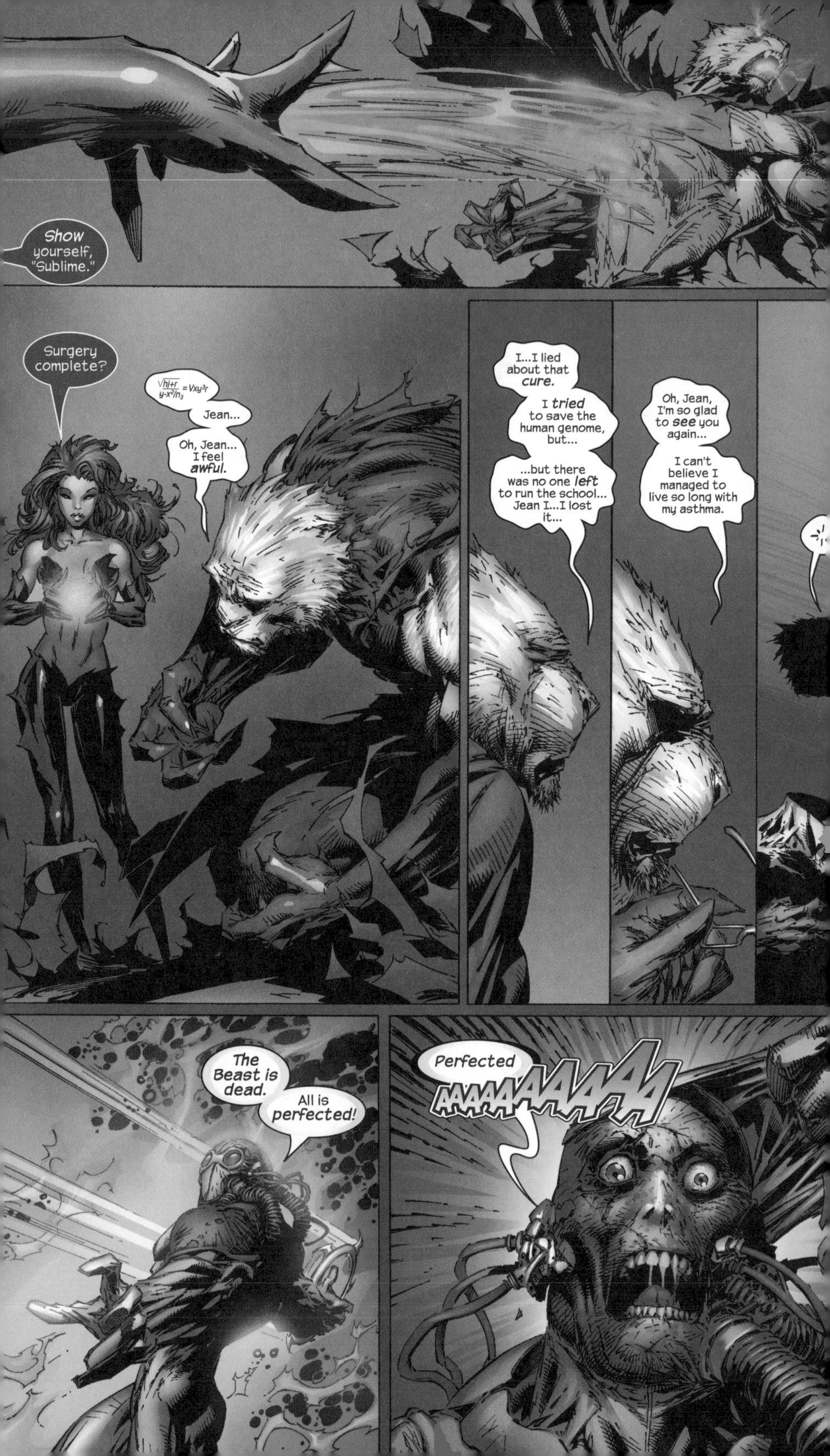

Show yourself, "Sublime."
Surgery complete?
$\frac{\sqrt{hj+r}}{y-x^2/n_3} = Vxy^3r$
Jean...
Oh, Jean... I feel awful.
I...I lied about that cure.
I tried to save the human genome, but...
...but there was no one left to run the school... Jean I...I lost it...
Oh, Jean, I'm so glad to see you again...
I can't believe I managed to live so long with my asthma.
The Beast is dead.
All is perfected!
Perfected AAAAAAAAAA

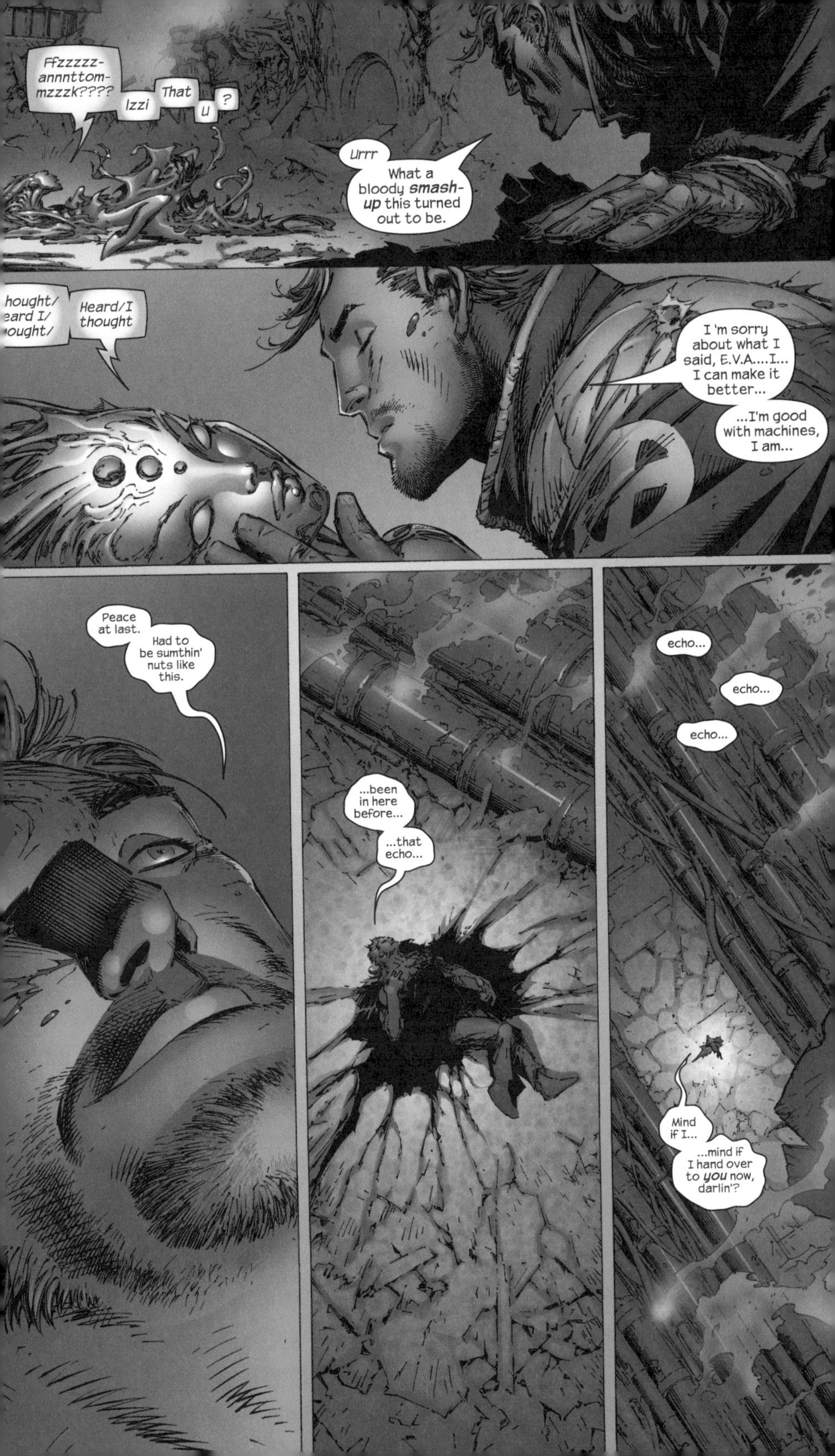

Ffzzzzz-annnttom-mzzzk????
Izzi
That
u
?
Urrr
What a bloody **smash-up** this turned out to be.
hought/ eard I/ ought/
Heard/I thought
I'm sorry about what I said, E.V.A....I... I can make it better...
...I'm good with machines, I am...
Peace at last.
Had to be sumthin' nuts like this.
...been in here before...
...that echo...
echo...
echo...
echo...
Mind if I...
...mind if I hand over to ***you*** now, darlin'?

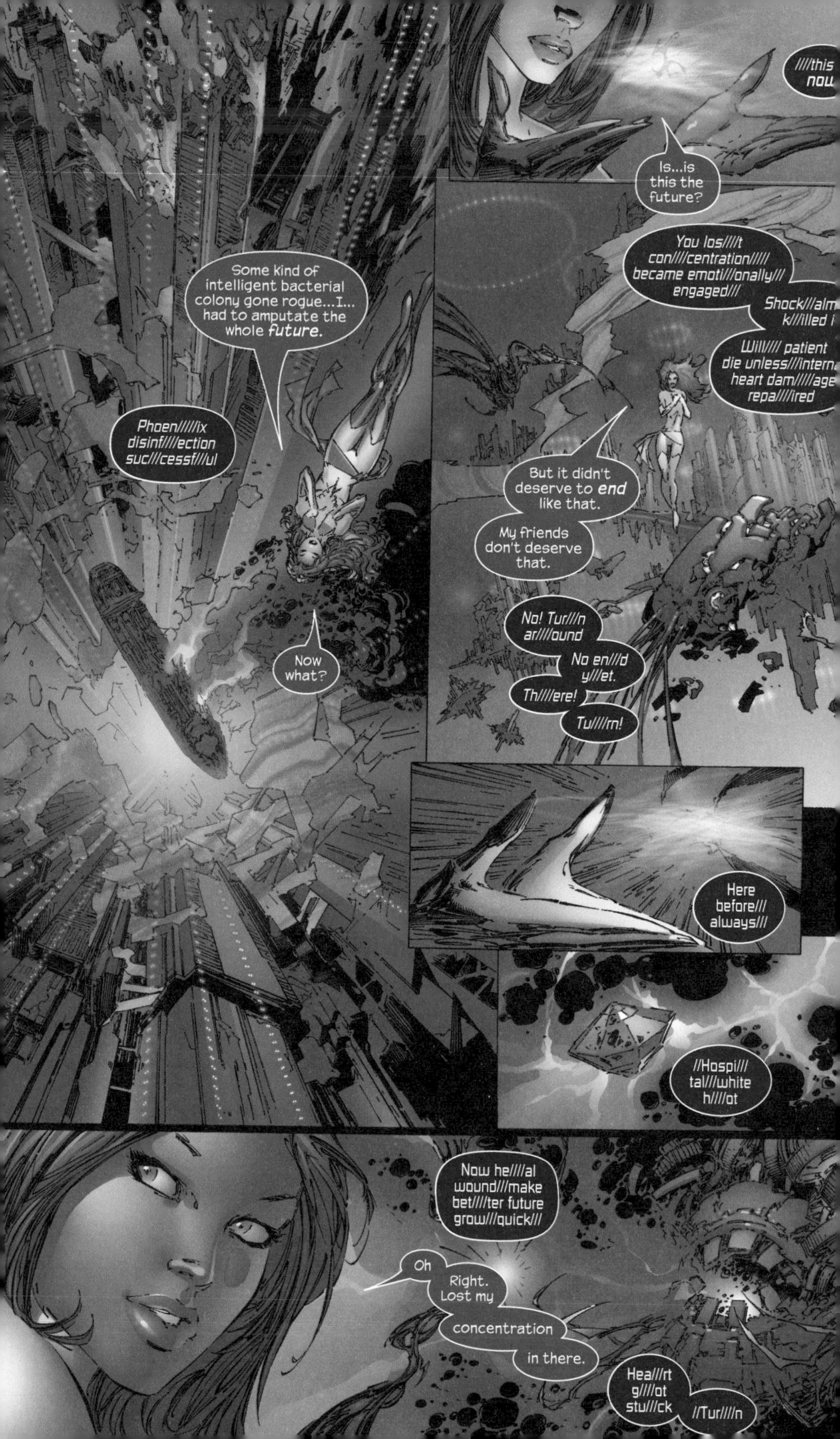

////this
nou
Is...is this the future?
You los////t con////centration///// became emoti///onally/// engaged///
Shock///alm
k///illed i
Will//// patient die unless///interna heart dam/////age repa////ired
Some kind of intelligent bacterial colony gone rogue...I... had to amputate the whole *future.*
Phoen/////ix disinf////ection suc///cessf///ul
But it didn't deserve to *end* like that.
My friends don't deserve that.
Now what?
No! Tur///n ar////ound
No en///d y///et.
Th////ere!
Tu////rn!
Here before/// always///
//Hospi/// tal///white h////ot
Now he////al wound///make bet////ter future grow///quick///
Oh
Right. Lost my
concentration
in there.
Hea///rt g////ot stu///ck
//Tur////n

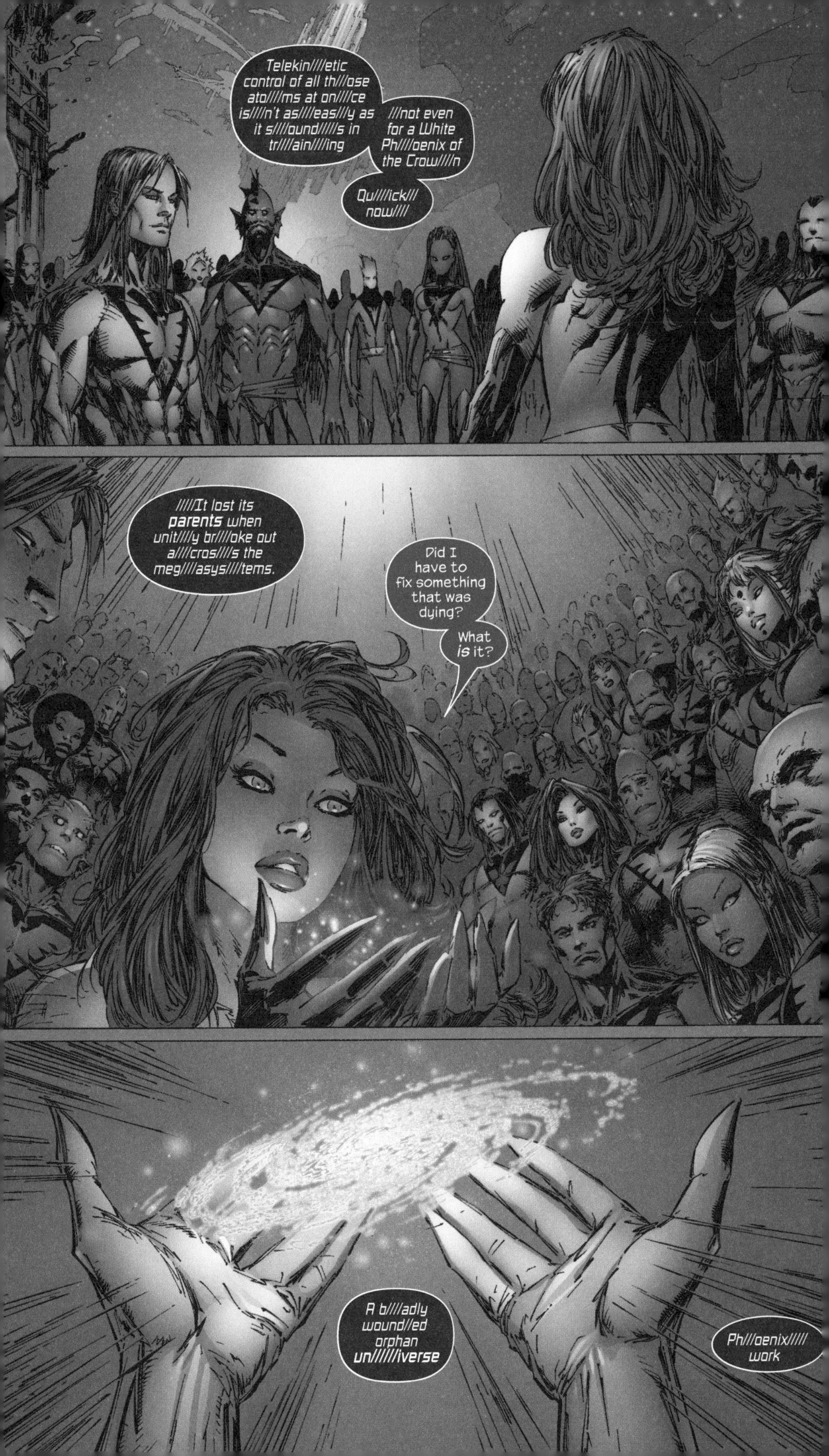
Telekin////etic control of all th///ose ato////ms at on////ce is////n't as////eas///y as it s////ound/////s in tr////ain////ing
///not even for a White Ph////oenix of the Crow////n
Qu////ick/// now////
/////It lost its parents when unit////y br////oke out a////cros////s the meg////asys////tems.
Did I have to fix something that was dying?
What is it?
A b////adly wound//ed orphan un//////iverse
Ph///oenix///// work

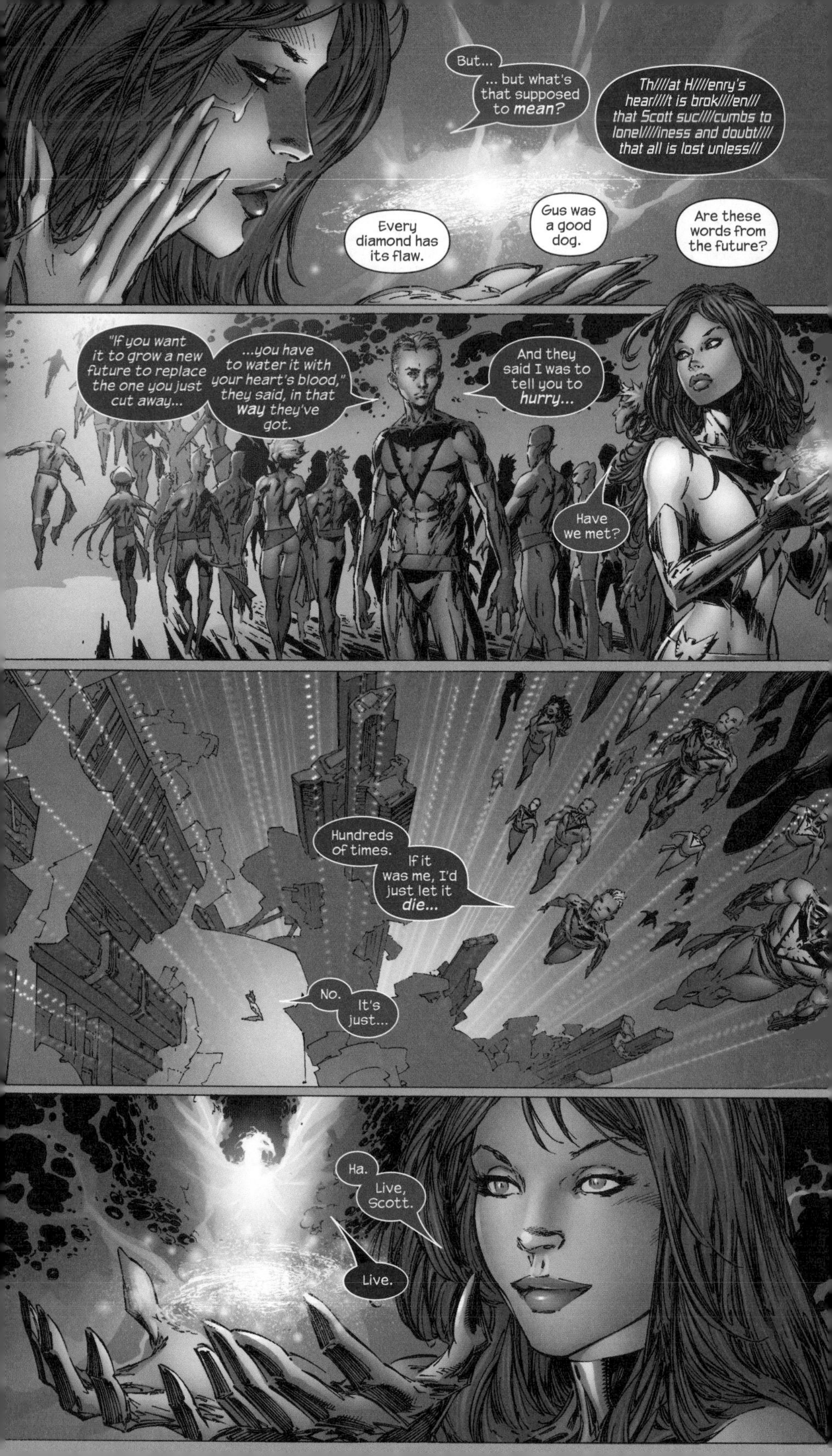
But...
... but what's that supposed to *mean*?
Th////at H////enry's hear////t is brok////en/// that Scott suc////cumbs to lonel////iness and doubt//// that all is lost unless///
Every diamond has its flaw.
Gus was a good dog.
Are these words from the future?
"If you want it to grow a new future to replace the one you just cut away...
...you have to water it with your heart's blood," they said, in that *way* they've got.
And they said I was to tell you to *hurry...*
Have we met?
Hundreds of times.
If it was me, I'd just let it *die...*
No.
It's just...
Ha.
Live, Scott.
Live.

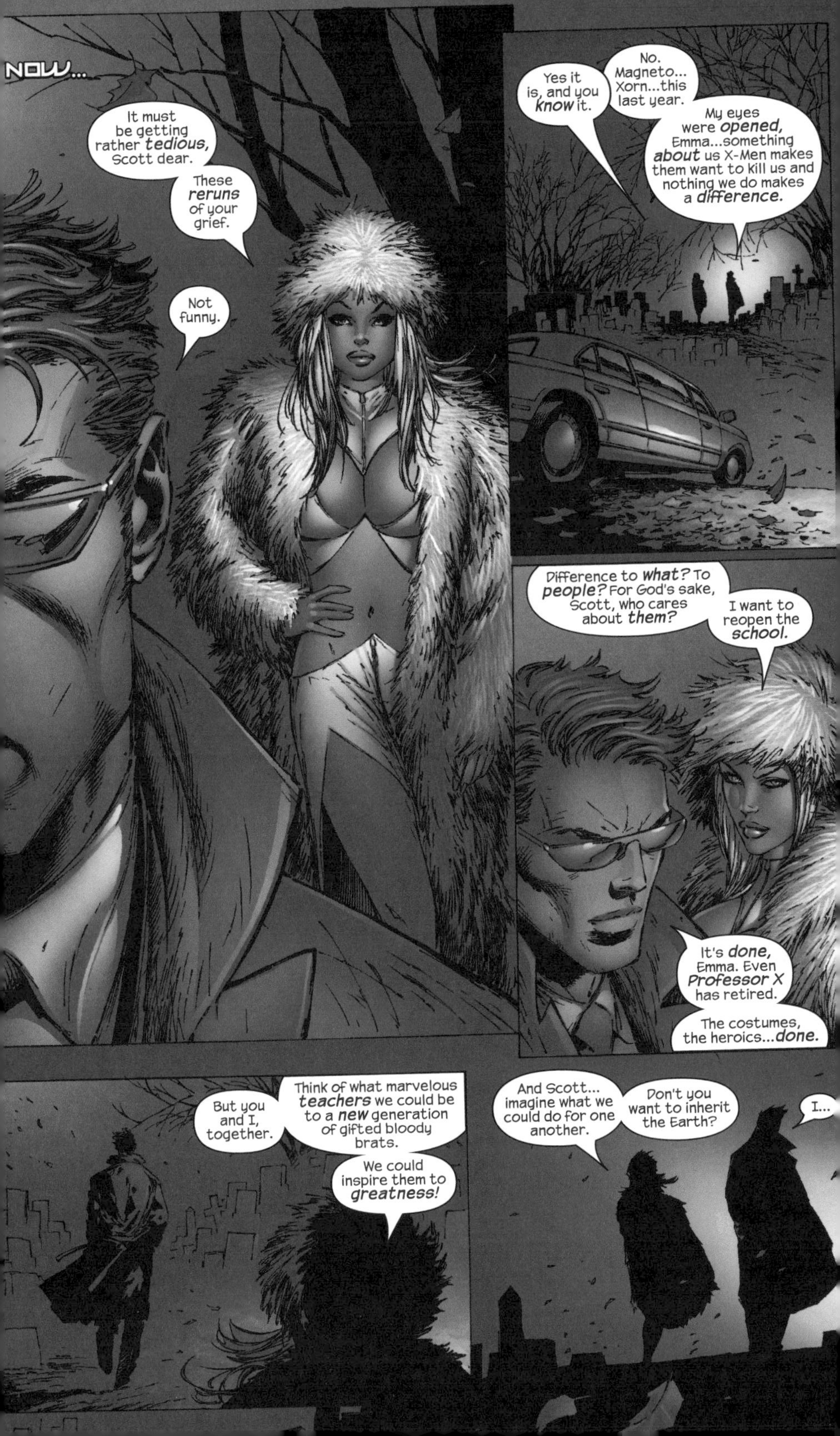
NOW...
It must be getting rather *tedious*, Scott dear.
These *reruns* of your grief.
Not funny.
Yes it is, and you *know* it.
No. Magneto... Xorn...this last year.
My eyes were *opened*, Emma...something *about* us X-Men makes them want to kill us and nothing we do makes a *difference*.
Difference to *what?* To *people?* For God's sake, Scott, who cares about *them?*
I want to reopen the *school*.
It's *done*, Emma. Even *Professor X* has retired.
The costumes, the heroics...*done*.
But you and I, together.
Think of what marvelous *teachers* we could be to a *new* generation of gifted bloody brats.
We could inspire them to *greatness!*
And Scott... imagine what we could do for one another.
Don't you want to inherit the Earth?
I...

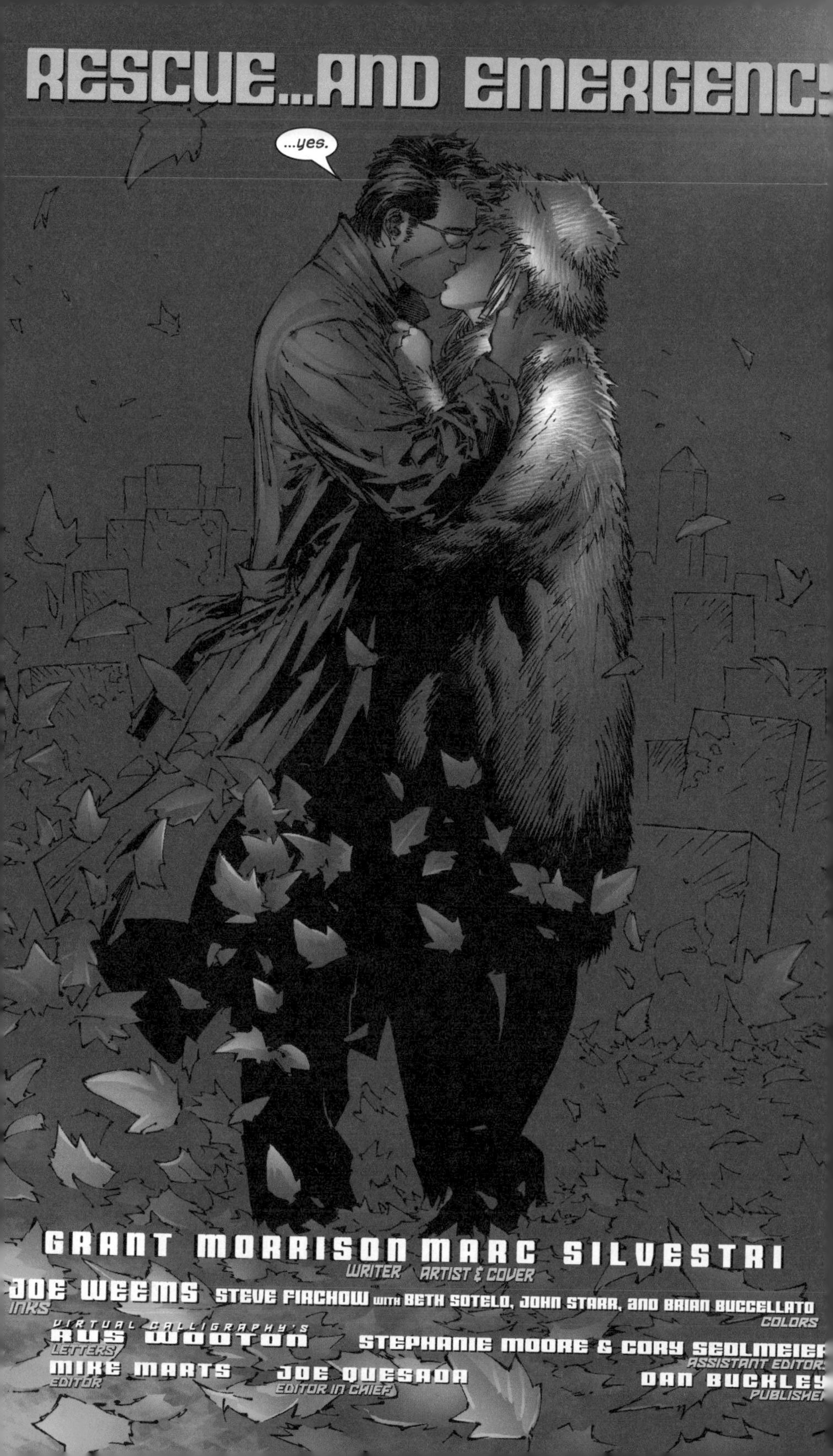
RESCUE...AND EMERGENC
...yes.
GRANT MORRISON WRITER
MARC SILVESTRI ARTIST & COVER
JOE WEEMS INKS
STEVE FIRCHOW WITH BETH SOTELO, JOHN STARR, AND BRIAN BUCCELLATO COLORS
VIRTUAL CALLIGRAPHY'S RUS WOOTON LETTERS
STEPHANIE MOORE & CORY SEDLMEIER ASSISTANT EDITORS
MIKE MARTS EDITOR
JOE QUESADA EDITOR IN CHIEF
DAN BUCKLEY PUBLISHER

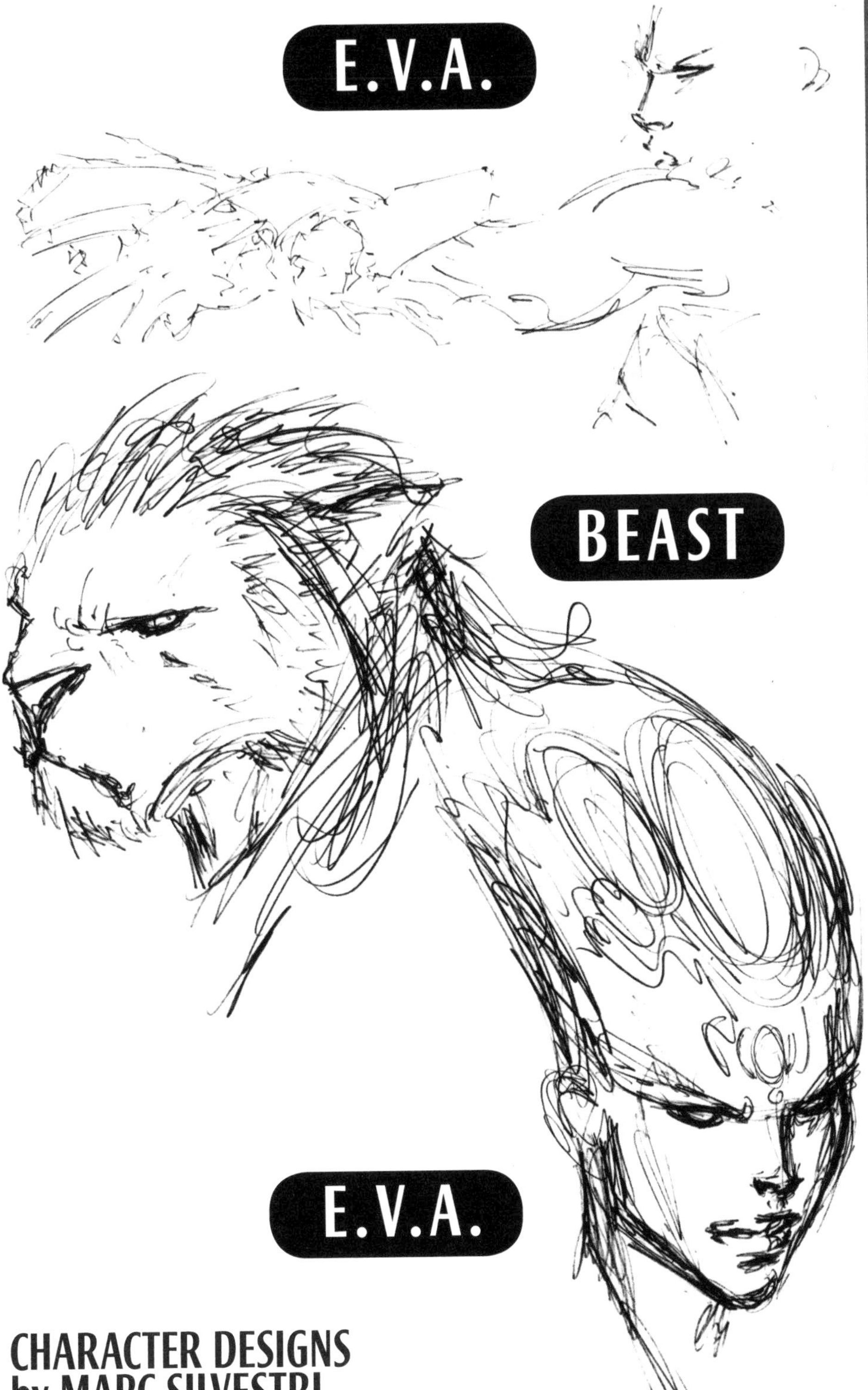
E.V.A.
BEAST
E.V.A.

CHARACTER DESIGNS
by MARC SILVESTRI

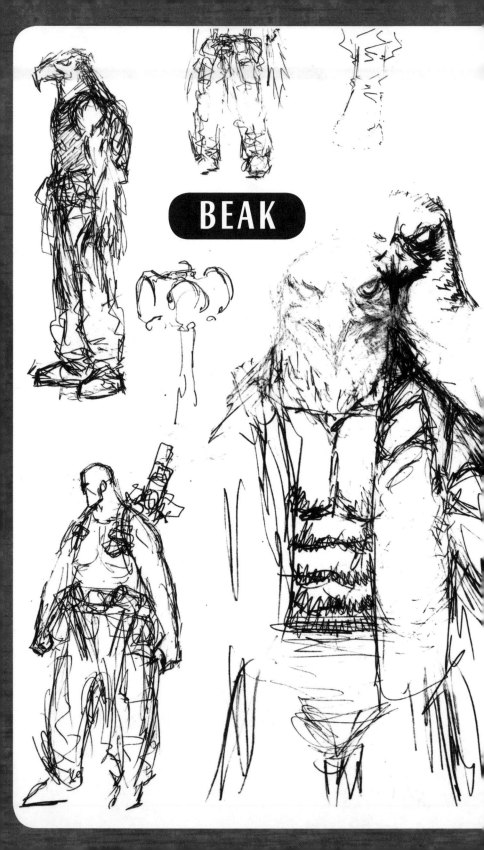

BEAK

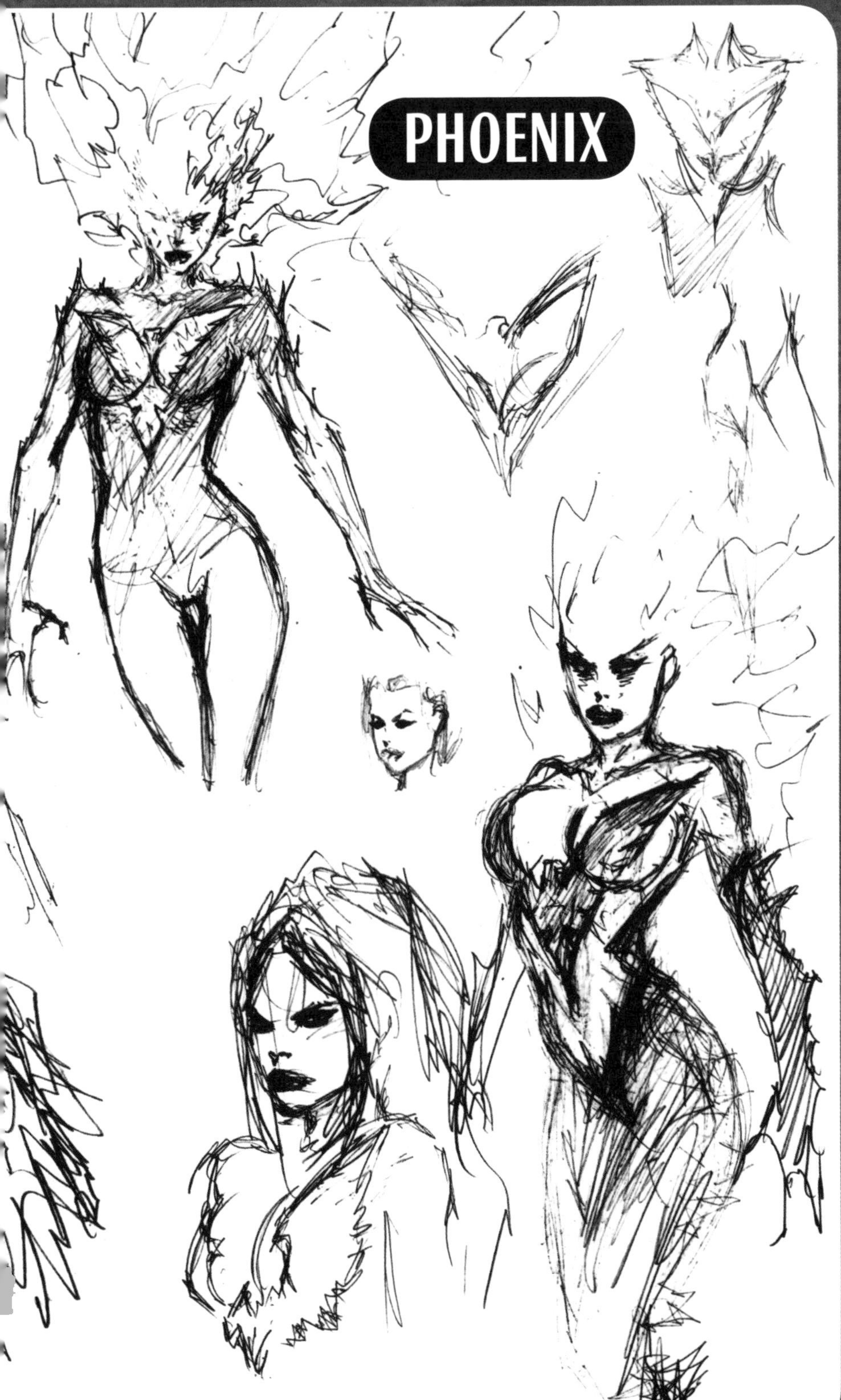
PHOENIX

New X-Men #154 layouts by MARC SILVESTRI

Page 3

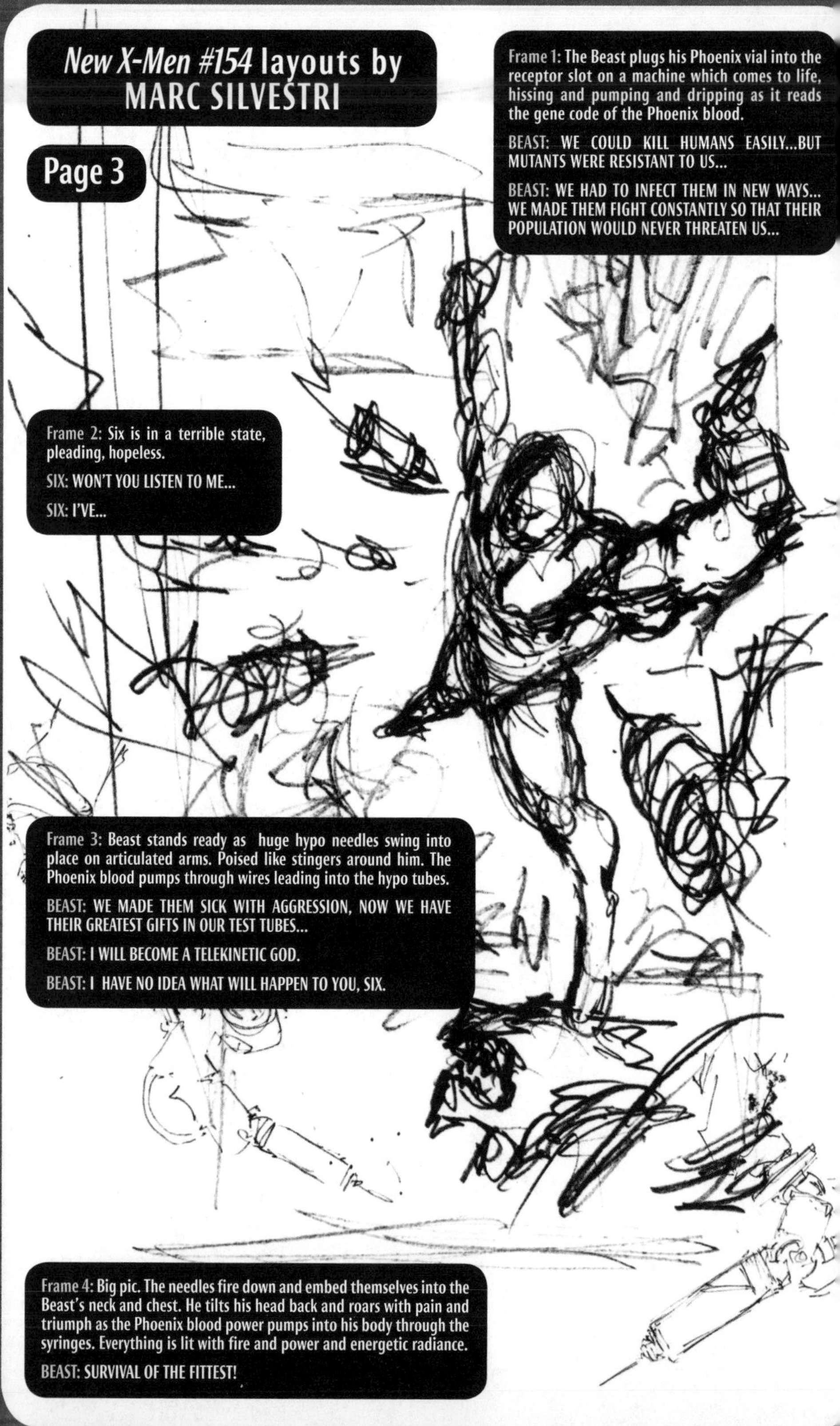

Frame 1: The Beast plugs his Phoenix vial into the receptor slot on a machine which comes to life, hissing and pumping and dripping as it reads the gene code of the Phoenix blood.

BEAST: WE COULD KILL HUMANS EASILY...BUT MUTANTS WERE RESISTANT TO US...

BEAST: WE HAD TO INFECT THEM IN NEW WAYS... WE MADE THEM FIGHT CONSTANTLY SO THAT THEIR POPULATION WOULD NEVER THREATEN US...

Frame 2: Six is in a terrible state, pleading, hopeless.

SIX: WON'T YOU LISTEN TO ME...

SIX: I'VE...

Frame 3: Beast stands ready as huge hypo needles swing into place on articulated arms. Poised like stingers around him. The Phoenix blood pumps through wires leading into the hypo tubes.

BEAST: WE MADE THEM SICK WITH AGGRESSION, NOW WE HAVE THEIR GREATEST GIFTS IN OUR TEST TUBES...

BEAST: I WILL BECOME A TELEKINETIC GOD.

BEAST: I HAVE NO IDEA WHAT WILL HAPPEN TO YOU, SIX.

Frame 4: Big pic. The needles fire down and embed themselves into the Beast's neck and chest. He tilts his head back and roars with pain and triumph as the Phoenix blood power pumps into his body through the syringes. Everything is lit with fire and power and energetic radiance.

BEAST: SURVIVAL OF THE FITTEST!